Daring Bureaucracy

Revelations and Ruminations

Attention Authors

'We Convert Fighters into Writers'. That has been the motto of Manas Publications, since more than four decades. Our message to the world is that India can win the battle, not only by the bullet but also by the pen. There is no dearth of intellectuals in our country, but their knowledge is confined to them only. No sincere effort has been made by any other publisher to channelise their knowledge in national interest. That is why the talent of a large number of intellectuals, remains latent. An author transforms his knowledge, into a manuscript, and it is our job to spread his/her knowledge by converting it into a beautiful book.

For over four decades, Manas has been motivating the intellectuals by publishing their manuscripts and would like to publish your manuscript too. If you or your colleagues have any manuscript, ready for publication or are working on it, kindly contact us with detailed synopsis and the list of contents. We would transform your work, into a valuable publication. If you wish, we can also suggest you, the suitable subjects for writing books, related to your area of expertise. Manas is known for its publishing quality and commitments. We take utmost care in production and give wide publicity to the book, as well as its author, through our national and international distribution network.

Daring Bureaucracy

Revelations and Ruminations

Vivek K Agnihotri, IAS (Retd)
Former Secretary-General, Rajya Sabha

Foreword by

Nripendra Misra, IAS (Retd)
Principal Secretary to Prime Minister of India

Manas Publications
(We Convert Fighters into Writers)
New Delhi-110002 (INDIA)

MANAS PUBLICATIONS

(We Convert Fighters into Writers)

(Publishers, Distributors, Importers & Exporters)
4402/5-A, Ansari Road (Opp. HDFC Bank)
Darya Ganj, New Delhi-110 002 (India)
Off. 23260783, 23265523, Res. 23842660
Fax: 011-23272766
E-mail: manaspublications@gmail.com
manaspub6@gmail.com

Website: www.manaspublications.in

ISBN 978-81-7049-536-9
₹ 995/-

Designed at Innovative Processors

Printed in India at
R.K. Print Service, Delhi and
Published by Mrs Suman Lata for
Manas Publications, 4402/5-A, Ansari Road (Opp. HDFC Bank),
Darya Ganj, New Delhi-110 002 (INDIA)

Dedicated to my visionary parents,
my wife Vijay, our two sons (Abhishek and Amitesh),
daughters-in-law (Meeta and Smita)
and their dear children
(Yash, Adya, Vedika and Ahan)

Foreword

I have known Vicky (the author) for over 50 years. Our association goes back to the year 1962, when we joined the Allahabad University as post graduate students and were accommodated in the A.N. (Amaranatha) Jha Hostel, earlier known as the Muir Hostel. Then only we could realize that our fathers were working in the same organisation (i.e. Kanpur Electricity Supply Administration). It speaks a lot about our life and times. We very often disagreed but shared the values of integrity, transparency and rich civil service traditions.

During a career in the civil services, as perhaps in several other services, there are many ups and downs. However, a peculiar thing about the civil services in general, and the Indian Administrative Service (IAS) in particular, is that, many a time, what appears to be an upward movement may not necessarily be so in actual practice. The uninitiated friends, relative and acquaintances actually commiserate with you, if you land a less 'respectful' job. But many officers are unaffected by such changes in fortune and try to do their best on the assignment at hand. Actually, very often, there is greater scope for original work on assignments which are looked askance at by officers in general. There is yet another aspect to the saga of postings and transfers. Certain positions that are the envy of officers in general are, in practice, really very taxing and not very enjoyable for the person occupying it. The author has had his ample share of all such civil service situations. Not being a seeker of so perceived key positions, Vicky is widely accepted as an ideal civil servant, who never compromised for petty career opportunities.

In this book the author has put together a variety of his experiences. He not only talks about various positions he has held but also those which he politely/diplomatically refused to hold. The richness of the fabric woven together is indeed out of the ordinary. The range of episodes that he deals with in this book is not only unusual but also covers the events of an era gone by as well as of most recent origin. The ethical dilemmas delineated in some of the accounts are in the nature of case studies and provide good lessons for the civil services aspirants. The life experiences recorded in the book give a good idea about how to deal with certain situations in reality. His memory of events and personalities is amazing and has been etched out in minute detail. The facts and anecdotes combined with personnel snippets or fragments, would ring a bell in the minds of those who figure in these exquisite pieces or narrations. Several of his experiences recorded in this book, however, sound true for all of us, especially those who belong to our generation. If there is some advice for the older generation, there are also lessons for the young.

I have read several autobiographies over the years. I find this one quite unique in its concept, design and execution. It is not a chronological account of events of his life from birth till date; but a discerning reader can identify the important milestones in the author's life and the key features of his attributes as (s)he goes through the book. The events of early childhood, student days and, more particularly, of his career spread over more than 40 years have been arranged under different section headings. Some of the articles are quite enlightening and are likely to raise the information quotient of the reader up a few notches.

The author wields a facile pen, has an engaging style and a rare turn of phrase that makes the mundane look fascinating through humorous delineation of reality. He has an ability to give a comical touch to even things which have provoked extreme reactions. The trials and tribulations of the common man have been jocularly described. There is twist in the tail of several articles, which will amuse the readers from all sections of our society. Also at display is author's ability to laugh at himself, which is not very common.

Nripendra Misra
Principal Secretary to Prime Minister

Vivek Agnihotri with his family (2010)

Preface

This book is largely a recollection of interesting experiences, viewed through a distinctive kaleidoscope. It is an en-crypted autobiography: various articles being pieces of the jigsaw puzzle of my life. It comprises some interesting events as well as some reflections. It is different from usual biographies the same way as an epistolary novel is from a normal novel. There is, of course, some chronology in the episodes, by way of travelling in time, back and forth. But most of the time, it is an interlinking of some events from my life and career presented in the form of modular capsules. The incidents, again, are official as well as taken from personal life. They attempt to highlight the fads and foibles or weaknesses of human nature as well as the latent humour in and the ironies of the human condition, particularly in the life of a career civil servant. There is also a sprinkling of random introspections resulting from a life time of largely sedate but varied experiences. It is, of course, impossible to compress a life-time of experiences into 300-odd pages.

Let me confess that I have not been, by any chance, subjected to serious traumatic experiences either in my personal life or during my career. There are a few revelations here, but none so momentous as to rock the establishment. But there have been several encounters that have, occasionally, left me stunned or stumped; and I can now sit back and mull over them with a detached sense of humour. There is God even in small things; and one thing leads to another. My career progressed from the executive to post-retirement semi-judicial assignment in the Central Administrative Tribunal as well as the position of the Secretary General, Rajya Sabha, which is equivalent to the Cabinet Secretary to Government to India, at least in terms of the emoluments.

My encounters, which have fashioned the framework of the episodes in this book, have impacted significantly on my career. I have had my ups and downs. My 'ups' have occasionally made me take unusual decisions; and the so-called 'downs' have taken me to greater heights. God has been merciful.

This book has been divided into five sections. In order to engage the attention of the readers, I have described some event clusters in the first section titled 'Amusing Episodes', which have one or more twists and turns in the tail. Learning is a life-long phenomenon and I have had ample share of my trials and tribulations. Some of these have been described in the section 'Learning Episodes'. And there are 'Other Episodes', which have a moral of their own.

I have come across several individuals, who have left a lasting impression on me. Some of them have contributed to the richness of my life through their selfless contributions. My 'Tributes' to them have been documented under a separate section. The final section on 'Musings' is a collection of sundry thoughts on a variety of subjects, which may amuse you and, may be, at times, disturb you. Bear with me, there is more in store.

I am not sure what you will be led to think of me as a person after reading the book. Am I a civil servant by accident? Am I an 'academician', as some of my colleagues never tire of calling me, and, therefore, not fit to be a hardcore 'real-politik' bureaucrat? Or am I a story teller, spinning some yarns? Or am I a person who loves reading and writing and suffers from a compulsive obsessive desire to see his name in print? Am I a good learner? Or am I a fool who has walked the path which angels fear to tread? I leave it to the readers to decide.

My CV projects me as a process expert, who has written / 'put together' several professional books and articles. As far as this book is concerned, I consider myself an 'associationist' of ideas (in a familiar psychological sense), mixing memory with desire and the present with the past. I blame my creativity in this book squarely on this syndrome.

If you are a civil servant, some of the episode may strike a familiar chord. If you are not, you may enjoy the fads and foibles (i.e. weaknesses) of 'babus' as well as confessions of a fellow human being. Some of the experiential tips may be found useful by the young officers. And if you are an aspiring civil servant, it may forewarn you about what is in store for you.

Vivek K Agnihotri, IAS (Retd)

Acknowledgments

First and foremost I would like to put on record my grateful thanks to Shri Nripendra Misra, Principal Secretary to the Prime Minister, for agreeing to write the foreword to this book. It is indeed a gesture I shall delightfully reminisce for the rest of my life.

I would like to thankfully acknowledge the permission given by Mr. Rajiv Shankar for publication of earlier version, of the following articles in this book, which had first appeared in domain-b, an e-magazine: So What's in a Surname; Tea for the President; Pulse Rate: Collateral Benefit; Protected by Naxalites; My Take Away from Emergency (On a Merry go Round in the Civil Service); An Arsenal of Political Allegations; A Tale of Two Ministers; Drama at the Airport; Electricity for All (Power and Telephony: How things Have Changed); Talking Aloud; An Investment in Character Building (The Tricky Question of VVIP Visits); Bachua Tewari: Voting Day Tamasha (Voting Day Tamasha); Taking the Road Less Travelled By; Make in India: What An Idea!; and Fate Accomplished.

I also thank Mr. P Jacob, for the permission accorded for reproduction of the earlier versions of following articles, which were first published in the 'Open Page' of the *Hindu*: The Consultant (An American, at home in India); Four Saturdays in a Week?; A Whistleblower's Dilemma; Which God Should I Pray Today? (These gods are hard to please) and Fighting Demons of Demonetisation (The Demons of Demonetisaton).

My thanks are also due to Mrs. Manju Shukla, my poetic cousin, who has polished the only Hindi poem I have contextually incorporated in this book.

The publication of the book would not have been possible but for the gracious acceptance of the manuscript by Manas Publications.

Contents

Foreword 7
Preface 11
Acknowledgments 15
Abbreviations and Acronyms 21

Part I: Amusing Episodes

1. So, what's in a Surname? 29
2. A South Indian Bet 32
3. Tea for the President 36
4. Pulse Rate: Collateral Benefit 45
5. Protected by Naxalites 49
6. My take away from Emergency 52
7. An Arsenal of Political Allegations 56
8. My first trip Abroad 61
9. A Tale of two Ministers 66
10. Transparency in Government 70
11. Drama at the Airport 73
12. Bonding over the Boss 76
13. From Delhi to Bhubaneswar 80
14. Hard of Reading 84
15. The Consultant 87
16. Electricity for All 90
17. Four Saturdays in a Week? 94
18. Three Episodes and three Telephone calls 98
19. Oxford Idyllic: A Refugee's Shibboleth 101
20. Language Barrier 104

21. Contextual Recognition 107
22. Monkey Business: The Eighth Wonder 110
23. My Beautiful Teeth 114
24. Talking Aloud 118
25. Collateral Benefit of Unsolicited Calls 121
26. In Quest of Help: An Anguished Account 125

Part II: Learning Episodes

27. Learning English 135
28. Driving Lessons 141
29. Learning Telugu 145
30. Learning Computer 149
31. Japanese Lessons 153

Part III: Other Episodes

32. Astrology @ Work 161
33. A Whistleblower's Dilemma 165
34. Family Values 168
35. Doing Ph. D. 172
36. An Investment in Character Building 178
37. Bachua Tewari: Voting Day Tamasha 182
38. Taking The Road Less Travelled by 185
39. Make In India: What an Idea! 191
40. The Ideas that did not Work 194
41. Unexpected Administrative Reforms 199
42. Beware of Dog: A Requiem 203
43. Fighting Demons of Demonetisation 209

Part IV: Tributes

44. Intelligence Test 225
45. A Fresher's Friend 229
46. My Adorable Dictator 232
47. A Personal Touch 236
48. Fate Accomplished 240
49. The Halcyon Handloom Days 243
50. My Benefactors 249

Part V: Musings

51. Senior Citizens in e-Land 257
52. Humble Samosa on a High 262
53. How to be an Intellectual 268
54. An Ode to South Indian Savouries 274
55. Distinguishing Marks 278
56. Skill Development: A Parable 281
57. Ten Commandments of Weight Management for Dummies 285
58. My Name is Vijay and I am a Woman: As told by my Wife 289
59. From a House to Home: The Final Resting Place 294
60. Which God Should I Pray Today? 299
61. Retirement is a Full Time Job 302
62. What are the Options? What a Way to Go! 307

Index 313

Abbreviations and Acronyms

ACASH	Association of Cooperatives and Apex Societies of Handlooms
ACR/APAR	Annual Confidential Report/Annual Performance Appraisal Report
ADC	Additional Development Commissioner
afap	As Far As Possible
AIDS	Acquired Immune Deficiency Syndrome
AIIMS	All India Institute of Medical Sciences (New Delhi)
AP	Andhra Pradesh
AP AGROS	Andhra Pradesh Agro-Industries Development Corporation
ARC	Administrative Reforms Commission
ASCI	Administrative Staff College of India (Hyderabad)
ATM	Automated Teller Machine
BA	Bachelor of Arts
BDO	Block Development Officer
BHK	Bedroom House Kitchen
BHIM	Bharat Interface for Money
BHU	Banaras Hindu University (Varanasi)
BMI	Body Mass Index
BNSD	Bishambhar Nath Sanatan Dharma
CBI	Central Bureau of Investigation
CBM	Confidence Building Measures
CD	Compact Disc
CDM	Collector and District Magistrate

CEO	Chief Executive Officer
CFL	Compact Fluorescent Light (bulb)
CGHS	Central Government Health Scheme
CJAPHC	Chief Justice of Andhra Pradesh High Court
CMC	Computer Maintenance Corporation
CNG	Compressed Natural Gas
CPM	Critical Path Method
Cr. P. C.	Criminal Procedure Code
CRR	Cash Reserve Ratio
CSOI	Civil Services Officers' Institute
CSS	Central Secretariat Service
CV	Curriculum Vitae
DARPG	Department of Administrative Reforms and Public Grievances (Government of India, New Delhi)
DAV	Dayanand Anglo-Vedic
DC	Development Commissioner
DD	Door Darshan (TV Channel)
DfID	Department for International Development (Government of UK)
DG, AEPC	Director General, Apparel Export Promotion Council
DMAIC	Define, Measure, Analyze, Improve and Control
DND	Do Not Disturb/Delhi-Noida-Delhi (expressway)
DTH	Direct to Home
DVD	Digital Video/Versatile Disc
ECIL	Electronic Corporation of India Limited
ECIR	Enforcement Case Information Report
EPZ	Export Processing Zone
ERP	Enterprise Resource Planning
EVK	Motor Van 4 Wheeler (A type of railway wagon used for transporting four wheelers)
FAO	Food and Agriculture Organisation
FC	Foundation Course
FEMA	Failure Mode and Effect Analysis
FIR	First Information Report
FIT	Fashion Institute of Technology (New York)
FM	Frequency Modulation (radio)

GAD	General Administration Department
GoI	Government of India
HLEG	High Level Expert Group
HQRS	Headquarters
http	Hyper Text Transfer Protocol
IAS	Indian Administrative Service
IFoS	Indian Forest Service
IIPA	Indian Institute of Public Administration (New Delhi)
IIT	Indian Institute of Technology (Delhi)
IPS	Indian Police Service
IQ	Intelligence Quotient
ISM	Interpretive Structural Modelling
ITO	Income Tax Officer
JNU	Jawaharlal Nehru University
KES-PS	An artificial intelligence based decision support system
KGB	Security Agency of Russia
KSA	Knowledge, Skill and Attitude
LBSNAA	Lal Bahadur Shastri National Academy of Administration (Mussoorie)
LDC	Lower Division Clerk
LED	Light-Emitting Diode (bulb)
LPG	Liberalisation, Privatisation, Globalisation/ Liquid Petroleum Gas
MD	Managing Director
MISIDICI	Make in India. Skilled India, Digital India and Clean India
MLA	Member of Legislative Assembly
MoU	Memorandum of Understanding
MPIN	Mobile Personal Identification Number
NAA	National Academy of Administration (original name of LBSNAA)
NCR	National Capital Region
NDA	National Defence Academy / National Democratic Alliance
NGO	Non-Gazetted Officer / Non-Government Organisation

NHDC	National Handloom Development Corporation (Lucknow)
NIFT	National Institute of Fashion Technology, New Delhi
NOIDA	New Okhla Industrial Development Authority
NOOC	North Oxford Overseas Centre
NPA	Non-Performing Assets
NPA&M	New Public Management and Administration
NPS	New Pension Scheme
NPV	Net Present Value
NRI	Non-Resident Indian
NTC	National Textile Corporation
OB Van	Outside Broadcasting Van
ODA	Overseas Development Administration (Government of UK)
OR	Operations Research
OSD	Officer on Special Duty
OT	Officer Trainee
OTP	One Time Password
OUP	Oxford University Press
PA	Personal Assistant
PDCA	Plan, Do, Check, Act
PE	Preliminary Enquiry
PERT	Programme Evaluation and Review Technique
PGI	Post-Graduate Institute (Chandigarh)
Ph. D.	Doctor of Philosophy
PIN	Personal Identification Number
PMO	Prime Minister's Office
PoS	Point of Sale
PWD	Public Works Department
QEH	Queen Elizabeth House (Oxford, UK)
QFD	Quality Function Deployment
QR Code	Quick Response Code
RBI	Reserve Bank of India
RML	Ram Manohar Lohia (Hospital, New Delhi)
RO	Reverse Osmosis
RPF	Railway Protection Force
RS TV	Rajya Sabha Television

SAARC	South Asian Association for Regional Cooperation
SAP	Systems, Applications and Products
SDM	Sub-Divisional Magistrate
SLR	Statutory Liquidity Ratio
SP	Superintendent of Police
SPC	Statistical Process Control
STS	Single Tender System
SWOT	Strength, Weakness, Opportunity, Threat
TCS	Tata Consultancy Services
TPM	Total Productive Maintenance
TQM	Total Quality Management
UK	United Kingdom
UP	Uttar Pradesh
UPA	United Progressive Alliance
UPSC	Union Public Service Commission (New Delhi)
URL	Uniform Resource Locator
USA	United States of America
USSR	Union of Soviet Socialist Republic
VAT	Value Added Tax
VIP	Very Important Person
WHO	World Health Organisation

PART I

Amusing Episodes

1 So, What's in a Surname?

Almost since my birth, I was brought up in a city called Kanpur in Uttar Pradesh. Being kept busy with my 'studies', under the watchful eyes of my parents, I did not have many opportunities to travel, especially outside Uttar Pradesh (UP). I knew that we, sort of, 'hailed' from another city called Nagpur, as several relatives living there used to visit us. However, I first time placed my foot on the soil of Nagpur when I was 20 years old. In between it had changed hands, in the sense that from being the capital of the erstwhile Central Provinces, one fine morning, it became a 'cornertown', so to speak, of the state of Maharashtra. I then used to pity my relatives settled there, as I thought they had been short-changed.

Our family name is Agnihotri; and most of the Agnihotris I had met in my early life were either from erstwhile Central Provinces or Uttar Pradesh. As a matter of fact, our original native village was part of Kanpur district. I, therefore, grew up in the belief that all Agnihotris were *Kanpurias*.

At the ripe and mature age of 23 years, when I joined the civil services, I had an experience which altered one of the basic features of my identity. After being selected for the Indian Administrative Service, I reported for training at the National Academy of Administration in Mussoorie, one rainy day of July, 1968. When I reached the allotted room, my room partner was already there. The moment I entered the room, he started talking to me animatedly in a language that I understood only vaguely. His name, as I had noted from the slip inserted into a panel on the door of our room, was Abhyankar. I, therefore, surmised that he was talking in Marathi. In no uncertain terms, I told him that I did not know Marathi. He was aghast. 'How could it be?' he queried. 'Don't you know that the top two brahmin clans of Maharashtra are Abhyankars and Agnihotris?' I said that, frankly speaking, I didn't. Apparently, like me, he too hadn't travelled much. I heaved a sigh of relief for my orphaned relatives settled in Nagpur, who had found themselves virtually shunted overnight from Central Provinces to Maharashtra. They had actually been sent home.

After that I have taken many such revelations in my stride. Upon disclosing my surname during certain train journeys, I have been spoken to in Kannada, Oriya, Punjabi, and Telugu. As a matter of fact, being allotted to Andhra Pradesh, I regularly used to receive invitations addressed to me as 'Agnihotrudu'. During a particular posting in Visakhapatnam, which is close to the border of Odisha, an official of the Odisha government called Mr. Hota (he regularly used to visit Visakhapatnam during weekends to dispose of files) confided in me that Hotas were actually Agnihotris. Once I had gone to Trivandram (now Thiruvananthapuram) for the inauguration of an exhibition. The chief guest was the Chief Minister of the state. After my customary welcome address, the Chief Minister gave an impassioned speech in Malayalam to an audience in excess of 3000. Suddenly, I heard the name Agnihotri being pronounced twice in succession, and once with a suffix. I asked a local officer sitting next to me as to what the Chief Minister was saying. He said that the Chief Minister was thanking me for organising the exhibition, and was, at the same time, recalling the greatness of a Malayalam poet of a similar sounding name. In all these instances, whenever I stated that I did not know the language, as I was not from that part of the country to which the speaker belonged, the language of communication used to switch automatically to English, *except once*. This time, the speaker happened to be from the Punjab. No sooner had I said that I did not belong to the Punjab, he shot back that I did not perhaps know that my ancestors were from the Punjab.

Another of the beliefs I grew up with was that somehow my surname was unpronounceable. On innumerable occasions, trying to leave a message on phone with the house attendants for the absentee 'callees', I had the discomfiture of having to repeat and break up, twist & turn the syllabi of my surname to make it understood. Still it did not work on most occasions. Actually, I could have developed a literacy rating system on the basis of whether a person was able to pronounce my surname or not. Then one day it all changed. The film *ek duje ke liye* was released. Rati Agnihotri became the instant heart-throb of millions of people. My unpronounceable name suddenly, at least for a few following years, became delectable. Acquaintances started looking up at me with a new sense of respect, particularly since the film was shot in Visakhapatnam. That, of course, was before I was posted there.

The inhabitants of the erstwhile USSR, especially of the Central Asian variety, have always had a great fascination for Indian films, thanks to Raj Kapoor's *awara*. Once I went to Moscow along with another colleague, as part of a team sent to organise the Festival of India. One day, as we were sitting in the lobby of Hotel Russia, a few young girls spotted and approached us assuming, from our appearance, that we were Indians. They started speaking to us in chaste Hindi. They introduced themselves as students of Hindi language from the University of Georgia. In the course of our conversation, they asked us to introduce ourselves. Being brought up in an Indian middle class family (which is, at times, unknowingly prudish), I said that my name was Agnihotri. My colleague, however, replied that her name was 'Rati'. 'Rati Agnihotri' they chanted and clapped.

Somewhere, in the cosmic time frame of the Stephen Hawking variety, I met Kamal Hasan, the male lead *of ek duje ke liye* fame at a film award function. When I was introduced to him, he winced, went pale in the face and said in a conspiratorial whisper, "I hope you are not related to Rati Agnihotri."

2 A South Indian Bet

Learning is a lifelong process. It is more so when it comes to understanding the culture and practices of different societies. The basic problem always is that we cannot help but pass judgment on or make assumptions about others, based on our limited knowledge, often relying on hearsay.

Let me start with myself. Being born and brought in the State of Uttar Pradesh as well as having lived there for the most part of my early life, till I joined the Indian Administrative Service and reached the National Academy of Administration (now Lal Bahadur Shastri National Academy of Administrations: LBSNAA), I did not know the difference in the language and culture of Meerut and Gorakhpur in the State of Uttar Pradesh itself, let alone the rest of India or the world beyond it.

Even the day to day experiences hold a testimony to this dichotomy. Take, for example, the people who ring my call bell or just lift the latch of the outer gate of my house to enter, without realizing that we have a dog. They run a serious risk of being given an extremely unfriendly treatment by the dog and often react with consternation.

Let me give another example from my family circle. My sister got married to a person who moved to the USA soon thereafter. They had a son, who, as a young child, came to attend a family function in which all his cohorts in the family were present. One of his cousins showed him that it was very easy to eat a raw green chilli. What she did was to pluck a chilli from the plant in the garden and swallow it, without biting into it. My sister's son did not quite see the trick and bit into another chilli given to him by the cousin. Having been brought up in the USA, and also in view of the family culinary habits, he was not used to the experience. All hell broke loose thereafter and senior intervention, short of hospitalisation, was required to retrieve the situation.

Against this back drop, let me recount a couple of my experiences after joining the IAS. I was allotted the Andhra Pradesh cadre. As part of our training at NAA. We were required to undertake *Bharat Darshan* (All India Tour), i.e. to visit a few states of India and observe the administrative system and culture in different parts of the country. It was an exercise that was carried out over a period of about two months. The total batch of trainees was divided into about eight group based roughly on the State from which they came and the State to which they were allotted. The idea was not to show them things which they had either already seen or were going to see, in any case, in the days to come. I and some other officers, who were allotted to Andhra Pradesh Cadre, found ourselves in a group which was to visit UP, Bihar, West Bengal, Assam, Manipur and Nagaland. I, of course, got to see parts of UP, which I had not seen earlier but was ironically also shown Allahabad University of which I had been an alumnus. So be it.

In the course of the long train journey, we really got to know each other. During this period, I and certain other officers, who came from the northern states and were allotted to Andhra Pradesh, had to undergo close scrutiny of the officers who were from Andhra Pradesh and were also allotted to Andhra Pradesh. On the lunch table one day the conversation veered round to the culinary habits of the people of Andhra Pradesh. I was told that the people in Andhra Pradesh were fond of hot food and, therefore, I would have to learn to enjoy dishes which contained a lot of chilli powder. In my home, we did not use too much chilli powder in daily dishes, but we did relish green chillies with our food. I was, therefore, not too daunted by the prospects and said so. There was a bottle of chilli sauce on the table. One of the Andhra-types said that if I was not worried about hot food, could I eat a spoon of chilli sauce to prove my credential? I did it with aplomb and the group was quite impressed. It was like an initiation ritual and I had passed with flying colours.

Another topic of conversation was the amount of rice that the people of Andhra Pradesh could eat in one sitting. One of the officers who belonged to Andhra Pradesh casually picked up a glass kept on the table for drinking water and said that a person could eat as much rice as a measure of raw rice that glass would hold. This analogy was somewhat difficult for me to swallow. In our home I had seen my mother, day after day, use a measure smaller than that glass on the table to take out rice to be cooked for the six of us in the family. How could one person eat more rice than six members of my family taken together? I wondered. We, of course, also ate *chapattis* too along with rice, but still. It was a huge exaggeration, I thought, and said so. They laughed in unison at my ignorance and let the matter pass.

We returned from the *Bharat Darshan* much wiser and more congealed than ever. Soon we landed up in Andhra Pradesh, each one of us in a different district, to undergo another long spell of practical training, before we were considered ripe enough to hold the reins of administration. After a while, we again assembled together; it was time for a State *Darshan* now. We were taken to different districts of the State to acquaint us with different aspects of administration and make us aware of various developmental schemes and projects. In the course of this trip, we landed up in the heart of the Andhra region, namely, Rajahmundry in the East Godavari district.

One day, our 'native' colleagues decided to visit a reputed local eatery for dinner. We sat at a table and a large banana leaf was placed in front of each of us. A waiter came and placed different types of vegetables and other accompaniments from a multi-bowl on the periphery of the banana leaf in an appetizingly decorative fashion. He went back and returned with a large metallic plate filled with steaming rice to the brim. In another hand, he held a quarter plate as a serving instrument with which he doled out portions of rice. One serving of it, I thought, would have been sufficient for my family, but before I could voice my reservations, a mountain of rice had already been stacked up on my banana leaf. I was aghast. According to the rate list of the restaurant, the customers paid for a meal and not for individual portions; which meant that a person was allowed to eat as much as he could, while he was at it. I saw some of the other customers being served second and third helpings of rice with the quarter plate, from out of the huge metallic disc. I knew I had lost the bet taken about a year ago during the *Bharat Darshan*. But my colleagues somehow skipped pointing this out to me.

3 Tea for the President

The first posting of an IAS officer as a Sub-Divisional Magistrate (SDM), also termed as Assistant Collector, Assistant Commissioner *et al* in some States of the country, is somewhat like the filmy first love or infatuation, which one always fondly or, sometimes even obsessively (of *Darr* genre), remembers. The aura of independent authority, within certain limitations, of course, is like a heady wine. It creates a sobering sense of responsibility in most of us; but sometimes it goes to the head of others. There are sagas of yeoman service to the community rendered by young and dedicated (I am wary of using the word 'committed') public servants; there are also stories of abuse of power and other types of misdemeanours. Careers have been made and lost during that brief stint of about two years. Be that as it may, the experience gathered during the district training, which precedes the first posting as well the SDM-ship itself, provides invaluable learnings, particularly because one is practically unabashedly free to learn from one's mistakes.

My first posting as SDM (in the then united Andhra Pradesh) was as Assistant Collector, Hyderabad (East). Frankly speaking, I was delighted when I got the news after more than a year and a half of district training. My posting was also the envy of my several batch-mates, particularly non-Andhraites, so to speak. They were going to rough it out in some far off sub-divisions across the State, whereas I was going to have a supposedly cozy and comfortable time in the State capital! So be it.

However, things turned out to be quite different when I reported to duty. I stayed in the State Guest House for several months, since there was no earmarked accommodation (let alone a palatial bungalow), which most of my colleagues posted in the so-called mofussil areas had. Actually, I had to rent a private one-BHK accommodation at almost equal to one-third of my the then salary in a multi-storeyed apartment (close to my office), after having surveyed several other properties, which were way beyond my means. Since I did not want to misuse my official jeep for my ever inviting private forays into the city, I bought a second-hand car with the loan, which the government so graciously provided. Soon enough we had a son, who prides himself on being a 'mulki', that is resident of the State (now Telangana) by birth. No green card here, of course. Till today, he has a smattering of Telugu, in which we converse when we want to have a private conversation among us in the company of strangers.

But my monthly budget went totally haywire. Out of my take-home salary of about Rs. 500/- in 1971, Rs. 125/- went to paying the rent and another Rs. 125/- went into paying the monthly installment of the car loan. Milk for us, particularly with a small child, was a priority. That too accounted for a princely sum of about Rs. 100/- per month. Most of the months, therefore, we were hand to mouth by the end of the fourth week of the month (we were happy with that because there are not many months in a calendar year, which have five weeks). Actually, we had a long empty talcum powder box in which we used to keep loose coins (we had paise: 5, 10, 20 25, and 50, of course); the not much revered rupee coin of today was extremely precious then. During the last week of the month, we used to move around in our Standard Super Ten (1956 model) car with that box tucked under the armpit. Once we were on the road when one of the back doors of the car flew open, and my wife, who was sitting on the back seat with our child, screamed. But there was help at hand. A cyclist behind our car kicked the door closed. Thank God. Today, after retirement, with my children having settled down, I am hard put to it to spend my monthly pension, which is half of my salary last-but-one drawn.

On the house front, as per the prescribed procedure, upon arrival in Hyderabad I had duly applied for government accommodation, hoping that the plight of the junior most and vulnerable IAS officer in the state capital would get some attention. I did the rounds of the General Administration Department (GAD); and after a wait of about 6 to 8 months, I was told that in the normal course, being the junior most, I had practically no chance. If I could meet the minister and make a 'personal' request to him, then, of course, things could brighten up. I did not consider it appropriate and asked as to what were other options. I was told that I could be given a Section Officers' quarters, which was much below my so-called status. I plumbed for it because my monthly budget was bursting at the seams. I moved into the first floor of a double-storeyed set of apartments occupied mostly by the orthodox and seasoned bureaucrats, almost twice my age and with daughters, who were cohorts of my wife. We had no problems and made friends with several of them. But they had a big one coming. When my batch-mates posted in *dur-daraz* (far-off) sub-divisions came to know about it, they were delighted (not that I had been spared during the occasional, though isolated, trips of some of them to Hyderabad when I was staying in private accommodation, which was an additional burden on my telephone budget), because the Annual Collectors' Conference was scheduled to be held shortly and they were sure to be asked by their bosses to tag along; it was the trend, if not 'trending'. All hell broke loose on the eve of the conference when the jingbang lot (rag tag and bobtail) started trooping into our first floor one-bedroom apartment to celebrate 'our reunion', at my cost. There was a lot of drama played out alongside beer, to the accompaniment of guitar, which one of them had unhelpfully brought along. We sang old Bollywood songs [they are still hugely popular (Kishore Kumar, Mohammad Rafi, Mukesh, Manna Dey, Hemant Kumar, *et al*: we were all men, you must appreciate, no ladies in our batch)] to our hearts' content, accompanied by soft strumming of the guitar. At the end of it all ('the day after' as they say), I became a *persona non grata* in my colony of Section Officers. They forbade their daughters from visiting us; some of them hastened to get them married to their *mamas* (mothers' brothers) post haste.

But it was the official role and responsibilities that took the greatest hit. I do remember my first substantial engagement as Assistant Collector. [One got designated as Sub-Collector after passing the final departmental examination, which included a tough test in Telugu language and conversation with a ryot (farmer), overseen by a senior officer. More about how to pass such an exam without tears, some other time]. It was April (the 'cruellest month' according to T. S. Eliot) of 1971. (I wish my daily/weekly diaries kept in those days had survived, to tell the exact date). It did not breed lilacs; it did not mix memory and desire, either. It brought a hailstorm which destroyed huge tracts of agricultural crops in my jurisdiction. My task was to distribute the taccavi (gratuitous) relief to the farmers, in cash, going from village to village on a fixed date and time in order to maintain transparency. I am sure I did it to the best of my ability because there were no complaints and it endeared me to my immediate superior (a very hard task master). We actually became 'family friends' and ended up watching movies together, including Rajesh Khanna starrer 'Anand'.

At this point I think it would be fair for me to define my 'jurisdiction'. Even though my office was located in the heart of Hyderabad (near *lakdi ka pul*, to be exact), my entire jurisdiction was in some of the rural areas on the outskirts of Hyderabad city. (It was subsequently made part of the Ranga Reddy District, comparable to several metropolitan cities which have been divided into rural and urban segments.) I, therefore, was a nobody in Hyderabad (proper) where I had an office and somewhat of a residence. Once my old rickety car stopped on the prestigious Tank Bund. I opened the bonnet of the car and was trying to figure out the problem, when a cop appeared on the scene. His first straight and obvious question was whether I did not know that it was a 'No Parking' zone. I, of course, said yes and tried to explain my predicament; but to no avail. I tried to impress the cop by giving him my official designation and address, when he started preparing the challan for a traffic offence. "No, no, your residential address", He said.

I sheepishly gave him the number of my Section Officers' quarters. I could see a smirk on his face. But the things did not end there. After a couple of months, sure enough, I got a summon from the court. I sought divine intervention then from a gem of Police Commissioner in Hyderabad (Dora garu), and the matter was luckily sorted out. Amen!

As regards my role and responsibilities, less said the better. Soon after I joined, there was a Non-Gazetted Officers' (NGOs') strike, which lasted a couple of months. During that period, I had the keys to my room, with which I used to open my room every day. I used to dust my table and chair. I mostly dealt with the *tappal* (dak) and was also able to carry out a modicum of official duties with the help of a few conscientious objectors. The strike ended, but it did not bring any relief in terms of performing my normal duties. When my batch of IAS officers reached Hyderabad in 1969, after completing the training at NAA, 'Pratyeka' (separate) Telangana Movement was in full swing under the able leadership of Dr. M Chenna Reddy, who later rose to become the Chief Minister of Andhra Pradesh. [The history has recently implemented itself and Telangana is a separate state now, under the stewardship of a new leader.] There were police firings all around and we saw agitationists burning tyres at road crossings. When I later joined as Assistant/Sub- Collector of Hyderabad East in 1971, I was saddled with the inevitable responsibility of enquiring into deaths that occurred due to police firings. These magisterial enquiries took a heavy toll of my time. Instead of doing the normal work that a new SDM does, I was doing court work of a different type. In any case, I was not required to do the normal court work under the Cr. P. C. on account of the Police Commissioner system having been put in place in the then Hyderabad District as a whole.

I lost out the most in terms of learning to be fluent in the Telugu language. While my other non-Andhraite colleagues, particularly those who were posted in the heart of the Andhra Region of Andhra Pradesh, had ample opportunity to try out their *tuti-phooti* (broken) Telugu on the unsuspecting and tolerant ryots, my attempts to do the same in the rural areas of Hyderabad district met with the stock response: "Why do you trouble yourself, we can understand Urdu". Actually I was complimented for my excellent command over Urdu, by which they, of course, meant Hindi.

But the most embarrassing and, therefore, memorable experience of that 'posting' was my attempt to serve tea to the President of India, who happened to be passing through my rural jurisdiction. One day, late in the evening, I received a letter from the GAD that the then President of India (Late Shri V. V. Giri) was going by train from New Delhi to Madras (now Chennai) and, on the way, his train will have a stop of about an hour at 6 am at a station called Ghatkesar, about an hour's drive from Hyderabad. It ordered me to make 'necessary arrangements'. I did not know what to do! It was too late in the evening for me to contact any one in or rush to the GAD to get the 'necessary' clarification. I called my Tahsildar of the concerned taluk, a venerable old gentlemen brought up in the traditional *nizami* culture. We poured over the near-inscrutable script of the letter and tried to decipher its implications. Why was the President stopping at a god-forsaken place like Ghatkesar for an hour? How come a measly Sub-Collector was required to make arrangements for it? Weren't the Chief Minister and the Chief Secretary, with other big-wigs in toe, required by the protocol to be present to receive and see him off? These were some of the questions we asked ourselves. The seasoned Tahsildar said that it was not for us to question the wisdom of the State government. We have been asked to be there so we should be there and attend to whatever was required to be done on the spot to the best of our ability. Then *que sera sera,* that is. The idea came to us in a flash. Six a.m. was the time for the arrival of the train. Eureka! Surely the President would like to have a cup of tea. That was it! Since we could not have offered Railway platform tea to him, I asked my wife to prepare half a dozen cups of tea to carry in a thermos flask. I was nervous and couldn't sleep well during the night. How would I, the lowest (senior) functionary of the State Government in Hyderabad, converse with the highest dignitary of the country? How should I address/salute him: Your Honour? Mahamahim? Soon the alarm clock rang. It was

4 am. I got ready and the Tahsildar arrived at 4:30 am. He had helpfully brought a couple of nice packets of biscuits. Armed with tea and biscuits, we reached the non-descript Ghatkesar railway station by about 5:30 am and waited with bated breath for the train to arrive. To our surprise, apart from us and the Station Master and a few members of the railway's staff, there was no gathering on the platform. Surely, the President was not so unpopular that nobody wanted to meet him. Punctually, at 6 am the train arrived on the platform. We waited for the doors to open and the President to alight. It was summer time and, in spite of the early hour of the day, I was sweating profusely in my woollen *bundgala*.

A large contingent of RPF and other security personnel got down from various bogies of the train and took their positions along the platform. Nothing happened for about 10-15 minutes thereafter. The President was nowhere in sight; and our patience was running out. We enquired from the security personnel as to when the President would alight and what was his programme. They were clueless. As a last resort, we asked a person who had got down from the train but was not wearing any uniform. He informed us that the train had stopped in order to enable the Hon'ble President to visit the loo in the train, because it would not have been very convenient for him to do so in the moving train.

We waited till the train had departed and had a cup of tea, with a variety of biscuits, in the august company of the Station Master. The pleasantries exchanged among us about the entire episodes are best left untold.

In the long run, I got more than even with the President. Instead of carrying tea for the President, I have had the privilege of having tea with the President on several occasions. It all started a long time ago when, as trainees, my batch called on the then President in 1969. Subsequently, on 15 August and 26 January every year, the officers, among others, are invited for tea in the evening by the President's secretariat. Whenever I was posted in Delhi, I made it a point to attend the President's tea. The last occasion was when in 2012, as Secretary-General, Rajya Sabha, I was appointed the Returning Officer for the

Election of the President of India. After I had declared the result, I went to the house of the President-Elect (Shri Pranab Mukherjee) to hand over his election certificate. I was feasted.

I got even with the President on another score too. When I was appointed to the IAS, I received a communication from the Government stating that the President was pleased to appoint me. At the end of my career, I had the pleasure of handing over the President's appointment certificate to him.

Hopefully, I may get an opportunity to have a cup of tea with the new president too, since His Excellency Ram Nath Kovind was an alumnus of BNSD College, Kanpur like me.

I never had the opportunity to work with a President. Having worked with a Vice-President as Secretary-General of Rajya Sabha, I have a better chance of having a tea-meeting with His Excellency M. Venkaiah Naidu garu since I belong to the erstwhile Andhra Pradesh cadre of the IAS.

The Prescient Watchman

Once upon a time, not very long ago, there was a president of a multi-national company, aged about 40 years, who, along with the substantial wealth of his father, had also inherited a very loyal, devoted and dedicated watchman (aged about 60 years) for guarding the household. Being a senior member of the household, the watchman was respectfully addressed as Kaka (uncle); he had actually looked after the businessman (let us call him Mohan for convenience), since his birth, as if he was actually his own nephew.

One day, as was quite common, given his wide-spread business empire, Mohan was scheduled to catch a flight to go abroad, late in the evening. However, very early in the morning that day, the venerable watchman, immediately after he had finished his night duty, came running to the house and knocked at Mohan's bedroom door. Because of his advanced age, he was out of breath when he called out "Mohan babu, Mohan babu!"

(*Contd.*)

(*Contd.*)

Though a bit annoyed at being woken up at an unearthly hour, Mohan opened the bed-room door and looked groggily at the flustered watchman.

The watchman, to Mohan's utter surprise, fell at his feet and holding them firmly with his two hands said "Babu! please cancel your trip abroad; do not go in that aeroplane".

"Why?" asked Mohan in great astonishment.

"Because, I just had a dream that the plane is going to crash."

"What nonsense"? said Mohan, "I don't believe in drcams, Kaka."

"Sir, I shall not leave your feet, until you concede my request".

After quite a few exchanges in which Mohan's wife too joined in to support the watchman's plea, the businessman agreed.

The plane did crash; the watchman had done more than the call of his duty.

Next day, Mohan called the watchman, gave him rupees one lakh (about one crore in today's value) in reward. Mohan also told the venerable watchman that he was being retired from his assignment as a watchman for having been found sleeping while on guard duty.

4 Pulse Rate: Collateral Benefit

In the days gone by, there used to be an aphorism in a Hindi dialect, viz. *ghar kee murgi dal barobar*. It meant that no value is attached to a thing that is easily available. However, an unprecedented increase in the prices of pulses (particularly the Indian universal *tuvar dal* or split red gram) has sent the pulse of the common man racing, spawning, in turn, a host of jokes and cartoons, at the cost of once humble lentils, of the 'dal banam murgi' (pulse versus chicken) genre. At this point, for the uninitiated, it may not be out of place to throw some perfunctory light on the mind-boggling range of pulses and/or lentils in use, particularly in India. Local names of some of these, along with their English equivalents, are given in the table below:

Tuvar/Toor dal	Split Red gram/Pigeon Pea
Sabut Urad	Black gram
Urad dal/Kali dal	Split Black gram
Moong	Green gram
Moong dal	Split Green gram
Chana	Bengal gram/Chickpeas (brown)
Chana dal	Split Bengal gram
Hara Chana/Cholia	Chickpeas (green)
Kabuli Chana	Chickpeas (white)
Masoor	Red Lentil
Kulthi	Horse gram

Rajma	Red Kidney Beans
Lobhia/Chawli	Black-eyed beans

The governments (State as well the Union) have *inter alia* gone into the customary overdrive against the so-called hoarders; because if hoarding happens, can raids be far behind. It has reportedly resulted in a huge haul of more than one lakh and thirty thousand metric tonnes of lentils across the country, over ten times, the quantity imported as well as proposed to be imported by the government, and practically at no cost; it is yours for the taking. However, according to one estimate; it is still only about 1/10th of the likely demand for it in the country.

These operations remind me of a couple of anti-hoarding and anti-smuggling drives, which I was part of during early part of my career. Actually, that is the carefree phase in the calling of most of the civil servants, when they hoof it, where angles would be wary of treading.

The year was 1972, when I had just completed my first year in my first posting as Sub-Divisional Magistrate (called Sub Collector) in the then State of Andhra Pradesh. The culprit on that occasion was not *dal* but fertilizers, a more precious and politically charged commodity in the so-called Rice Bowl of the country. Our *khabri* (informant) told us that in a local godown there was a stock of fertilizers, which had been diverted from its legitimate destination and hoarded for purposes of black marketing. I, along with my entourage of local Tahsildar, Block Development Officer (BDO), some village functionaries and a modicum of constabulary, reached the place unannounced. Actually, while congregating, I had not informed any member of the retinue the exact purpose of our getting together. It was around 12 noon of a working day; but the godown, which belonged to a cooperative society of which the local MLA was the President, was locked and no caretaker was in sight. We made inquiries but got no wiser. I then ordered the locks to be broken following the prescribed procedure, known as *panchnama*. The Tahsildar and the BDO got apprehensive and advised me against it. The President of the Cooperative Society happened to be a Minister of the State government. In the first flush of youth and idealism, I directed them to do what I had told them. The locks were broken and, sure enough, a huge unauthorised stock of fertilizers was unearthed, along with some innocuous material. An inventory was drawn up and the godown was sealed following the *panchnama* procedure. I returned to my office, prepared a report under the Essential Commodities Act and sent it, along with the concerned documents, to the Collector of the district for further necessary action. My job in that case was over and I proceeded to undertake other similar indiscreet mis-adventures.

Those were days of scarcities. Everything was scare and, therefore, under the 'command and control' regime (direct regulation of an industry or activity by legislation that states what is permitted and what is illegal) to a great extent. It was applicable not only to food grains and fertilizers, but also to cars, of all things. For example, if I wanted to buy a new fiat car (one of the two or, at the most, three options at that time, and the most popular, at that, for private use), the waiting time was about 18 months, even if I had the money. The 'controlled' price at that time was about Rs. 14,000 (a big sum in terms of purchase power, though). It was approximately 28 times my monthly take home salary; today the price of a decent car is only 6 times my take home pension and is available off the shelf.

Coming back to my mis-adventure, having done my job, I forgot about it till I was told by my Tahsildar that the Collector had released the seized stockpile of fertilizers. I forgot about that too, till I came to know through the grape wine that the Collector had been made an out-of-turn allotment of a fiat car. The Minister concerned was the Minister for Transport.

A few years later, I was posted as Joint Collector (Additional District Magistrate) in a district, which was facing food grains scarcity (particularly rice), but was surrounded by the legendary 'Rice Bowl'. It had little rice production, but was blessed with a slew of rice mills, some of them conveniently located at the district borders. In order to ensure that the rice millers delivered the 'levy' quantity of rice to the administration, there were restrictions on inter-district movement of paddy (un-milled rice). No paddy from other districts could enter my district for milling (of course), without a certificate from my counterpart that the levy on it had been delivered/deposited. Since most clandestine operations take place during the night, it was the duty of my team to petrol the borders and catch the trucks entering our district without the necessary certificate and *vice versa*. Occasionally I accompanied my team on these nocturnal sojourns. It was perhaps a festival holiday, and, expecting a huge haul, we went on petrol to porous points with a large team. At the dead of night, we accosted a caravan of trucks, stopped and seized them for want of necessary certificates. The trucks were brought to the district headquarters and parked in the Collectorate compound, with ample security arrangements. Next day, as expected, my subordinate staff started receiving desperate calls from local big-wigs, including the rice millers, for release of the trucks. The officers came to me for instructions; I told them to proceed as per law and get the rice milled for realization of levy and sale of the rest in the open market.

A couple of days later, one of the senior officers came to me and said: "Sir, there is great pressure. What should I do?" I told him that we were in the Chief Minister's district. If he is not bothered, why should you bother? And that put all doubts to rest.

5 Protected by Naxalites

For quite some time, there has been considerable talk, off and on, about 'good' and 'bad' terrorists/Talibans. While certain countries, in their own narrow self-interest, attempt to make a razor-fine distinction, many others, including objective observers feel otherwise. I would, however, like to recount my simultaneous encounter with 'happy' and 'unhappy' naxalites.

Naxal movement in Andhra Pradesh (AP) has had a chequered history. It began as an off-shoot of Telangana movement, which had its origin in the poor living conditions and the barbaric zamindari system in that region during the Nizam's rule. It came into its own in 1960s. The movement was considered to be strongest in Adilabad, Karimnagar, Warangal, Khammam, East Godavari, Visakhapatnam and Srikakulam districts. I happened to be posted in Khammam district in the early 1970s, when naxalism was quite widespread there.

Khammam District is a unique blend of Telangana and Andhra regions of the erstwhile Andhra Pradesh. It was carved out of Warangal (Telangana Region, now Telangana State) and East Godavari (Andhra Region, Now Andhra Pradesh State) districts. Two of its Sub-Divisions (Khammam and Kothagudem) were part of the Telangana region, while Bhadrachalam Sub-Division belonged to Andhra Region. It is the only district of erstwhile AP which has been divided between the two states after the creation of Telangana State in 2014, with a part of Bhadrachalam Sub-Division being taken over by the residual Andhra Pradesh and merged with East Godavari district. Another important feature of Khammam district is that it has extensive forests (about 47% of its total geographical area), which provides excellent hideout for covert naxal operations. The revenue systems of the two regions are quite distinct since the Telangana Region subscribes to the Nizam system while the Andhra region follows the Madras Presidency system. I had quite a tough time trying to master two different systems in order to perform my supervisory functions of *jamabandi*. Summer, particularly the period after harvesting of the Rabi crop and closing of schools, is the time when the 'operation *jamabandi*', i.e. annual reconciliation of revenue accounts of the villages, takes place. The farmers are free and the school buildings are also available for holding the *jamabandi* meetings. My responsibility as the District Revenue Officer, as the post was then named (the nomenclature has since been changed to Joint Collector), was to do a random check of the village accounts, which had already been checked by the concerned Tehsildar. The summer in Khammam could be really hot. In the revenue Division of Bhadrachalam, where I did the *jamabandi* some time earlier, I had experienced 50°C temperature. I have had other, only one of its kind experiences, in various places during my district life; another one in Khammam was watching in shock and awe the movement of an iguana on the wall of a guest house in Wyra Tehsil Headquarters.

Returning to revenue matters at hand, it was the height of summer of 1974 and I had gone to Sattupalli, along with my family (wife and two small kids aged about 3 and 1 years), for *jamabandi* operation. It was an erstwhile Taluk HQRS of Khammam District, before 'mandalisation' (through which the Taluks were replaced by smaller and a larger number of 'revenue mandals' and made co-terminus with the development Blocks, in order to take administration closure to the people) and much before the bifurcation of the composite State of Andhra Pradesh.

We were accommodated in the guest house of Public Works Department (PWD). After my work during the day, we had dinner by Petromax (a brand name for a type of pressurised paraffin lamp). Since it was hot, we decided to sleep in the guest house lawns, which were circumscribed by a thick hedge for privacy. Two beds were laid out and were covered with mosquito-nets. Late in the night, my wife woke me up to tell me that she had heard some movement on the other side of the hedge. I was aware that the *patwaris* (village accountants) from the villages, the *jamabandi* of which was due next day, used to arrive at odd hours during the night. I told my wife not to worry and go to sleep.

Next day morning, when my wife and I were sitting in the portico having our morning cuppa, she spied a figure moving suspiciously behind the pillar. My wife got scared thinking that the naxalites had come to attack us in the morning time. It was actually the Tehsildar, who did not want to come in the open, so long as I was in the company of my 'family'. I, however, persuaded the Tehsildar to come out of the hiding, which he did with great reluctance. We discussed the schedule for the day. My wife then enquired of him about what she thought was some suspicious movement in the night around the hedge of the guest house lawn. After some humming and hawing, he told us that there were some naxalites in his area who were happy with my work; but there were others who were in any case unhappy with everything. The 'unhappy' ones were keen on bumping me off. The 'happy' ones had, therefore, formed a ring around the lawn where we were sleeping in the night in order to protect us. The news was received by us with a great deal of shock and relief.

In the course of the discussion that followed, the Tehsildar told us that the police had identified the hideout of the 'unhappy' naxalites and also found out who among them was their leader. This they were able to do because their informant had taken a photograph from top of a tree of the group having its lunch in a forest clearing. The photograph showed an assembly of men sitting in a ring formation. Each one of them had in front of him a platter, in which a pile of rice and other eatables could be seen clearly. All except one were seen eating out of a banana leaf. But there was one who had a stainless steel *thali* (a metal plate for serving Indian food) before him. He obviously was the leader.

Sometime later, a gory incident took place at the district government hospital of Khammam, when the heads of the Medical Superintendent and his wife were chopped off, because he refused to treat the gun wound of a naxalite without informing the police.

6 My take away from Emergency

As we mourn the 42nd anniversary of emergency, I am reminded of my days in government during and immediately after it. On 25 June, 1975, I was in a quiet and non-descript place called Khammam, eponymous headquarter of a district in the erstwhile state of Andhra Pradesh, awaiting a posting to Delhi. My wife's medical condition at that time required treatment, which was not locally available. On request, the Government of Andhra Pradesh had agreed to sponsor my name to the Central Government for a posting in Delhi. Finally, I landed up in Delhi on a fateful day in September, 1975. Having spent past several years in the backwaters of various districts of Andhra Pradesh, I, my wife and two small kids, who had yet to go to a proper school, were completely taken aback by the hurly-burly of the metropolis. "Dub-deck, dub-deck", my younger son would chant and clap, when he saw a double decker bus.

I was posted as Under Secretary in the Department of Health, Ministry of Health and Family Welfare. When I received my posting orders, I considered it a very thoughtful gesture on the part of the Government of India, since my wife needed specialized medical treatment. Much later, I realised that it was a fortuitous occurrence and happened as part of a routine exercise; except that one of my instructors in the NAA in Mussoorie, where I was trained, happened to be the Officer on Special Duty (OSD) to the then Minister of Health and Family Welfare (Dr. Karan Singh) and had picked up my name when a panel of names was sent to the Ministry. Had he not been there, perhaps my name would have gone on doing the rounds of various Ministries, and God only knows when it would have been picked up, as actually happened a few years later, when the need arose on account of my promotion. However, my posting in the Department of Health did not help me much as far as my wife's ailment was concerned; but it came in handy when one of my sons had an accident.

It was my very first posting in a secretariat, and that too happened to be the Central Secretariat. For the first few days I sat in my room in a trance, not knowing how to deal with the files that kept on piling up. The problem was compounded because the post I was assigned, had been lying vacant for over a month; so there was no one to 'hand over charge' to me and pass on the baton, in a manner of speaking, as had been the practice in all my previous assignments in the districts thus far. I literally sat at the feet of my juniors to get the hang of it.

The emergency had cast its shadow in my room in the shape of a poster stating in Hindi: 'batein kam kaam jyada' (talk less, work more). The corridors were quiet; the officers and employees were largely to be found in their rooms. At a personal level, I remember my car being stopped ostensibly for a traffic offence one night by the Sanjay Gandhi Brigade for having turned left from Connaught Place outer circle into Kasturba Gandhi Marg (Curzon Road) while the traffic light was turning amber. I was allowed to go after some discussion. Given the chaotic nature of traffic on Delhi roads these days, I wish government would appoint such traffic wardens officially.

During emergency, there was a lot of urgency and many heretofore unacceptable ideas were being tried out with élan. One such idea pursued by the Department of Health was to post Administrators (in lieu of the existing Hospital Superintendents) at its two prestigious hospitals, namely the Wellington (subsequently renamed Ram Manohar Lohia) and Safdarjung hospitals. I and a doctor from PGI, Chandigarh, were selected for this purpose. We were deputed to attend a Course for Senior Hospital and Health Services Administrators organized by the International Hospital Federation at the

Kings Fund College for a period of 10 weeks in July-September 1977. Things were turning out rather well for me. First came my promotion as Deputy Secretary, albeit on an *ad hoc* basis, dot on the due date (1 May, 1977), when a temporary vacancy arose on account of a south Indian Deputy Secretary helpfully going on long home leave. (He conveniently returned only after I had departed for the training programme). Then came my very first trip abroad, that too to 'dear old Blighty', for 10 weeks!

But I shall spare the reader details of my trip abroad for the time being, because what followed was a unique pendulous movement in my career. The Government had changed even before I went to UK; but the wheels of government move slowly, though they grind fine. My mentor, the OSD, had moved out with the Minister. Given the twin facts of lifting of emergency and the change in government, the 'administrator move' had perhaps been challenged by the medical fraternity of the concerned hospitals while I was away. So when I returned, not only the 'southern' Deputy Secretary had come back and nicely taken his position, but there was no posting as Administrator of any of the hospitals waiting for me either. The new government had scrapped the decision. I, therefore, returned and joined back on the lower post of Under Secretary. To rub salt on my wounds, the additional allowance of the post of Deputy Secretary, paid to me for the period I was abroad, was recovered from me, since I did not join as Deputy Secretary on return from UK. To bring some cheer, I had a few interesting encounters (direct as well as indirect) with the new Minister of Health and Family Welfare. More about it elsewhere.

Since there was no possibility of a vacancy of a Deputy Secretary arising in the Ministry of Health and Family Welfare in the near future, a proposal was sent to the Department of Personnel to find a berth for me elsewhere. Days turned into weeks and weeks into months, but there was no news. In the meanwhile, the Department of Health, helpfully, promoted me to the post of Deputy Secretary, as and when an officer went on leave. So I underwent cyclical and iterative interchanges between Under Secretary and Deputy Secretary, from time to time. To add to my woes, my younger son (all of 4 years in age) decided to take a short cut from our second floor flat in Asia House, Kasturba Gandhi Marg, to the ground floor, by sliding down the railing of the staircase (as he had seen some older children doing it). He fell in no time, came crashing to the ground and broke his crown. We were in and out of hospitals (Ram Manohar Lohia and AIIMS) for next three months. I was on leave and, occasionally, visited the Department of Personnel to check the developments relating to my career's progression. I met the Secretary, Department of Personnel too in my desperation; he was a senior colleague from my cadre of Andhra Pradesh. He promised to do his best and get me a 'good' posting. He told me that a useless post of a Deputy Secretary had been lying vacant in his own Department for over seven months, but he would not advise me to take it.

A little over a year after this saga began on 1 May, 1977, I got two letters from two different divisions of the Department of Personnel, almost on the same day. One of them informed me that my three year tenure as Under Secretary to Government of India was coming to an end soon, and wanted me to apprise them whether I would like to report back to Government of Andhra Pradesh immediately or I would like to avail of some leave before reversion. The other letter gave me the good news that I had been posted as Deputy Secretary in the Department of Personnel, on the same post which the Secretary of the Department, a few months ago had described as 'useless', namely, Deputy Secretary (Vigilance-II). My tenure too had been extended by one year. Detailing my forays on that post would need another article.

When I joined the Department of Personnel, the Secretary had changed. Later, through a fortuitous coincidence, I happened to see the file relating to my posting in the Department of Personnel and found that my benefactor had already signed the file approving the proposal to post me as Deputy Secretary (Vigilance-II), when he was describing the post as 'useless' and promising to get me a 'good' posting.

7 An Arsenal of Political Allegations

If Dickens were alive today and in India, he would be smiling like a Cheshire cat and muttering, under his breath, of course, "What the Dickens!" Because in 2015, as we celebrate 200th anniversaries of the Battle of Waterloo and Charles Dickens' family moving to London, we are indeed living in the best of times and the worst of times. Some consider it as a spring of hope, but others are convinced that the winter of despair is not far behind.

Allegations and counter allegations are flying thick and fast, all around us. While the past regime has been hopelessly cornered, the new one, after raising high hopes, has got mired in several controversies; the latest among them being the episode variously described as Lalitasana/Raga Lalit/ Lalitgate. And this is when we thought we had woken up in the heaven of freedom, leaving the '-gated' community far behind. One uncanny observer has described it as 'women-gate', as suddenly four prominent women politicians are allegedly involved in various, some common and others differentiated, imbroglios.

Of course, as is to be expected, skeletons are tumbling out of cupboards kept so far safely locked in the corridors of power. There is a spate of cases being filed against the high and mighty for corruption, causing wrongful loss to the state, accumulation of assets in excess of known sources of income, misuse of office, so on and so forth.

In June 2015, the Enforcement Directorate has registered two Enforcement Case Information Reports (ECIRs) under the Prevention of Money Laundering Act (PMLA) against Shri Chhagan Bhujbal, the NCP leader, suspecting illegal transactions to the tune of Rs 900 crore in all. It has been reported that Enforcement Directorate has simultaneously conducted searches at multiple locations pertaining to the former Minister of the Government of Maharashtra.

On 17 June, 2015, the CBI registered an FIR against former Union Textile Minister Shri Shankarsinh Vaghela, and others in connection with an irregular land transfer of prime mill land in Mumbai to a private developer that allegedly led to a loss of around Rs 709.27 crore to NTC.

On 18 June, 2015 CBI registered a Preliminary Enquiry (PE) against Shri Virbhadra Singh, Chief Minister of Himachal Pradesh, to probe disproportionate assets acquired by the former Minister of Steel, Government of India, and his family members. FIRs have been filed by the Lokayukta of Karnataka against two former Chief Ministers, namely B. S. Yeddyurappa and H. D. Kumaraswamy (belonging to two different parties opposed to each other) in a land scam relating to denotification of a prime plot to benefit Kumaraswamy's relative.

Amidst all these revelations, with Delphic as well as Orwellian prescience, comes the news about Shri Lal Krishna Advani stating that the country's political system has still not come to terms with the Emergency of 1975. Since the imposition of Emergency during 1975-77, "I don't think anything has been done that gives me the assurance that civil liberties will not be suspended or destroyed again. Not at all," Advani told an English daily. "Of course, no one can do it easily. But that it cannot happen again — I will not say that. It could be that fundamental liberties are curtailed again," he added.

A case in point, which prophetically came to light a little after Shri Advani's observations, is questioning the loyalty of the Rajya Sabha TV channel on the ground that it did not give adequate coverage to the Rajpath event on the World Yoga Day. The channel authorities, of course, responded by stating: "We are not obliged to be the mouthpiece of the government".

Earlier a BJP General Secretary had questioned the absence of the Vice President of India and the Chairman, Rajya Sabha at the same event, irrespective of the fact that he had not been invited.

Observing this amalgam of events in a kaleidoscopic whirl, my mind went back in time to the year 1977, when in a major turn of events, the ruling Congress lost control of India. The hurriedly put together Janata alliance of parties opposed to the ruling Congress party, for the first time in independent India, came to power winning 298 out of 543 seats in the Lok Sabha (Lower House) of the Parliament of India. Morarji Desai was chosen as the leader of the alliance in the newly formed parliament and, thus, became India's first non-Congress Prime Minister on March 24, 1977. The scenario was somewhat similar to Indian Government, immediately after independence. The ruling party had no trust in the existing system and was eager to expose the misdeeds of the party, which they had uprooted, during its rule in the past three decades. It is another matter that the dream of heaven did not last very long.

Be that as it may, the Desai government proceeded to establish inquiry commissions and tribunals to investigate allegations of corruption and human rights abuses by members of Indira Gandhi's government, political party and the police forces. Specific inquiries were instituted on Sanjay Gandhi's management of the state-owned Maruti Udyog Ltd., the activities of the former Minister of Defence Bansi Lal and the 1971 Nagarwala scandal. Both Indira and her son Sanjay were charged with allegations of corruption and briefly arrested.

Several inquiry commissions were set up under the Commissions of Inquiry Act, 1952. The mother of all commissions was, of course, the omnibus Shah Commission appointed by Government of India to inquire into all the excesses committed during the emergency (1975-77).

Prominent among other Commissions of Inquiry were those set up to inquire into the alleged misdeeds of three Chief Ministers: J. R. Vimadlal Commission to enquire into the charges levelled against Shri J. Vengal Rao, Chief Minister of

Andhra Pradesh; A. N. Grover Commission to enquire into the allegations made against Shri Devraj Urs, Chief Minister of Karnataka; and P. Jaganmohan Reddy Commission to enquire into the allegations levelled against Shri Bansi Lal, Chief Minister of Haryana. In each case a detailed memorandum had been presented to the Prime Minister leading to appointment of the Commission of Inquiry.

In mid-1978, when I joined the Department of Personnel, Ministry of Home Affairs as Deputy Secretary (Vigilance-II), various Commissions of Inquiry were firmly in the saddle. While the Shah Commission was being serviced by the officers of the main Ministry of Home Affairs, I had the responsibility *inter alia* to provide requisite support to the others inquiring against the three Chief Ministers.

One day, we received a request from one of the Commissions to forward to it, any other petitions received and pending against the concerned Chief Minister or relating to the terms of reference of the Commission. I called my Under Secretary to delve into the Record Room in order to dig out the information required. A few days later, I was presented a set of about 10 files relating to pending petitions/memoranda against various VIPs, including present and former Chief Ministers, former Union Ministers and so on. Upon carefully going through these files, I discovered a minefield of very well orchestrated and meticulously documented set of allegations in each one of them. There was none relating to the Commission which had sought the information, but, belonging to the then Andhra Pradesh Cadre of the IAS, I distinctly remember the memorandum relating to K. Brahmananda Reddy, former Chief Minister of Andhra Pradesh and the preceding Home Minister of Government of India. He was indeed, a stalwart among politicians of his times, and a maverick at that. The memorandum was indeed of gargantuan proportions, and specificity and precision of the allegations made me believe that it must have been drafted by someone very closed to Mr. Reddy, perhaps under duress.

All the petitions pertained to stalwarts and satraps of the Indian political system of those days were received during the previous regime, from time to time, and were kept in the cold storage in the best Kautilyan tradition. You behave and keep the secrets or else we know how to go after you. That is another facet of the events leading up to the emergency of 1975.

8 My First Trip Abroad

By the standards of a person who had moved to Delhi straight from a sprawling bungalow in a district headquarters, the two-room tenement in Asia House was an apology for accommodation. But it was, on the whole, much better than a slightly bigger accommodation in RK Puram (a locality farther away from central Delhi) for various reasons. First, comparatively, it had much more storage space on account of built-in cupboards and lofts. Being a recent construction, it was also spic and span, with sparkling bathroom fittings. But most importantly, it was in close proximity to my small children's school.

Being a mere Under Secretary in the Government of India, it was a harsh grind. I was not eligible even to a modicum of facilities I enjoyed in the district, including transportation to and fro the work place. Luckily, I had a rickety old car (Standard Super 10, an almost 20-year old model) to ferry myself. But providence decreed otherwise, when some electrical parts of the car were stolen and it cost me a fortune to get them replaced. I, therefore, decided to dispose it of when I got nominated for a foreign training programme for 10 weeks. If it could be vandalized when I was there, I shuddered to think the shape I would find it in on my return from my longish absence. I got a princely sum of Rs. 2,500/- from the sale of the car. I dipped into my shallow pockets to add another Rs. 2,000/- to it in order to buy a black & white ECIL TV in order to provide some entertainment to my nuclear family by way of weekly *chitrahar* (selection of film songs) and a movie, the best they could get.

Naturally, I was excited. I may have had the best of country life in the district; but going abroad, that too for the first time, was a different matter all together. A decision had been taken by my Ministry of Health and Family 'Planning' (which was subsequently changed to 'Welfare') to send two officers to UK to get them trained in Hospital Administration in order to take over as administrators of two prestigious hospitals, namely Wellington (since renamed RML) and Safdarjung, on return from training. I was to be one of them; the other was a doctor from PGI Chandigarh. Of course, it is another matter that by the time we returned from training, a new government was firmly in saddle and the proposal was shelved for good.

But go abroad, I did; in right royal style because the whole programme was funded by the British Government. One early morning, I boarded a British Airways flight with foreign exchange (in dollars, as advised) equivalent of Rs. 50/-. The flight had started from Dhaka and was to fly to Heathrow via Delhi and Doha. It was a small plane (by the present-day standards) with a seating capacity of about a hundred. When I entered the plane, there were very few passengers in it. It being a Saturday in the month of July, only a few passengers boarded it from Delhi. With only Doha to come before the plane landed at its destination, I wondered about the logic of the stoppages. It must be a loss-making route, I thought. But come Doha, and the plane filled up in no time with raucous youngesters being carted right up to the gates of the plane in their big limousines. Soon after the plane took off and the seat belt sign was switched off, there was a sudden spurt in activities, with the young men going on a spree of ordering liquor to sooth their scarcely parched throats. I gathered that they were all rich and dandy, perhaps going to London for a few days to paint the town red, as they say. It was my first encounter with the oil rich. I would have loved to have an afternoon beer myself, but with very little money in my pocket, I avoided the temptation. We reached Heathrow with the boisterous crowd giving no sign of a let up. I was wrong; the route was a very profitable one indeed, by any standard!

At the Heathrow, a couple of things stood out. My friend had brought with him some mangoes for his friends and relatives in the UK. The customs authorities, however, did not take very kindly to it. They were pulled out from his baggage and simply binned. Imagine a couple of kilos of precious alphonsos being chucked out just like that? My mouth watered; given a choice, we could have polished them off at the airport itself. Be that as it may, my colleague's discomfiture was soon dispelled when we came out of the airport and he was mobbed by a motley crowd of his friends and relatives, who had come to receive him. I noticed several of them stuffing his pockets with one Pound notes, to equip him for the days ahead. The importance of the gesture could be gauged by the fact that for the duration of the training programme, our daily allowance was going to be two Pounds per day. A person from the institute where we were going to be trained had come to receive us; and he guided us to our hostel *via* a journey by the tube in order to explain to us the intricacies of travelling by that mode. The accommodation was very nice, and I did not have to share it with anyone. The fittings and fixture were indeed of a very high quality and looked so fresh, bright and clean, unlike what I was used to in India.

In the hospital administration programme, we were a motley crowd of persons from Asia, Africa and South America. The authorities kept us quite busy with classroom instructions and field visits. The daily allowance of £ 2 turned out to be quite inadequate, since during a trip to a nearby Indian restaurant a few days later, I had to cough up £ 1.75 for a plate of chicken curry and one Nan. We survived because we were provided a working cold lunch during the working week days at the institute; in the evening we made do with bread, butter, jam, cucumber, and tomato. There were a few nurses in the group and, occasionally, we had a pooled lunch in which the ingredients brought from the market were cooked by them in the community kitchen. Towards the end of the programme, we were invited by a faculty member for dinner to his home (the castle of every Englishman), where after the meal was over, I found the female members of our group helping the hostess in doing the dishes in the pantry.

The daily routine was quite monotonous, except that one day my colleague went to meet up with one of his umpteen friends and relatives and was mugged in an alleyway during his return in the night. Of course, none of his acquaintances ever came to look him up in the hostel, having done their duty at the time of receiving him at the airport. Walking the streets, day in and day out, occasionally in the rain, my shoes gave way. I had not brought a spare pair, so I went looking for a shoe repair shop. I found one and, with great trepidation, asked whether he could attend to my shoes. He took one look at me and quoted an exorbitant sum of perhaps £ 2 (equal to my daily allowance), which I could ill afford. In India, it would have cost not more than a rupee at the most. I moved around with a somewhat cracked shoe for the remainder of my stay. Towards the end of my stay, I had saved some money with which I was able to buy a couple of Marks and Spencer shirts @ £ 4 each for myself, a cassette player and a mixie for my wife and some Lego-type games for my kids.

All good things must come to an end, as they say. The Course Coordinator, who was the master of ceremonies in the concluding session of the programme, thanked each one of us individually. Suddenly, I was asked to respond on behalf of the participants. I was quite unprepared and at a loss because I did not remember the names of all those who had interacted with us. In order to wriggle out of a tricky situation, I, *inter alia*, said that I too would have liked to thank the faculty and the support personnel individually, but that would have taken a lot of everyone's precious time. This understatement generated a murmur of approbation; I wouldn't like to call it a laugher in deference to the British sense of humour and their way of appreciating its presence in others.

On return to India, as I entered my one bedroom flat in Asia House, New Delhi, my eyes chanced on the wash basin in the lobby-cum-dining area. Compared to its earlier spic and span appearance, it now looked a little off colour.

Columbus at Crossroads

In 1492 a Spanish trans-atlantic maritime expedition by Christopher Columbus led to the Discovery of America, a new continent previously unknown in Europe. Columbus was an Italian navigator sailing for the Spanish Crown. He sought a westward route to Asia, which led to the discovery of a New World. Believing he had arrived in Asia or the Indies, he coined the misnomer 'West Indies' for the Antilles, where he had reached. Ultimately, the American continent and collection of islands of the Western Hemisphere came to be known as the Americas. It was serendipity at its best.

After about 6 months' voyage, Columbus landed back in Barcelona, to a hero's welcome. However, as usual, there were some sceptics. All he had done was row; what was so great about it? In any case, he had not reached Asia, to which he had set out to find a westward route.

Columbus, the toast of the town, was sitting in a pub recounting his experiences to an admiring group of friends. One of the sceptics, somewhat inebriated, came up to the bar and said in a loud voice: "What's so great? You just rowed and rowed and arrived at some place you had not even set out to reach in the first place."

Suddenly there was pin drop silence, in the midst of joviality. After a little while Columbus asked the bartender to get him a boiled egg. When it arrived, he asked the sceptic to make the egg stand on the table. He tried and tried, as best as he could with his unsteady hand, but failed. Columbus asked him to give the egg back to him. He picked a knife and broke and cut one end of the egg and made it stand on the table top.

"Wha's so great? I too could've done it" The sceptic said.

"Then, why didn't you do it?" said Columbus.

9 A Tale of Two Ministers

Occasionally in one's career, an employee gets to work with two different bosses in succession, who are as strikingly different as chalk and cheese or, as they say, 'poles apart'. I have had my quota of such bosses, while in the same job. For the most part, my tenures on various positions were comparatively stable; in the course of which, I changed bosses two to three times, in a manner of speaking. 'A happy go lucky boss' was, in quick time, replaced by a reticent and 'committed' officer, who, in turn, was succeeded by a 'street-smart' and extremely voluble sample, who didn't allow others to get a word in edgeways. It requires tremendous capacity to adjust with changing circumstances, because an act or observation which may go down well with one, may get the other's goat. It may also, sometimes, require fine tuning of one's biological clock. I had one Chief Minister, who started serious work late in the evening and, occasionally, one got home by 2 am; his successor's office dished out appointments beginning at 4 am. But it was in the Ministry of Health that I had the most extraordinary experience of 'boss diversity'.

My posting in the Ministry of Health and Family Welfare in the mid-1970s was fortuitous, but peppered with some exciting experiences. In the course of my stay of about three years there, I had the opportunity to watch the performance of two ministers, mostly from the sidelines. The first minister was suave and scholarly. The second one was down to earth; actually, he had been pulled across the floor of the Parliament on a couple of occasions as an MP during the previous regime. One was born great and the other had achieved greatness.

I was extremely grateful to the first minister, even before I met him, for having signed the file which gave me a posting in his Ministry. In retrospect, it turned out to be a blessing in disguise. I had occasion to listen to his scholastic discourses on a couple of occasions. However, the most memorable event in which I played a minor role was the passing of The Cigarettes (Regulations of Production, Supply and Distribution) Act, 1975. It made mandatory statutory health warnings on all tobacco products, including those of the chewable variety like *gutkha* and *pan masala*. The warning text, written in English but in small letters, said "STATUTORY WARNING: CIGARETTE SMOKING IS INJURIOUS TO HEALTH" and for chewable tobacco, it read, "TOBACCO IS INJURIOUS TO HEALTH," written in both English and Hindi. At that time, the issue was the size of the lettering, today it is the size of the graphic pictorial warnings. In the course of the speech introducing the Bill, the minister admitted that one special reason for his passionate advocacy of the ills of smoking was the fact that he had been a passive smoker since his marriage.

There was a sea change in the work culture of the Ministry with the change in guard, which brought with it a new minister. The personal staff of the Minister did not comprise seasoned bureaucrats; it consisted of persons who had his trust albeit without any administrative experience. Instead of preparing succinct and cryptic answers to Parliament questions as of yore, we were directed to provide complete details on the topic from the beginning of time. During Parliament sessions, it was my responsibility to ensure that all the replies relating to my charge had been received by the Parliament Section of the Ministry, duly approved by the minister. One day, it so happened that a particular file did not come back from the minister. It was very late in the evening and the minister had already gone home; his staff too was not around. With great trepidation we went to the minister's residence and requested the staff there to check whether by any chance the file was there. After a lot of search, the file was located in the washroom and we breathed a sigh of relief.

There are several other incidents that come to mind, some of which I was a witness to; others are apocryphal. I distinctly remember one day when we were involved in a serious discussion on some topic in the minister's chambers. As the clock struck one, an attendant entered the room with a large aluminum tiffin carrier and announced to the minister that his lunch had arrived. He got up from his chair and went to the table on which the tiffin was kept. He opened the carrier, smelled each one of the containers and expressed satisfaction with the contents. He then returned to his chair and the discussion was resumed.

Being new to government, neither he nor his personal staff was familiar with the intricate filing system of the central government. In brief, each file has two parts, kept, most of the time, within the same folder. The right side is called 'Correspondence', which contains the letters and other documents on the subject. The left side contains what is called the 'Notes', in which are recorded the notings on the subject by the multifarious hierarchy of bureaucrats, from time to time. One day, a very senior lady officer was sitting in front of the minister and explaining the details of the case dealt with in a file. Upon being asked to show a particular letter, first the officer requested the minister to turn to a specific page in the file. When the minister was unable to locate the paper, the officer went round the table and, standing next to him, helpfully tried to turn the pages of the file to get to the relevant correspondence. The minister was not pleased and asked the lady to go back to her chair, while muttering something about the sleeveless blouse that she was wearing.

India was on the verge of being declared a small pox free country. A big function was organised on the occasion by the WHO to make a presentation about how the certification was achieved. The minister was the chief guest. He had gone to his constituency and was to return on the day of the event. He came a little late and was looking a bit under the weather after a long and tiresome road journey. The lights were switched off in the hall and a video presentation started. After about 10 or 15 minutes, a snoring sound was heard, but it stopped after some time. When the presentation was over, the lights came on and we saw the minister resting his head, circumscribed by his hands, on the table, fast asleep. His private secretary goaded him and he woke up. He read out his acceptance speech, first in Hindi and then in English, in deference to the foreign audience present on the occasion.

Talking of foreigners, an apocrypha comes to mind. After lunch, the minister as well as his personal staff was used to having a siesta. For the minister, a very low wooden cot was kept on the floor of his chamber with a modicum of linen. One day, an appointment was given to a couple hailing from a Swiss NGO to meet the minister immediately after lunch. The couple arrived in time but there was no one to attend to them in the minister's office. Since the door to minister's office was not locked, they pushed it and, upon finding no resistance, went in. They saw the minister sleeping in his bed on the floor. They were wondering what to do next when the minister opened his eyes and squinted at the phenomenon hovering above him. Being a bit groggy, he remained fixed in that posture for a few seconds. The lady smiled and, after making a brief gesture of lifting her skirt ever-so-slightly above her knee, said: "No, Mr. Minister; it is not what you think. I am wearing undies."

10 Transparency in Government

There is a lot of stress these days on transparency in government. But it was not always so. Not so long ago, we had the Officials Secrets Act rather than the Right to Information Act, which is now a very important instrument of making information about the working of the government transparent and accessible to the citizens.

The year was late 1968 or may be 1969. It was an informal interaction between the current batch of trainees with a Secretary to Government of India in the common hall of the NAA (as the present LBSNAA was then called). A questioning hand was ever so tentatively raised. The visiting dignitary stopped and graciously gave an opportunity to the owner of the hand to make his intervention. The question was blunt and stunned all of us:

"How is it that probationers with connections get the cadre of their choice, while others' requests are not at all considered?" Or something to that effect.

The oblique reference was to the dignitary's daughter, who was one of the probationers in the batch. There was that expected pin drop silence in the room; it was definitely a misdemeanor, if not an outright sacrilege. The Director made an attempt to divert the attention by trying to move on to other raised hands. The guest, of course, thought otherwise. He suggested to the questioner that he should come to Delhi where he would be explained the cadre allotment procedure in detail. The officer went to Delhi and came back apparently satisfied, because the matter was not raised again.

It is difficult to imagine the scenario; but it was an unusual response to a difficult proposition. All credits to the sagacity of the senior officer, who understood the concern of a young recruit and wanted to ensure that he did not lose faith in the system.

Cadre allotment has always been, a contentious issue and cause of much heartburn. Even though the IAS, IPS and IFoS call themselves All India Services, the desire to work in one's homestead, is always strong. Over the years, officers have applied for change in cadre for various reasons, including being the only son of a family with a large landed property to be managed. There have been marriages of convenience between officers of two different cadres in order to get (if not the home state) at least a state near the home state. My reaction to my own cadre allotment was somewhat different. First, I did not have a real home state, since my father was the first among the family members to move to UP for higher studies and then took up a job there. Secondly, we did not have 'landed' or any other property in UP. Finally, given the cadre allotment system then in vogue, my rank in the IAS examination was not high enough to deserve the so-called home cadre. I was informed about my 'cadre' by my newly acquired cadre mates, who were 'in the zone'. My immediate reaction was: 'Oh, so I shall get to see a new place'. Having not travelled very much so far, the desire to see new places was strong. Further, I was assured by the 'cadre mates' that it was a good state to be in, though I needed no such assurance, being ignorant of the cadre environment and its impact on one's official and personal life; which I came to know much later.

About a decade later, I happened to be posted in the Department of Personnel and Training, one of the functions of which is cadre allotment to IAS officers. The concerned Deputy Secretary narrated to me an interesting episode over our daily luncheon meeting. One day, he got a call from the reception that a young man was there to see him. On further enquiry, he was told that the man had recently cleared the civil services examination and was on his way to the Lal Bahadur Shastri National Academy of Administration, Mussoorie. As regard the purpose of his visit the Deputy Secretary was told that it was personal. Even though a little intrigued, he gave the go ahead for the meeting. The man came. He appeared to be very suave as well as ingratiating from his conversation. After the initial small talk, the man said that he wanted to find out about cadre allotment. The Deputy Secretary told him that the exercise was under way and the cadres would be made public after a couple of months. The man did not seem satisfied. The Deputy Secretary thought that perhaps he wanted to know the procedure for cadre allotment. He proceeded to painstakingly explain the broad features of the guidelines prescribed by the government for the purpose. The man listened to him patiently. Having heard him out, in the end, he said:

"Sir, I haven't come to find out how cadre allotment is done, but how it can be done. How can I get the cadre of my choice?"

Understandably the Deputy Secretary was shocked to hear such an indecent proposal and proceeded to dispose him of as nicely and as soon as he could.

11 Drama at the Airport

"Sir, the Finance Minister wants to speak to you". My PA told me over the intercom.

"Please give me the line", I said.

In a little while, I heard the Minister's voice: "Agnihotri garu", He said firmly but politely in Telugu, "Please don't hand over charge of the District Collector". He went on to explain that a move was afoot to cancel my transfer orders.

"*Chustam*, sir", I replied after hearing him out. It was a standard and stereotyped, albeit much abhorred, reply of a typical bureaucrat in situations in which he did not want to commit himself. It meant, "I shall see".

I had been in Visakhapatnam as the Collector and District Magistrate (CDM) for about 6 months when a Minister (a different one) had landed up to review the functioning of his Department in the district. According to the statutory division of work between me and the officer next in command, the Joint Collector, the subject of review was part of latter's jurisdiction. There was, in any case, a whole retinue of staff belonging to the Minister's own Department stationed in the district. But the Minister insisted that he would like me to be present for the review. The Minister had been briefed well. At the start of the meeting he reeled out data about the shortfalls in the performance of his staff in the district. At the end he asked me to explain. I suggested that, with the Minister's permission, I would ask the Joint Collector to respond. The Minister did not permit, he wanted me to reply. Being broadly aware of the problems and issues in the district I tried to make out a case in defence of his staff. The Minister was not satisfied and got up and left the meeting in a huff, saying "*chustam*" as he left.

And "see" he did. A few days later, rumours started floating around that I was going to be shifted. A month or so later, I had to go to Hyderabad to attend a meeting convened by the Chief Secretary. It was the month of May. At the end of the meeting I sought an audience with the Chief Secretary. I met him in his private chamber and asked him whether there was any move to shift me. If there was, I would do the rounds of schools in Hyderabad for the admission of my children in the new session that was about to begin. The Chief Secretary smiled and said that there was no truth in the rumours and that I should not worry. At the end of the brief interaction, while leaving, I said: "Sir, your predecessor was gracious enough to post me to Visakhapatnam for my first assignment as District Collector. In case the government decides to shift me, please do not post me to another district, because it would be a demotion. I would like to have a posting in Hyderabad." According to a well established convention in Andhra Pradesh those days, officers were posted as CDM, Visakhapatnam, only after they had been CDM of at least one other district. It must be said to the Chief Secretary's credit that he honoured this request.

The orders came in September. I waited for the officer who was to replace me in order to hand over charge to him. He had been the CDM of Visakhapatnam earlier. Actually, in a sense, he was a victim of local politics. The district had two groups of the ruling party, ably lead by two MLAs. Depending on which group was in the good books of the Chief Minister of the day, the concerned MLA used to become a Minister in the cabinet and used to dictate local politics. One such leader had earlier favoured the outgoing CDM, when he happened to be a Minister. The Chief Minister changed and the mantled passed on to the MLA, who was the leader of the other group; and he sought and obtained a change in the CDM. I succeeded his successor. But again the tables were turned and the previous MLA came into favour and sought the return of the CDM, who had earlier been unceremoniously removed. I happened to be in the seat at that moment and, therefore, became an unwitting victim of the political drama. But the path to glory was not smooth, the group which was temporarily out of favour had some well-wishers among the ruling elite and attempted to stall the move to bring back the earlier CDM.

Several days went by but there was no sign of my replacement. I was in touch with the happenings in Hyderabad political circles. The news came that the new CDM had come to the airport but was not allowed to board the plane by the supporters of the local group, which had got him removed earlier. I thought that enough was enough. I did not want to be a pawn in the murky game of political chess. I spoke to the Chief Secretary and sought his permission to hand over charge to my next in command, the Joint Collector. He permitted and I started to complete the formalities for my departure to facilitate the arrival of the officer posted to replace me and thus avoid the embarrassment to the Chief Secretary of having to retract the orders issued. The Finance Minister, who had spoken to me earlier, spoke to me again, but I had handed over charge by then.

I reached Hyderabad to take charge of my new assignment, leaving my family behind, in order to make my posting a *fait accompli*. As I came out of the arrival lounge at Hyderabad airport, I could hear some commotion in front of the adjoining departure lounge. I was later told that the supporters of the group that did not want CDM-designate back in Visakhapatnam were raising slogans, even as the police stealthily escorted him to the aircraft.

12 Bonding over the Boss

The All India Services, the Indian Administrative Service in particular, are somewhat unusual when it comes to maintaining human relations. The officers shift not only from one location to another but also from one type of assignment to another, often a very different one, say, from health to finance. In each assignment, one makes friends with his/her colleagues; some relationships become quite strong, but most of them fade away over time with the change in location and/or department. I can recall several such close friendships, the objects of which are nowhere in the horizon now. I do not know where they are and what they are doing. Names of some of them, I have difficulty in recollecting.

The most frequent and perhaps the strongest bonding with a colleague occurs at the workplace when you share an obnoxious boss, who tends to be the biggest fixer of them all (call it Fevicol, Quickfix, Fevikwik, Araldite, All Fix or whatever). And such relationships last and last for no other rhyme or reason.

My first such bonding took place in the first decade of my career, when I and a junior officer had a particularly eccentric boss as the collector of the district in which we both were posted. The collector had a great love for the written word. He wanted a detailed report on all administrative events, big or small. Thus most of our time used to be spent on producing reams and reams of written (typed in those days) paper rather than in solving the actual problems of the citizens, whom we are mandated to serve. The boss really loved paper. 'He must have been a termite in his previous life', we used to joke among ourselves. He was changed sooner than expected and the new boss knew the problem we had been facing. He was actually sent by the Chief Minister (whose district it was) with the direction that a lot of paper work had been done, he should now go and do some work. My junior colleague, with whom I shared the travails of the 'paper boss', not only became a close lifelong friend, but almost a member of my family over time. Such was the hard bounding we got into!

A few years later, another bonding took place when I and another colleague were at the receiving end of the ire of our common boss, due to an unfortunate misunderstanding. It was the fastest fix, and started on day one when we together (having only recently met for the first time) called on the boss, who too had recently joined. She had wanted us to brief her about our programmes and priorities before she formally called on the Chief Minister. But we were late for some reason (which is a little vague at this point of time: it could have been traffic on the way or confusion about the location of her office room or even the time at which she wanted us to meet her or even the fact that she was called in by the CM's office earlier than scheduled) and, therefore, she was ushered into the CM's chamber before we had an opportunity to brief her. All hell broke loose when she returned to her room and found the two of us waiting there. She chided us no end for our unprofessional and careless attitude. And since this was the first impression, it was stored away permanently in the deep recesses of her mind. We failed to gain her confidence for quite some time thereafter. It was only after several successful ventures, for which we duly gave her all the credit, that we got into her good books and also, perhaps, got good annual confidential reports from her, if the progression of our future careers is any guide. But that apart, in the meanwhile, my friendship with my co-sufferer grew by leaps and bounds. We continued to be in touch irrespective of changes in locations and departments. One example of it was that during my study leave in 1991, when I was cut off from the rest of the working world for all practical purposes, I got a phone call (prior to the mobile era) from this colleague, who was then posted in Washington, to inform me about the unfortunate demise of Rajiv Gandhi, who was killed by a human bomb. This again was the period prior to the proliferation of TV channels; and we had access only to broadcasts for a limited time on the national channel (Doordarshan) and, therefore, would have had to wait for quite some time to get that news.

The bonds have continued, even though the atrocities (if we may describe our treatment by those bosses with this obnoxious word) have been long forgotten. Someone I met several years later who, going by my friendship and camaraderie with one of these junior colleagues, thought that I was that 'bonded' colleagues' batch-mate, even though, in fact, I was five years his senior. It made me feel much younger.

But I had a very different type of bonding with the paper loving boss described earlier. His love for the written word had continued unabated. Several years later, I succeeded him on the post of secretary to a committee, which was set up to advise the government about changes to be brought about in the Panchayati Raj System in the State, following the recommendations of a committee set up by the central government. The chairman of the committee, in my first meeting with him, told me that a lot of paper had been collected during the past year and a half, but the report of the committee was nowhere in sight. He gave me three months to produce the draft report. I found reams and reams of bound volumes comprising material collected from various sources. It took me quite some time (including several sleepless nights) to get a hang of it; but the draft report was prepared and presented to the committee within the stipulated time.

In the Indian Administrative Service one not only moves from post to post but also from perks to no-perks. As a District Magistrate, one has an almost Maharaja-like existence, with a retinue of helps and other facilities. If the same officer then moves to a secretariat, specially the central government secretariat, as an Under or a Deputy Secretary, all those amenities and conveniences vanish in no time like the objects of an illusory world. As a District Magistrate, my paper loving boss used to boast that he had not touched his new born son even once, because he was being looked after by the servants. A couple of years later in Delhi, I saw him holding, with one hand, his newly born daughter (without an underwear) close to his waist, while in the other hand he held a milk can, as he stood in a queue to get milk from a recently opened milk booth of Mother Dairy in a multi-storeyed apartment complex.

I have made some friends late in life. But their is an unwritten code of conduct. Keep away when they are with their bonding-over-boss friends.

13 From Delhi to Bhubaneswar

It was perhaps the most horrible air travel experience of my life, and also the most forgettable, although not in a hurry; otherwise, I wouldn't have cared to write about it after almost 42 years, as the clock started ticking in the Orwellian year 1984.

I distinctly remember. It was end of May (in the Orwellian year), a scenario of sweltering heat in Delhi; you know what I mean. I had joined as Additional Development Commissioner (Handlooms) in the Government of India about a month ago. I had come to Delhi on that post because of the confidence that my boss had reposed in me. He asked me to go to Sambhalpur in Orissa (Odisha now) to check out the problems of the renowned weaver community there, famous for its exquisite 'Ikat' fabrics. It happened to be the constituency of one of the Ministers in the Government of India at that point of time. I have a creeping suspicion that the boss was testing me out. In international (WTO) parlance (oblivious of the hoary or grayish Indian textiles tradition), for your information, Ikat means fabric made using an Indonesian decorative technique in which warp or weft threads, or both, are tie-dyed before weaving. The Indian Ikat tradition is spread far and wide, but is largely associated with Pochampalli, Patan Patola (double Ikat), and Sambhalpur.

It all started at Varanasi, the constituency of the present Prime Minister. I was on an Indian Airlines (now Air India) flight that was to take me to Bhubaneswar, via Varanasi. It had begun very well. But a task well begun need not necessarily have a good ending. The flight reached Varanasi well in time but the aeroplane developed a snag there. The passengers were required to wait in the plane and, after some time, naturally, they got impatient. The air-conditioning in the plane was petering out and the passengers were getting restless. We waited and waited, but nothing happened. We waited for more than two hours inside the plane, but there was no sign that any progress had been made. We were then asked to go and wait in the lounge. More time passed, while afternoon turned into evening; then it started closing in onto night. While the 'authorities' were on 'long-distance', 'negotiating' about the future course of action (about which we were not aware, since no announcements were made), the passengers decided their own course of action. Some of them came out of the lounge and lay down in front of the wheels of plane because there was a rumour that we were going to be taken back to Delhi!

We were told that an attempt had been made to accommodate the passengers in the local hotels for the night, but it did not materialize because, given the number of passengers, adequate accommodation was not readily available. After a lot of persuasion, the passengers agreed to go back to Delhi on the promise that they shall be taken to Bhubaneswar, *via* Calcutta (now Kolkata) the next morning. I thought the ordeal was over; but I was mistaken, as it turned out.

We reached Delhi by about midnight. The nightmare started thereafter. Checking out of the airport was a problem because we had not arrived by a regular Delhi-bound flight. We were taken to Centaur hotel (a government hotel, since privatized), near the airport. We were told to report to the airport at 6 am to catch the flight to Calcutta. There was not enough time for me to go back home to get a sleep. In any case, we had come to Delhi only a few months ago and were living in a 'transit accommodation' 'borrowed' from a friend, who was abroad. I had no landline connection and, of course, there were no mobiles at that time. So I was in Bhubaneswar as far as my family was concerned and it had no idea about my fate, even though I was back in Delhi.

At the Centaur hotel we queued up at the reception as unexpected guests. We were not told or perhaps we did not hear the announcement, if any was made, that couples as well as those willing to share the room should come up first. When my turn came, I was told that there was no single room available, because it was assumed that I did not want to share a room with a stranger. My protestations to the contrary, the pre-dawn argument continued *ad infinitum*, till the confusion was sorted out and all similarly placed passengers, who had not heard the 'pairing' announcement, were doubled up at random.

Finally, at about 1:30 am I got into a room with an unknown NRI of Orissa origin, who was travelling to India to visit his home town near Bhubaneswar. We had hardly any time to get introduced to each other before we hit the bed. When I woke up a couple of hours later for morning ablutions, the washroom door was locked and there was no response to my knockings. I wondered what had happened to my NRI co-occupant; I till today do not know. I went down to the lobby and requested to be shown to a washroom in another room. I shall skip other details and move on.

We somehow reached the airport just in time and boarded the plane to Calcutta. The flight from Delhi to Calcutta was smooth and, with the grace of God, we reached our intermediate destination; but again as unwelcome guests: and turbulence was waiting for us there too. The nerves of the passengers, over a 100 of them, were on the edge because of the trauma they had to go through over the past several hours. When they queued up at the counter of the rescheduled flight, which was to take us to Bhubaneswar, they were a bit impatient, to say the least. The airlines staff at the counter was not sensitized to the situation and was dilly-dallying the proceedings, which made the passengers see red. Some of them moved up the queue and started arguing vehemently with the person who was issuing the boarding cards. In Calcutta, you cannot do that. The operative closed the counter and left us in the lurch. It took some persuasion from the higher ups to restart the proceedings. Finally, the boarding cards were issued and we got in the plane which took us to Bhubaneswar.

At the end of the day, of course, what mattered was whether I accomplished the task assigned to me by my boss. Decades later, his autobiography released on April 12, 2016, and a copy of which I acquired on the spot, carried the endorsement: "To Vivek, a very dear friend and a tower of strength – whose advice I always value." I am eternally grateful to him because his decision to get me to work with him gave a new turn to my career as a civil servant. I ended up doing a Ph. D. in Handloom Technology from IIT Delhi, which unfortunately earned me the sobriquet "Oh, that academician!" It considerably dampened all prospects of my getting any of the so-called 'practical' assignments.

14 Hard of Reading

All of us are familiar with the phrase *hard of hearing*. I have had, perforce, to coin the phrase *hard of reading* in the bureaucratic context, after over 34 years of experience in the Indian Administrative Service. A person who is *hard of reading* is not illiterate, by any stretch of imagination. He or she, however, just does not make an attempt to read the document or whatever is placed before her/him.

In bureaucratic circles, it is common knowledge that the boss often asks you for a detailed note on the subject under consideration. After a detailed note has been provided, the boss invariably asks for a brief note on the subject in order to have a quick overview of the situation. After that, it is CATCH 22 all the way. If you send a brief note first, knowing that the boss will not have the time or the inclination to read a detailed note, you will be asked to put up a detailed note; if you send both, you will be chastised for burdening her/him with too many papers. Of course, you have an option of choosing your own route to chastisement.

Once, and only once, I had the doubtful fortune to work with a boss who initially never bothered me about any notes, detailed or brief. I was surprised but, of course, somewhat circumspect and at the same time relieved. By that time, however, I thought I had become a wee bit wiser. I always used to maintain a repertory of detailed as well as brief notes on all possible topics relating to my assignment. In any case, these notes were required for the briefing of the minister as well as for preparing *Notes for Pad* in the context of Parliament questions, particularly the starred (*) ones.

Then, one day, my boss surprised me with a question. He said, "Where is the detailed note on the topic xxx?"

"I shall send it to you straightaway", I said. I went back to my room, retrieved the note on it from my computer archives and sent it to him. He later called and asked me to come to his chamber. I went with great trepidation, expecting to be given a dressing down for some unimaginable mistake of fact or figures or an error of judgement in the detailed note sent to him earlier in the day.

"Where is the brief note?" He asked

"Sir, you never asked for one", I replied

"Please send the brief note at once", He said.

I went back and fished out the other one from my computer and sent it to him. After some time, he asked me again to appear before him. I didn't know what had gone wrong this time. I was a little exasperated and somewhat annoyed. The brief note was just a summary of the detailed note. If there was nothing wrong with the detailed note, what could have gone wrong with the brief one, I wondered.

I entered his room with a scowl. I was prepared to pick up a fight with him for his irrational behaviour. I, of course, remembered what a senior colleague had once told me. All persons, including all officers, particularly all bosses with their juniors, behave rationally only after they have exhausted all other routes. Upon entering his room, he apparently noticed the traces of agitation on my face.

He asked me to sit down as I stood glowering at him. He asked me whether I would like to have tea or coffee. I could barely disguise my anger and said that I did not feel like having either at that point of time. He called his orderly and asked him to get cold drinks for both of us. I knew I could never forgive him ever for his temerity in taking my consent in the matter for granted.

He kept looking at me while l looked at my copies of the detailed and the brief notes, I had already sent him, trying to mentally frame my replies to whatever questions he could shoot at me. After the drinks arrived, he took a sip of his bottle and said, "Don't you know that after sending both the notes, you are still required to appear in person and explain what is contained in them?" And he smiled.

15 The Consultant

I took an instant liking for him. First, because of his essentially American hail-fellow-well-met disposition. Also because I could empathise with him, an administrator in the midst of a daunting coterie of fashionistas, since I was facing a similar predicament in my job. His stock response to the traditional greeting "How do you do?" was a wry "surviving", which nicely summed up the situation. He had a business-like no-nonsense attitude.

It all started with the signing of a Memorandum of Understanding (MoU) between the National Institute of Fashion Technology (NIFT), Government of India and the Fashion Institute of Technology (FIT), New York, in the mid-80s. In terms of this MoU, FIT was required to provide all necessary assistance to establish NIFT and make available the services of an administrator as well as its faculty on secondment for the purpose. The indigenous faculty recruited for NIFT was to be trained at FIT; and till such time as it became fully functional, the FIT faculty would help conduct short term courses in garment design, manufacturing and marketing, in India.

He came to India on a two-year tenure; and it must be said to his credit that during that period, we were able to start short term courses in all the three disciplines, albeit from a temporary accommodation, viz. the Shopping Plaza of Samrat Hotel, New Delhi. The first batch of Indian faculty was also trained and were conducting the programmes in collaboration with the FIT faculty. The Indian garment industry, which was initially quite skeptical about government's ability to run a 'fashion institute', came forward and started sending their executives to attend the programmes.

But this is not a piece about NIFT; it is about its consultant. Let us call him Robert (Bob, for short) Cunningham. After the signing of the MoU, and before his arrival in India, we were in touch on long distance. Given the time difference between India and the US, the calls from him and his boss came at odd hours, mostly at mid-night. We did not have the convenience of mobile phones those days and my sole landline instrument was kept in the drawing room. This required being able to 'hear' the ringtone in deep sleep, getting up and scurrying to the drawing room to receive the calls, which disturbed my wife no end. She did not take very kindly to the whole arrangement. Once Bob landed in India, the mid-night calls stopped. But then the phone rang again well past mid-night after several months. This time, he was calling up from Leh (Jammu & Kashmir), where he had been detained at the airport for want of adequate papers. His American joviality did not cut much ice at 15,000 feet above sea level. Frankly, I was not aware of his surreptitiously adventurous streak, and he had gone there without our explicit knowledge (I would not use the word 'permission' in the current-day liberalisation, so to speak). But in retrospect, I think I should have known better. With some help from the right quarters (pre-liberalisation), we were able to extricate him from a tricky situation and get him back in one piece. That put an end to his in-country sojourns for some time to come.

He chain-smoked unprotected (un-filtered) Camel brand of American cigarettes. He had brought the permitted quota with him, but it did not last very long. When I or some of my colleagues went abroad, we had a standard request from him to replenish his ever diminishing stock. Perhaps as a return gift, he presented us with a kitchen knife set on the New Year eve, preparatory to his departure. He must have brought it with him when he landed in India, because the MoU had no provision for a trip to US during his stint in India. This, perhaps to some extent, assuaged the feelings of my wife about the mid-night calls. If any gift was given to him by us, in return, on Diwali, New Year etc. he used to rip open the cover almost instantaneously and display the item to all present with a beatific smile on his face. Sometimes, it appeared a bit put on; but all of us enjoyed the antics of the open American.

On his arrival Bob was accommodated in a suite in Samrat Hotel, where the initial programmes of NIFT were also conducted. In due course, we hired a bungalow for him in one of the posh colonies of New Delhi. He moved in there with great panache and hired a retinue of servants. He had a girl friend back home. He tried to persuade her to pay him a visit by telling her that he had a palatial house and was living like a maharaja. Initially, she didn't believe him; but relented in the end. During Xmas holidays, she came. She was so impressed with his current life style that she said "yes" to the question he had popped up two years ago.

When his tenure was coming to a close, we arranged a gala farewell party in his honour. We had several dignitaries, including the glitterati of Indian fashion world. It was also attended by the FIT faculty in India at that time, the newly recruited Indian faculty and staff of NIFT and the alumni of the Institute. At the end of the party, at the thought of termination of more than two-year association, I became sentimental and started recounting some of our memorable experiences. I asked Bob to tell me one thing that he would always remember about his stay in India. "The stink in the common washroom of your office complex", he said with a wry smile.

16 Electricity for All

On 4 September, 2015, on the eve of 125th birth anniversary of Dr, Sarvapalli Radhakrishnan, the first Vice-President of India and Chairman of Rajya Sabha, Prime Minister, Shri Narendra Modi, while interacting with the students of India in the course of a video conference, announced that by 2022 all villages of India will have 24×7 electricity supply in all the villages of our country, i.e. *Bharat*.

In the same news coverage of the event, during a break, there was an advertisement. It showed a grand-father telling his grand-daughter to study hard for her examination, at which point the lights suddenly go out. The ad goes on to show that the son (father of the child) leaves his food, despite the old man's protestations, and says that his daughter's future is more important than his dinner. He goes on his motorbike and, at the end of it, we see a tree illuminated with CFL/LED bulbs and a number of tables and chairs under it for the students, in general, to sit and study under glaring lights. He is a Hero! The ad has been replayed, intermittently, thereafter.

I am sure this and other advertisements of its ilk will become irrelevant in 2022. It happens; things, which are very critical and important at a given moment, have a tendency to become irrelevant with the passage of time. But you would be wrong to write them off altogether.

A generation ago, I attended a conference organized by one of our business community associations. During a session one of the participants recounted his experience as a member of a delegation led by the then Minister of Telecommunication (by whatever name it was known then). In the course of the ministerial exchange, the Minister from India asked his counterpart from Japan as to how many 'tries' did it take him to access the telephone number he was dialing.

The Minister of Japan had a perplexed expression writ large on his small face. He asked the interpreter to repeat the question put to him by the Indian Minister; but to no avail. He consulted his civil servants, but they too were at a loss. The Japanese Minister then informed the Indian Minister that it would take some time for him to find the appropriate answer and the discussion veered round to other topics. The Japanese bureaucracy in its Ministry of Telecommunication was in a tizzy. They tried various sources to get the hang of the question. Finally, they rang up their ambassador in India, who had little difficulty in explaining what the Indian Minister meant because he was facing the problem himself day in and day out.

When the time came for the Japanese Minister to bid good bye to his Indian counterpart, he had a beatific smile on his face. His reply to the postponed question was simple: "We dial to get the number we want". Soon we were taken over by the mobile revolution, which, after some initial hiccups, made the question asked by the Hon'ble Minister from India, look irrelevant. But a couple of decades later, we are back with the reincarnated problem of call drops, about which too, the Hon'ble Prime Minister has expressed great concern. The land or fixedline telephone is back in demand, as is home cooked food.

Coming back to the promise of 'electricity for all', I am reminded of an incident which happened with me when I, along with my family members, went to Kashmir for a vacation in mid-1980s. From Srinagar we drove down to Anantnag to enjoy the scenic beauty of somewhat interior Kashmir. We reached the circuit house in the evening when the Sun was about to set. We found that there was no power in the circuit house. Power-cuts were no great shake in those days. We had them all the time, mostly unscheduled. I asked the caretaker as to when the electricity was likely to be restored. He smiled and said: "*abhi to gayee hai sahib*" (sir, it has just gone). Meaning thereby that it will take time and God alone knew when it would come back. We stayed at Anantnag for two days; and sure enough there was no electricity during that period. Of course, given the weather conditions in Kashmir during autumn, we did not feel greatly inconvenienced and enjoyed going through our chores in candle and paraffin lamp light.

Several decades ago, there came into focus, what was then known as Haryana model of electrification. Almost overnight the government announced that electrification in Haryana was 100%. The trick was to take the high tension wires to the four corners of the state, without ensuring to connect the people to the poles. The same problem of last mile connectivity was repeated several decades later under the rural electrification scheme (Deen Dayal Upadhyay Gram Jyoti Yojana). The case in point being the Nagela Fatela village of Hathras district in Uttar Pradesh, which became the centre of a row between the centre and the state.

Thing are, however, much better now. In Greater Noida, we built a house in 2002-03, but shifted there only in 2012. In the intervening period, we heard horror stories about power supply from our tenants, from time to time. Six hour outage was the norm; but it could be much more on a day to day basis. When we were moving in, we had to take a major investment decision regarding power back up: inverter (Rs. 40k) or generator (Rs. 1.5L+). We went around seeking advice from a few friends, who had already settled down. Some had installed generators others inverters, and both categories appeared quite satisfied. We were confused, till the realisation dawned upon us that the generator-wallas were those who had settled down 10 years ago, when we had built the house. The inverter-wallas were comparably recent settlers. We went ahead and installed a double battery inverter. But after about 4 years of happy inverting, we began to regret the decision on account night time outages during peak summer period.

"Street Lamp is here"!

A man was searching for something under a street light at night. A passerby stopped and asked him as to what was he searching.

The Man said: "I am searching for a coin that fell out of my pocket".

The passerby asked:"If you tell me where exactly it happened, may be I can help you with the search".

The man pointed towards a place quite some distance away up the street.

"Then, why are you searching for it here?"

"Because the street lamp is here", the man replied.

17 Four Saturdays in a Week?

The refrain of a popular song being played out on music and other FM radio/TV channels some time ago went thus: "*hafte maein chaar shanivar honein chahiye*" (there should be four Saturdays in a week). It is indeed a laudable idea and music to the ears of all those who toil day-in and day-out to earn a living and do all other things that they are required to do: men, women, children and all other variants of the human species. It is definitely the stuff, dreams are made of! As a matter of fact, the languid intoxication of a late Saturday morning is obliterated only by the inevitable languorous hangover of a Sunday morning. 'Oh to wake up on a Saturday, with three more of them ahead' could be the refrain of another song yet to be composed. I am ruling out the revelries of the Friday evening because they do not behove the somewhat old-fashioned, hardworking, metropolitan middleclass middle-aged people working from distances, which takes two hours or more to reach their homes. Their young and not-yet-adult children, therefore, of course, perhaps have no option.

A long time ago when I visited the then USSR in the mid-eighties, I was pleasantly surprised to learn that the common man there had a three-day working week. More about it a little later, but first let us get the scenario right.

I was the Development Commissioner for Handlooms in the Government of India then and was deputed to visit the then USSR (cities of Moscow, St. Petersburg and Vilnius, in particular), as a member of a delegation sent to oversee the arrangements being made for organizing the 'Festival of

India' in that country. Much later, after the Baltic States gained independence and the formation of CIS, I realized that I had visited not one but two countries; Vilnius now is the capital of Lithuania, an independent country on its own.

The reception for us arranged at the Moscow airport by the Indian embassy was smooth, business-like and friendly. (We were taken through a separate exit to expedite completion of our arrival formalities.) But as soon we entered the apology of an arrival lounge to collect our baggage, there was a bit of commotion, with a couple of men being chased by the security personnel. On enquiry, we were told by our embassy personnel that the men being chased were touts, who wanted dollars in exchange for roubles from the arriving foreigners; four roubles to a dollar, as against the official exchange rate of 0.67 rouble to a dollar or thereabouts. Sometimes later, the value of a rouble went steeply down and one could get a bagful (2,500, if I'm not wrong) in exchange for a dollar.

Subsequently, we saw government sponsored Dollar Shops, where all types of imported goods were available; but, of course, one had to make the payment in dollars there. Eagle-eyed touts were hanging around there too. I have kept a paper rouble of those days with me till today, as a souvenir. Its size is smaller than the Indian Rupee, when we saw it last or may see it again in its revised version.

For most part of our stay in the USSR, we stayed in Hotel Russia in Moscow (except for a couple of trips to visit the other cities), the counterpart of our Ashok Hotel in New Delhi. I remember a huge box kept in the hotel room, which we were told was the TV. We hardly had time or inclination to watch programmes on it, since it had only local language channels. But its size was really awe-inspiring, although not as big as the first computer.

As per the mutual agreement between the two countries, we were provided free accommodation and food, leaving us with a daily allowance of next to nothing (25% of the normal). A part of the dining area in the hotel was cordoned off for our 'free-food' delegation, where we assembled for breakfast, lunch and dinner. The delegation was divided into groups of official with similar responsibilities. Each group was provided the services of an interpreter.

We had one middle-aged, quiet, friendly, and somewhat absent-minded professor of English from Georgia University as our interpreter. He used to come usually around the time when we were about to finish our breakfast. He always carried a small briefcase with him. I often saw him stuffing his briefcase with boiled eggs left behind by some of us who were vegetarians. One day, it was pretty hot in the afternoon and we saw a streak of oil down one of the side-pockets of his synthetic fibre pant. One of us had spotted him stuffing pieces of ham in that pocket in a hurry, when we were leaving after our breakfast. Throughout the day, when he was with us, he did not change his clothes, including the pant which had this oily patch below his pocket. Then there was a spritely young man, who used to strut around giving instructions to the interpreters and guides in the local language. Later, we came to know that he was from the KGB (the Russian secret service). During our stay, we became quite friendly with our guides and interpreters and used to exchange pleasantries and personal information about families, hobbies and so on. Almost every second person we met was a divorcee.

In the course of our stay we were taken for sight-seeing, including ancient monuments, most of which were old churches. Some of them were renovated and, in a couple of cases, the renovation was actually rebuilding the monument from about 5% of the original structure. We, of course, saw an excellent ballet at the Bolshoi theatre and a performance by our own maestro Uma Sharma.

But what surprised us most, were huge queues in front of certain shops, comparable to the queues one got to see in front of banks and ATMs in India in late 2016 after demonitisation of 500 and 1000 rupee notes, or the ones that used to be there, in good old days, in front of ticket counters of single screen cinemas at the time of release of a Rajesh Khanna starrer. On inquiry, we were told that those were ration shops. The biggest queues were in front of Vodka vending shops. (Which reminds me of another rap doing the rounds: *"char bottle vodka, mera kaam roj ka"*: four bottles of Vodka, my daily routine.) There is definitely a 'four'-connection here. It was, therefore, on account of the time required by the people to obtain their daily ration that the common man had a three-day working week, four days being devoted to standing in various interminable queues. I cannot, however, be sure whether it was really true or cooked up by the feverish and effervescent imagination of the starved professor, who was our interpreter.

Move forward to 2015. As winter season approaches, there comes the news that the present Russian Government is contemplating banning booze or wine once a week in 2 cities, namely Moscow and St. Petersburg. Ironically again, the odd-even policy of the Delhi Government to restrict the number of vehicles on the road, has the potential of four holidays in a week. Come 2016, there is news that President Nicolas Maduro of Venezuela has announced that millions of officials will now work only on Mondays and Tuesdays, taking the rest of the week off in a bid to save electricity! Then again, Carlos Slim, the richest man in Mexico, said that he wanted to introduce a three-day work week and a later retirement age to counterbalance changes in the way that civilization is living and working today. According to him, this would especially suit governments where productivity demands have led to excess personnel.

18 Three Episodes and Three Telephone Calls

There is always a great rush and, if I may say so, an unhealthy competition among a plethora of news channels to tell you the so-called breaking news. Actually, today every news item is a Breaking News, or a Big News or a Flash or Exclusive, so to speak. What, apparently, differentiates one channel from another is who broke it first; there are, of course, unverifiable simultaneous claims.

Let me take you back to a time in my life a little over four decades ago, that is in the 1980s. Television had just become expensively accessible. That too meant opening your black and White TV (a 'dabba' in today's advertorial parlance) in the evening to listen to the news on the Door Darshan (DD) channel, the only one legally available at that time. Other sources included the transistor, which one hardly ever accessed, having become enamoured of the personable TV news readers. Another source to so-called breaking news was the old faithful newspaper, which too was denied access, occasionally, so to speak, in those days.

The point I am trying to make is that 'live' (or 'breaking'/'flash'/'streaming') news was not easily accessible. I only, normally speaking, woke up to breath-taking events when I picked up the newspaper pushed under the door of our flat early in the morning, a little earlier or later than the delivery of the much awaited milk bottles.

Against the backdrop of this scenario, I would like to recount three episodes of receiving tragic news first hand, even before the transistor, the revered TV channel or even the morning newspapers had announced them.

I had returned to Hyderabad after a tenure in Delhi and had been posted as Joint Secretary in the Department of Panchayati Raj of the Government of the then united Andhra Pradesh. I had a very good-natured and cultured politician as my Minister. One day in the morning, in mid-1980, I was sitting with him in his room and discussing a file, when his landline telephone rang. His first greeting to the caller was a courteous "hello". I then saw the expression on his face change quickly to a blank look, followed by a guttural sound and then the word 'what?' said almost in disbelief. The conversation ended quickly. The Minister got up from his seat and was in a hurry to leave.

I asked him: "Sir, what has happened?"

His quick reply was: "Sanjay Gandhi has died in an accident."

Before this 'breaking news' could sink in, he was gone. It was 23rd of June 1980.

The second episode occurred a few years later when I returned to Delhi for another central deputation as Additional Development Commissioner (Handloom). I had been in Delhi for barely about six months, when I was required to go to Kanpur to negotiate a deal with the regional office of the National Textile Corporation (NTC) for supply of yarn to the recently set up National Handloom Development Corporation. I had flown to Lucknow from Delhi and then driven down to Kanpur early in the morning. The time was between 11 am and 12 noon, when I was sitting in the office of the regional Managing Director (MD) of the National Textile Corporation in Civil Lines, Kanpur and trying to strike a deal. The landline telephone rang and the MD excused himself to pick it up. The expression on his face changed quickly. I had seen it happen earlier and, instinctively, knew that some great tragic event had taken place. When he replaced the receiver, I asked him, cautiously, as to what had happened. He told me that Indira Gandhi had been shot and had been admitted to the AIIMS. We concluded our discussion quickly and I headed back to Lucknow on way to Delhi. The date was 31st October, 1984.

By the time I landed at Delhi airport, it was fairly late in the evening. With the weather moving from late autumn towards winter, it was pretty dark. I had had no news about what had happened apart from what the MD had told me. I had no way of getting in touch with anyone, including my family members, since there were no mobile phones or internet those days. There were no TV screens at airports either. Actually we were quite laid back those days and did not either expect or even try to get a live news update.

It was a hell of a journey from the airport to my flat in Asia House on Kasturba Gandhi Marg (another 'Gandhi' connection), near India Gate (Central Delhi). What I saw gave me quite a shiver. The streets bore a deserted look. There were cars and tyres burning at various places. When I reached home, I got the news that Indira Gandhi was dead. Next day's newspaper told me about the carnage that had followed the spread of news about her killing by her own two security guards. My wife, sensing more trouble, had taken the precaution to buy ration and other necessities to last us at least for a week or ten days.

My association with the Gandhi saga did not end with that. I had completed my tenure with the central government and taken a sabbatical (study leave) for two years to undertake a Ph. D. programme at IIT Delhi. Since I was not entitled to continue in government accommodation, we had shifted to a private accommodation in Vasant Kunj, an up and coming habitation at that point of time. The house belonged to my wife's sister and we were to be its first occupants. It was middle of summer. I had just got out of the bed and was sipping my first cup of tea, when the landline telephone rang. It was a long distance call from a long lost friend. I did not even know that he was posted in Washington. After the exchange of pleasantries and fixing of coordinates, in almost a conspiratorial tone he said: "Do you know?"

I enquired: "What?"

"Rajiv Gandhi is dead", my friend said. It was 21st May, 1991.

It is uncanny, that I was privy to three news items relating to the unnatural and sudden demise of three eminent members of a single family, considered 'the first family' in those days.

19 Oxford Idyllic: A Refugee's Shibboleth

My Oxford stint was an extended paid holiday and more. I had free family accommodation for me and my wife (in Indian real estate lingo it translates into 1BHK). The bursary (in rupee terms) was more than the salary that was being simultaneously credited to my account in India. In addition, transport, photocopying etc. were reimbursed. After two trips to Europe (one of them reimbursed by the ODA/DFID), and also after financing a holiday for my son in UK, I saved more money (in rupee terms, again) than the total salary credited to my account for that period of 9 months or so. In case you are wondering (with smacking lips) about the fellowship on which I went to Queen Elizabeth House (QEH), Oxford, sorry, it doesn't exist anymore. Tony Blair took care of it, so to speak.

At that point of time, I had been already working on my Ph. D. thesis for about two years at the Indian Institute of Technology, Delhi on a sabbatical. The subject of my thesis was Public Policy Analysis and Design. Those were the pre-internet days when access to foreign resources was limited. I could not find many books on public policy, particularly the latest ones, in the IIT Delhi or Delhi University Libraries. I had become a member of Indian Institute of Public Administration (IIPA); but its library too did not yield any encouraging results.

Since I was eligible for a government sponsored foreign training programmes, I applied for a short-term (3-months) training abroad to buttress my research work. Considering my seniority, I was sponsored to one of the prestigious fellowships going at that time, namely the QEH Visiting Fellowship. My request for a three months exposure had been converted into a nine month long sojourn. The letter of offer received from QEH was also very encouraging. It said that I was free to do whatever I wanted, during the period of the fellowship. To illustrate the point, it mentioned the work of two of the previous fellows from India. One of them had devoted the entire period to learning typing; the other one had written a book and got it published during his stay in Oxford. So that was the range on offer. On my part, I was able to 'finalise' (the word is an Indianese; and I prefer British 's' to American 'z') two key chapters of my thesis and get them published, to meet one of the Ph. D. requirements of IIT Delhi (in addition to the course work, which I had already done before reaching Oxford).

Having been an alumnus of 'Oxford of the East' (Allahabad University), a secondment to the Oxford University was, in a manner of speaking, a homecoming for me. I attended some of the courses on offer at Oxford University including one on developing Expert Systems, which resulted in the final chapter (an application) of my Thesis. My supervisor at IIT would describe it as 'icing on the cake'. I had free access to the Bodleian library, which helped me in collecting all the material I wanted to use for my thesis. In addition, I was provided the 'services' of a 'free' mentor (a regular Professor in one of the colleges in Oxford) all to myself. He facilitated my presentations of the drafts of my two key chapters ('aforementioned') to the faculty of his college, who provided excellent feedback to me.

I also had membership of the British Council, where we watched weekly movies. I was donated a TV by my predecessor at QEH from Andhra Pradesh. I had some resident friends from India who, otherwise, took good care of us, in terms of transport and Indian food (not that we needed it, really, since my wife was around). I too learnt a bit of cooking, in the bargain.

During our stay in Oxford, we had the opportunity to make many friends: Indians, South Asian and British. We actually stepped into several castles. ('An Englishman's home is his castle', as they say.) Along with the hosts, we washed utensils at the end of the meals. In return, we treated many of them at our modest accommodation with some Indian culinary delights.

But one person among them all was special. He was Victor Lal (his real name). His ancestors were among some of the early Indian settlers in Fiji Island. A journalist by profession, he had fled the country during a political upheaval, and had been given asylum by the UK government. He was one of the fellows in QEH.

QEH had a modest library; actually it was no bigger than some of the private libraries I have seen. It had a quiet and relaxing ambience, with a few small steel benches placed at convenient locations for the users to rest their limbs. One day I and my wife were sitting on one of the benches when Victor (whom we did not know then) came and occupied the corner of the bench, we were seated on. While we made small conversation among ourselves, we heard Victor muttering something to himself. At first, we ignored it. Apparently, my wife, who was seated closer to him, heard something which appeared familiar to her. She turned around and said something to Victor, which at that time, I could not really follow. Victor said something in return and soon they were running up a conversation. It turned out that my wife had heard Victor say something which to her sounded familiar because her grand-mother used to converse in a similar dialect of Hindi, akin to Bhojpuri.

Victor told us that he had been trying this gimmick with a couple of previous batches of fellows from India hoping that someday someone will recognize the language of his mutterings and tell him what actually he was saying. He knew the words, which he had inherited, but did not know what they meant. My wife had, at long last, come to his rescue. In due course, Victor recited his version of the *Hanuman Chalisa,* which too was part of the oral tradition. It was nothing like the one we were used to reciting and listening. It had been completely transformed over centuries of oral transmissions, and sounded like nothing on this earth. In his recitation, the feats of Hanuman were more in the nature of the battle-cry of a crusader than the sedate version we knew.

20 Language Barrier

'Oh! the Indians? They have an accent', the Brits would say. In my opinion, the Brits too have an accent (actually many accents) as my wife found out, to her consternation, when she took up a teaching assignment in a Primary School in Oxford. We spent about a year there in early 1990s. But yes, we too have not one accent, but many accents, depending on our geographical location. Some are just variations of local language accents; but a few others are out of this world. One of this 'other world' or huge accent, I had the good or bad fortune (depends on how you look at it) to come 'tongue to tongue' with during one of my assignments. In cricketing language, one could call it a wide ball of huge proportions, which gives a miss to even the most diligent of wicket keepers.

The location was Lal Bahadur Shastri National Academy for Administration (Academy, for short), which had, through the Union Public Service Commission (UPSC), advertised for a post in its Law Faculty. After due diligence, the UPSC short listed a candidate and invited him for personal talk (interview). At this point, I would like to highlight the trials and tribulations that the Academy has to go through when it comes to filling up the faculty vacancies. Tucked away in the foothills of the Himalayas, the small town of Mussoorie is a great place for short visits, especially during the summer as well early winter; it is not really a great place to live in. There are all kinds of hardships: the excruciating winter when the power often goes off, particularly after a snowfall; the vacationing crowds during the summer months; dearth of public transport and other city-life facilities; absence of any worthwhile social life or night life for the young, to name a few.

Actually one incident comes to mind to fix the scene. It was mid-winter and the place was quite deserted. There was nothing happening in the Academy either, on account of the winter break. It had snowed during the night and the power had been switched off to avoid any untoward incidents. My wife and I were sitting in the non-descript verandah of our modest accommodation, shivering to the core and watching the pile of snow in the small lawn in front of our house. A car emerged from nowhere and stopped in front of our house. Stray visitors to Mussoorie to watch the snow fall or see the snow upon learning about a snowfall on the previous night, were a common sight. A couple carrying a small child alighted and entered our lawn. For some time, they played with the snow and then we saw the young women remove the underpants of the child, who had perhaps relieved himself, and wash his bottom with a blob of snow. They then went back to their car and drove away, while we still sat shivering in the verandah.

Coming back to fixing the faculty position in the Academy, as per the UPSC requirement then, I was deputed, as a departmental representative, to attend the 'personal talk' of the person short-listed for the position. At the outset, the Chairman of the Selection Committee told me that I could brief the members but would not be allowed to ask the candidates any question.

The interview, in retrospect, was a bit of a farce and, in the course of it, I was often hard pressed to suppress my laughter. The candidate had a heavy Malayali accent and was also unable to follow the so-called North Indian accent. With the result, every question from the members of the interview board had to be repeated twice or more in order for the candidate to grasp its import. Similarly, his reply too had to be reiterated in order for the members to understanding what he meant.

At the end of it all I asked the Chairman: "How many marks have been awarded to the candidate, Sir".

51%", the Chairman said.

"What does it mean, has he passed or failed?"

"50% or more mean that he has passed, of course."

"But Sir, you saw the difficulty the interview board had in understanding what he was saying. How will the trainees understand his lectures in the classroom?"

"That's your problem not UPSC's. We select the best qualified people on all prescribed parameters. In the list of requirements mentioned in the recruitment rules, there is no mention that the candidate should be articulate or un-accented."

The gentleman was selected and he joined after a few days. He turned out to be a nice person with no angularities, despite his accent. But his teaching sessions were a disaster. In the weekly feedback forms of the trainees, which were compiled and copied to the faculty members for their guidance, there were always a large number of comments suggesting what we should or should not do with the gentleman. We had to carefully edit the comments before passing them on to the faculty because several of them were quite unparliamentary and would not have stood the test of civilized expression.

We observed the performance of the person for about three months, and then took him off active duty, so to speak. He was given coordinating and administrative assignments. Then the excruciating winter arrived. He did not like it one bit. He was visibly uncomfortable and also felt very lonely as his family was still in Kerala; he also perhaps had a bout of depression and fell off his bed one night. When the Academy reassembled in its full strength after the winter break, the gentleman expressed his desire to discontinue the assignment. In government, it is easy to join, but it is quite difficult to leave. Anyway, his request was forwarded to authorities concerned and, in due course, in consultation with the UPSC, of course, we were told that he could be relieved.

I am quite sure that in the UPSC they do not have any system of tracking the career of the candidates they select for various assignments. They deal with them only in fits and starts, that is to say in emergencies like the one we had in the Academy. But if they did, it would help them read the fine print of recruitment rules and avoid the kind of mismatch we experienced. Amen.

21 Contextual Recognition

I have a dog. It doesn't like anything going out of our house. It is particularly allergic to my handing over money to anyone. For these two very cogent reasons, it has singled out our washer man for especial treatment. It barks uncontrollably when he comes to pick up or deliver our clothes, and it goes berserk when I try to hand over money to him. Given half a chance, it would snatch the money from my hand before it is passed on to the washer man. Actually, the money-related ritual starts the moment I open my cupboard. I have to carry the money surreptitiously in my pocket and hand it over to the washer man over the house's boundary wall. But the dog refuses to recognize the same washer man when we meet him during my morning walk, because the context is completely different. There are no clothes and no money is changing hands and, of course, a park is different from the boundary wall of the house. Human beings too often tend to recognize persons in context. In other words, we fail to recognize them out of context.

It reminds me of an interesting episode that happened with me a couple of decades ago when I was posted in the LBSNAA, Mussoorie as the Joint Director. Apart from the Academy, Mussoorie is home to a large number of educational institutions; some of them are quite prestigious and get students from all over the country and even abroad. I used to often get invited to be the chief guest at their Founder's Day, Sport's Day and other events. *Inter alia* the institutional authorities thought that my presence would motivate the students to crack the civil services examination and join the ranks of trainees coming to LBSNAA.

On one such occasion, the Principal of a school came to invite me for the Founder's Day. After I had accepted the invitation, we had a longish chat on this-that and the other over a cup of tea. He promised to remind me a couple of days before the event. He visited me again to hand over a formal invitation card and renew his request. We spoke to each other on a couple of occasion to work out the logistics. Then I was there. He came down to the drive way to receive me when I alighted from the car he had sent for me. I got a good reception from the students too.

Several days later, my wife and I had gone to Kulri, which is located at the far end of the Mall from the Library Point direction. It was a summer weekend. The schools were closed on vacation. We were standing in front of a shop and sipping a coke, when I saw the Principal of the school I had been to alight from his vehicle. I tried to attract his attention with an ever so light movement of the hand to greet him. He looked at us vaguely and moved away. We were out of context and hence out of focus. I was in casuals and with my wife, whom he had not seen earlier. Again it was Kulri and not LBSNAA.

Actually, it is not the fault of that particular Principal. The problem is with our neural networks. I too have, sometimes, experienced a similar difficulty. The difference is that often I recognize the face but am unable to recollect the context in which I had met that person and what is his/her name. But once the context comes into the frame, the name and other details come tumbling out, like Jill after Jack.

During my stint in Mussoorie, one thing never went out of focus. And that was the presence of our 400 or more trainees every year. The faculty in the Academy had trained itself to spot the trainees, wherever they were, irrespective of the context. We never failed to recognize the trainees, in or outside the Academy; although they would have loved not to have been recognized out of context, especially when they were visiting the local hot spots. Upon seeing us, they would try to avoid us. Look away, turn their backs upon us and whatever else they tried to become invisible somehow, the faculty never failed to recognize them and give them a pleasant smile. Actually, it is we who should have felt embarrassed upon being seen by the trainees at those hot spots. However, continue to spot the trainees (-no-more) we do now even after two decades, albeit on different locations and in varying contexts.

22 Monkey Business: The Eighth Wonder

Mussoorie was a small sleepy town (before the formation of the Uttarakhand State in 2000 with its capital in Dehradun), which burst into frantic activity only during the peak tourist season, mostly in May-June of the year. The Bengalis and the Gujaratis always arrived early in April.

When I was posted to LBSNAA, Mussoorie as the Joint Director in 1992, I became part of a ritual called Weekly Faculty Meeting, in the course of which there was a free for all discussion on everything under the Sun. The ostensible purpose of these weekly meetings was to discuss the training programmes in progress or in the offing and get the views of all concerned on issues relating to those programmes. In actual practice, most of the time was consumed by day to day personal problems being faced by the faculty like water shortage, electricity outages, monkey menace, flooding of homes during the rainy season and so on. The main agenda used to be always hijacked and was usually rushed through. Having watched the proceedings on a few occasions, I suggested to the Director that we should have two separate meetings: one to sort out administrative issues and another to discuss only the academic matters. The Director agreed and an Academic Council was accordingly constituted.

LBSNAA, given its small town ambience, was a community of less than a hundred faculty and core staff members, if the trainees and the contractual employees were kept out of the reckoning. As often happens in such closed communities, everyone is an open book and everything happening on the campus or around it is not only known to everyone but is also automatically everybody's business. There are no secrets and everyone is well aware of all the goings-on, even though they may not talk about it in public. In many ways it is like a district posting, which the IAS officers have to go through during early part of their career; but without the aura or authority over the geographical area which the field officers command. I would like to illustrate my small-town-district-posting point with a few incidents I encountered during my stay at LBSNAA.

It was quite late in the evening. I and my wife had finished having dinner with the Director of LBSNAA and were engaged in a discussion relating to some political event of recent origin, when his landline phone rang. He went and attended the call. When he came back, he told me that one of our drivers had been arrested by the police. The employee who had rung up informed that the driver was a bystander at a students' agitation near a police out post, mid-way between the Library Point and the Academy. A girl student of a local college had been teased by some local goons and the students of the college were agitating because of police inaction. Our driver was in the age group of the college students and, along with the students, he too was rounded up. We decided to go to the police station in order to get the driver released. On reaching the police station we introduced ourselves and were given due respect but told that they had not arrested any driver of LBSNAA; only a few of the students who had been indulging in unruly behaviour had been put in the lock up. Knowing the likelihood of confusion, we requested whether we could take a look at the persons who had been arrested.

The Officer-in-Charge of the Thana said that he would bring them out of the lock up and parade them before us for identification. Five persons were shown to us; our driver was not one of them. We tentatively enquired whether there were any more. The reply was: "May be". A lot of five was again paraded before us; the driver was nowhere to be seen. The driver was found in the sixth or the seventh lot. The police personnel having told us in the beginning (perhaps because of our antecedents) that they had arrested only "very few" students, it required a lot of administrative acumen, accumulated over years of 'district experience', on our part to persuade them to produce the sixth or the seventh lot!

The Mussoorie rains, you have to see them to believe. It really pours, particularly during the monsoon season. As already mentioned, one of the staff grievances used to be regarding flooding of houses during the rainy season. On one particular night, an employee, who perhaps had one too many that day, rang up the Director past mid-night to complain to him that his house had been flooded. And since he couldn't sleep, he saw no reason why the Director should be sleeping peacefully.

Another mid-night operation related to a phone call received by me from a faculty member regarding another faculty member staying in his next door flat. He informed me that the other faculty member and his wife were engaged in a brawl, and the commotion was disturbing his sleep. I sent a watchman to ring the call bell of the flat in question and that is where the matter rested.

Monkeys, of course, were a real menace in Mussoorie. Quite often they destroyed our small patch of garden in the hoary old tradition of Hanuman devastating the Ashok Vatika. One early morning, a lady trainee officer got a knock on her door while she was getting ready for the classes. Thinking it was the room boy, she said: "come in." When she turned around she found a monkey at her door step. What happened next, I shall leave it to the reader's imagination; except to tell that, in the end, no harm came to either of them.

Be that as it may, let us get back to where we began. It was neither an Academic Council meeting nor a general faculty meeting to let off steam about their grievances regarding administrative apathy. It was a meeting convened by the Director of the Academy to discuss some administrative matters relating to an impending VIP visit or some such matter, with some of his senior colleagues. There were seven of us in his conference room, to begin with, three on either side of the Director, who sat at the head of a long oval table. There was an animated discussion. Suddenly the Director felt that an eighth faculty member was sitting opposite him with only the head visible above the table, and wanted to ask him to come closer. But on a closer scrutiny, he found it was a monkey who had surreptitiously sneaked into the room from one of the windows and quietly occupied the empty chair across the table.

I, of course, did know that monkeys could be mood changers too. In the late seventies, I was posted as Deputy Secretary (Vigilance-II) in the Department of Personnel of the Home Ministry housed in the North Block, which too was a prey to monkey menace. The Janata Government had come to power and the Shah Commission to enquire into the emergency (1975-1977) excesses had been appointed. One afternoon I was summoned by an Additional Secretary of the Home Ministry, who was neither my boss nor did he figure in the chain of command to which I reported. I was surprised, but had no option. He told me to proceed immediately to Calcutta (Kolkata now) to brief a government pleader, who had to appear before the Shah Commission. I was indeed concerned with a couple of commissions which had been appointed to go into the allegations leveled against a few chief ministers, but I was in no way concerned with the goings-on before the Shah Commission. I tried to argue with him, but to no avail. In the end, I told him that I shall check with my boss and act accordingly. When I made some enquires, I was told that the concerned Additional Secretary was in a bad mood that day because a monkey had entered his room and polished off his lunch in the tiffin career. I didn't bother to check with my immediate boss and I did not hear from the Additional Secretary again either.

Monkey Business

A monkey was sitting on a parapet wall. A dog on the street below was constantly barking at him. The monkey kept looking down for some time. He then looked right and left and spread himself out on the parapet. He yawned, and the expression on his face said: 'Dogs will bark anyway'.

23 My Beautiful Teeth

"Your teeth are beautiful", she said. It was a left-handed compliment, at best; because she had been a local beauty queen, and I was not handsome at all, by any standard. She must have been generally pleased with herself for some reason to have suddenly sprung this 'praiseulogy' on me amidst the general chatter of a group of friends. Moreover, the heartening observation was made in the gathering dusk on the University campus, when we could barely see each other. In modern times, it would be called the 'Happydent' effect. The important thing is that I was perhaps sub-consciously aware of it, the compliment of the fairer sex notwithstanding.

In support of the claim about my ugly duckling appearance, I must mention that in spite of my 'fair' acting abilities, the best roles I could muster were of the prisoner in (*The Dock Brief* by John Mortimer), and of an old servant in Chekhov's *The Proposal*, with a missing tooth. For the servant's role, in one of its productions much later, I painted my central incisor in the upper jaw black, for which I was chided by a female colleague because I was trying to look uglier than I really was; what she really meant was, 'Why bother, you look ugly enough'.

It must be obvious by now to the readers that my teeth were perhaps the most beautiful part of my appearance. They continued to be so till the age of 50 (except for the damage done to them by un-chained smoking and occasional removal of a few due to normal wear and tear) when I met with an accident.

Actually, the 'destruction' of my teeth began early, when due to lack of proper oral care, one of my molars decayed and had to be pulled out. For several years thereafter, I retained my residual dental attractiveness. But things began to happen in my late forties. My teeth have been much attached to each other, physically as well as emotionally. If I lost an upper tooth, for instance, the corresponding lower tooth would also pine away after some time in sorrow. As it sometimes happens in the case of an aged couple, if one of them dies, the other withers away. I have been thus, fighting a 'losing battle' for years.

Be that as it may, the real 'break through', which has had a cascading effect, came 'accidentally'. The year was 1995, date 30 December, time about 2:30 pm and location was the road from Hassan to Shravanbelgola, in the state of Karnataka. I was on an official trip to the State and that particular day, after completing the work in Hassan, I had decided to go to Shravanbelgola on way to Bangalore (now Bengaluru). I and my wife were cruising along in a car provided by the State administration; it had a huge metal plate in front announcing the ownership of the car along with the State emblem. It was about 12 metre wide tarmac road with hardly any traffic. We had covered more than half the distance to our destination, when I spotted a minibus coming from the opposite direction. My last memory of that encounter is the thought in my mind: 'Why is that bus swerving towards our car, when there is no other traffic, person or animal on the road?' There was an almost head on collision and I passed out. When I regained consciousness I was back in Hassan and in a hospital bed of the district hospital. My wife, who was the only one to remain in her senses after the crash, told me later that our driver had a serious chest injury (no seat belts or balloons then) and the accompanying officer who was sitting alongside had also passed out due to a head injury after he fell out of the door, which had opened due to the impact. This officer was the one who had the most serious injury and it took him more than a fortnight to come out of coma. I had hit my face against the back of the front seat, which not only resulted in temporary loss of consciousness but also loosened most of the teeth in my lower jaw. After first aid, I and the other two persons were shifted to Bengaluru civil hospital for further treatment.

A slight digression here to explain the accident and its aftermath. The accident apparently took place because the driver (who must have been overworked) had dozed off at that moment. The minibus too was heavily damaged, but its occupants were not seriously injured. My wife came out of the car and started looking for help. After a little while she spotted a state roadways bus coming from the same direction as we had come. Some good Samaritans in that bus agreed to take the injured back to Hassan, foregoing their onward journey, with the destination only a few kilometers away. I have, over the years, observed that somehow there is more humanitarianism in the villages and small towns than in the metropolises. Be that as it may, we reached the district hospital in gathering darkness. It being 30th of December, there were only a few doctors and paramedics in attendance. The local Collector and District Magistrate, who had seen us off after lunch that day, came to our rescue and not only arranged for emergency treatment but also ensured our escorted departure to Bengaluru next morning. God bless the kind lady!

About half a dozen of my teeth (mostly incisors) in the lower jaw had become dysfunctional, and they were removed during the emergency treatment. My wife had broken her shoulder and a few ribs. After recuperating for about a fortnight, we returned to the biting cold of Mussoorie, which caused no end of pain to my wife. I made several trips to a dentist in New Delhi to get my teeth repaired and a dental bridge (a sort of fixed denture) put in place. The initial estimates for the procedure put the price of the repair and reconstruction job at about Rs. 50,000/-, a huge amount at that time. Some of the members of the faculty of LBSNAA helped me to file an application before the Motor Accident Claims Tribunal. The order of the Tribunal provided quite a bit of relief through a compromise with the Insurance Company after about six months or so, but not before we had been put through some grueling and unsavoury cross-examination in the course of which not only was my relationship with my wife was made a matter of doubt but the purpose of my visit to Karnataka too was questioned. It made me appreciate the trauma that a rape survivor faces during the court proceedings, even when it is done outside the public view. In my opinion, the presence of the judge and the leering/sniggering advocates is bad enough and makes the victim feel not only ashamed but also unclean.

The contraption in my mouth lasted about ten years and was replaced by another more modern device. About ten years thereafter, I started having frequent gum trouble. A series of X-rays revealed that the previous contraption was not only outmoded but also of poor quality. I was advised to get the teeth fixed on a set of implants, if my aging jaws could support it. Being father of an army officer, I agreed to a six month long procedure, which started with taking out the previous device along with the remaining teeth in the lower jaw and a few of the upper jaw as well, which too had been adversely affected. That was the most painful part and the procedure lasted for about eight hours, with some rest periods in between.

But there was a collateral damage. My tongue was severally battered and bruised, with the result I could not chew or relish any food for the next ten days and survived on oats or porridge with cold milk. There was a collateral benefit too. I lost about five kgs of weight, a loss which I relished for the next few months and hoped that it would last. But losing weight through the implant route was very costly because it came with a price tag of Rs. 1.5 lakh! But the gain was lost (and the lost weight gained) in equally quick time and I was back to where I began, by the time I put pen to paper to write this article.

And my teeth, of course, are no one's envy now.

24 Talking Aloud

I was appointed an observer in Bihar during the general elections to the eleventh Lok Sabha (1996). Upon reaching the constituency allotted to me, the first time, for about three days, I went around visiting various Polling Stations in order to ascertain their location, spaciousness and suitability. I was provided with the services of Mahipal Singh (not his real name), a local officer, as a Liaison Officer. In a particular village I decided to speak to the *mukhiya* (village head-man) in order to take his opinion regarding arrangements made for the elections. I had to wait in front of his house as he took considerable time to put on a proper dress in order to make himself presentable, while Mahipal kept on taunting him.

During the course of our discussions, the *mukhiya* told me that everything was all right and that he had no suggestions to make. However, when I was about to leave, he suddenly remembered something and requested me to wait. He went inside his house and came out with the village map. With the help of the village map, he explained to me that during earlier elections, there used to be a Polling Station at the Gram Panchayat office, but had been shifted to another site during the assembly elections held the previous year. This had resulted in some of the electors having to walk 5 to 6 kilometres to reach the new Polling Station. He wanted *status quo ante* to be restored. All this while, he was talking in a distinctly loud voice. I told him that I would convey his concern to the District Magistrate for such action as he would like to take in the matter. I got into my car and proceeded to the next destination.

Once inside the car, Mahipal Singh told me that for a *mukhiya* to produce a copy of the village map meant that he was a trouble maker. He further said that I should not mind the loud tone of the *mukhiya,* since in the villages in Bihar people generally spoke in a loud voice. As a matter of fact, Mahipal said, conscious of my official status, the *mukhiya* had considerably toned down his normal pitch. Mahipal then took to talking about various facets of Bihar's social and cultural life with great enthusiasm. Inside the car, with glass windows drawn up due to the summer's mid-day heat, the loud pitch of Mahipal Singh's voice was a bit more jarring than the articulation of the *mukhiya* in the open air. As my patience wore thin and my ears could not take it any more, I had to subtly make him stop talking from time to time by pointing out some scenic features of the landscape outside, making it necessary for him to look out and observe in silence. But he would, time and again, return to describing, animatedly and in graphic details, the nuances of Bihar's rich cultural heritage. He had a post graduate degree in Indian History!

I returned to the constituency for my second visit lasting about fifteen days. In spite of his loud ways, I had taken a liking for young Mahipal who, in a way, represented the cream of Bihar's state civil service. This time, however, he was put on active election duty and I had another officer to accompany me. Rajendra Kumar (not his real name again), my new companion, met me with a vacuous smile and a cloying grin at Patna airport. He spoke in a peculiar, of course *Bihari,* accent and his enunciation was a little fuzzy. He too had considerable difficulty in following my UP-*wallah* Hindi as well as English accents. His general concerns were also of a different nature. He very excitedly described to me a run-of-the-mill village pond, saying in the end that it was 'circled'. In the beginning, I used to request him to explain his point; later, I started looking out of the window, the moment he tried to make an interesting observation in a loud voice. In short, we had a great time talking loudly at each other for about two weeks. Another colleague on election duty with me, not only started 'talking aloud' but even had the volume of the television in his room raised to a level which was distinctly uncomfortable.

Upon my return from election duty, when I was relating to my wife a particularly exciting event of the trip, she interrupted me, at one point, to ask: "But, why do you have to shout?" Earlier, ever since our marriage, that was the question that I used to put to her.

25 Collateral Benefit of Unsolicited Calls

If appropriate technology was there, I would have loved to hear the sound of a tight slap on the caller's face, delivered by his own mobile/landline, the moment his/her unsolicited promotional call was identified by me as such. As a softer alternative, a mild electric shock on the offending hand or crumbling of the mobile/receiver would have done the trick. Unfortunately, such a technology is not in sight nor is it likely to be available ever, for reasons of safety and privacy of the caller and, no doubt, the human rights activists. The 'called', of course, do not enjoy such privileges.

The current smart mobile phones have a call blocking facility for unsolicited calls. But their ceiling of 100 numbers is ridiculous. It should be raised to at least 10k, given the frequency and diversity of such calls. Luckily, promoters from Chennai, Mumbai, Kolkata, Hyderabad etc. don't bother about NCR; otherwise the ceiling would need to be revised to one million. But a Gurgoan based real estate agent does not think twice before calling me (based in a comfortable 'last' bungalow of my own in Greater Noida) to buy a flat on Sohana Road, as if I was just waiting to jump at such an offer. 'Bull dung', to say the least.

Then you have those insurance solicitors. They are the most regular callers. My stock response is: "Do you know my age?" And then I switch off. My wife's stock response is: "Oh, I too am an insurance agent, can you give me some contacts?" That too switches them off. We have developed several such stock responses to keep the unsolicited calls at bay. One method which I have been using is to say "sorry" and disconnect. It saves time as well as often wards off repeat calls.

I am reminded of the DND (Do Not Disturb) scheme launched by TRAI not so long ago with a lot of fanfare. The subscriber had to just register with it and all promotional calls originating from unknown sources would automatically stop. In those days it was considered a dream come true. I promptly registered myself with a huge sigh of relief. But, actually, there was no relief from unsolicited calls.

They continued to flood my mobile like the streets of Delhi after a heavy downpour. I had a 'contact' in Telecom Regulatory Authority of India. I rang up my friend there and told him about my predicament. He advised me to send him a complaint with details of some of the promotional calls and SMSs received by me. I sat down to write the details assiduously, with particulars such as the number from which the call or the SMS had originated, the time when the call was received and the text of the SMS etc. I sent the complaint with all the details, running into several pages, but nothing happened.

However, when I was noting down the particulars of SMSs, I found one peculiar SMS being repeated. It had a long number with the letters IMEI and the word 'Amma'. I was intrigued. I told my son, who is more literate in these matters, about it. He was quick to understand and link it with a mobile which had been stolen from our home some time ago. It was a programmed message generated on my mobile as when a new SIM card was used in the mobile we had lost, because my son had activated the tracking feature in that mobile, which I had gifted to my wife on her birthday. The word 'Amma' stood for my wife, because that is the expression our children use for her.

I forgot about the unsolicited calls and made a complaint to the nearest police station reporting the loss of the mobile and the tracking data, I had meticulously noted down earlier. A few days later, we got a call from the lost mobile (along with the SMS giving the IMEI number and the word 'Amma'). The speaker identified himself as a policeman, and said that he had tracked the mobile to a town bordering Pakistan. He requested me to speak to another person.

A female voice came on the line and said, "Uncle, I am Asha (name changed) speaking. How are you?"

"I am fine", I replied.

"I had bought a second hand mobile from a footpath vendor, and it seems that it belongs to you. I am handing it over to the person who spoke to you first. He says he would deliver it to you."

"Fine. But please hand over the mobile charger too."

OK, uncle."

The policeman was back on the line, "What should I do Sir?"

"Take the mobile, along with the charger, and bring it back to us."

"Do you want to pursue the case of theft you had lodged?"

"No", I said sedately and the conversation ended there.

Just before the mobile was lost, a new sari gifted by my wife to one of the guests was also stolen. And we had blamed our house maid for both. But it turned out later that the sari was stolen by another maid, who had come with another guest. As far as the mobile was concerned, as it turned out, it had been stolen by the wife of a senior army officer, who had come to attend a function organised at our residence to celebrate the birth of our grandson. She had gone into our bedroom on the pretext of changing the nappy of her child and picked up the mobile and charger from there. She was no other than the Asha, who spoke to me when my wife's mobile was tracked to her. That she had purchased it second hand from a road-side vendor was just a story cooked up by her to save her face. I did not want to pursue the police case because her husband was an honourable person and a friend of my son.

DND is now not the flavour of the day; it went out of fashion like many other consumer services have done from time to time, since it didn't quite work. The only DND we hear about today is DELHI-NOIDA-DELHI Expressway, which too is currently toll free under the orders of the court. Actually, we are a nation of no-payers and our prayers have been answered.

But there is a new and additional problem we are facing these days.

Cases of dialing of wrong numbers are on an increase. During my childhood the landline / fixed-line numbers had only four digits. Sometime later, it increased to five digits in bigger towns and then gradually to six and seven. And that is where it is today, except for metropolitan cities where the number of digit of landline phones is eight. But in the meanwhile the STD code numbers were introduced. Sometimes, they have five digits or more. The mobile numbers, of course, have ten digits. All this has made remembering phone numbers, which was very easy in good old days, an uphill task and hence, the menace of wrong number. These days, I keep getting wrong number emergency calls in the middle of the night, most of the time, since my landline number is very similar to that of a popular hospital nearby.

26 In Quest of Help: An Anguished Account

During the last few years, from around the time of my retirement from government service, perhaps we have been singularly, and unfairly, unlucky in finding a reasonably good live-in help. Of course, we have had our share of luck earlier over 40 years or so when, during my service career, on some appointments, I was provided with house help. On several other postings, particularly in Delhi, the attached servant quarter was a great boon. Prospective occupiers used to converge like bees to a honeycomb. We could afford to be choosy and even ask them to leave if they did not live up to our modest expectations. We are extremely grateful to all of them for being a real 'help'. We very fondly remember at least two of our official helps (not live-in though), namely Ramulu, who looked after our small kids in early part of my career (1982-84), when my wife too was pursuing her career as a teacher. The other one was Sinderpal, who was with us when we were in Lal Bahadur Shastri National Academy of Administration in 1990s. The first one we got in touch after over 30 years, following a strenuous search. As regards Sinderpal, we are still in touch. We are also extremely grateful to our two private live-in servants who stayed with us through our ups and downs at different points of time in our life: Names of both started with 'Ram', and calling out to them, first thing in the morning, made our day.

The real problem started when I was on the verge of my final retirement in 2012. We wanted to plan sufficiently in advance for our retired life away from Delhi, but in NCR.

We had built a house in 2004. There were two other critical requirements: a live-in help and a driver. Our search for them began at least one year in advance. We got a driver and, thankfully, he continues to be with us till today.

But before I proceed any further, let me first establish the scenario. We have never called our house helps 'servants', 'peons' '*kamwali*' *et al*, in public or privately. We always called them helps or assistants, depending on what we thought would appear respectful to them. We have always taken care to address them respectfully, by using the honorific '*aap*' (of which, unfortunately, there is no satisfactory equivalent in English; but there are several in Sanskrit and my third language Telugu). In order to avoid being dogged by bovine controversy, I refrain from naming some other species that I consider worthy of the pronoun *aap*.

We have given our helps much more than the promised salary, in addition to the traditional Diwali gifts. We have celebrated their birthdays and wedding anniversaries. My wife, who has been a teacher during her working life of close to three decades, has taught their children, when the opportunity came her way.

Post retirement, even though our search for a driver was successful, the search for a live-in help went through many ups and downs. In anticipation of being able to get a live-in help(s), we had built upstairs two additional guest-rooms (with attached bathrooms) and a kitchenette (with the use of an open terrace thrown in for good measure) in our post retirement house, almost 10 years ago. They are a ditto copy of the guest rooms downstairs. So the scene was set and we expected a flock of birds coming home to roost, if not bees to honeycomb.

During the search period of one year and after shifting to our post retirement abode, we have had several unfortunate experiences. Unfortunate, actually, is an inadequate word to describe the trials and tribulations I and my wife have gone through. The following narration will provide ample proof thereof.

The first one on the block was a boy of about 16 years with a very pleasant disposition. But my wife had a problem because he was innovative in extreme and would always try to do things differently, as Shiv Khera (the Management Guru) would say about winners. If he was asked to chop a vegetable, say carrot or radish, into big slices, he would cut them into small pieces. When asked as to why he did not follow the instruction, he would give an inscrutable smile. Over time, the smile turned into chuckle and then it became a snigger. After we had had enough of these subtle variations in humorous responses, we had no option but to say good bye. We parted like good friends who had never met.

The next one was a young couple, very recently married. He was very protective of his young wife and used to look at all male helps around our house with suspicion. In a month or two, we discovered that the wife was pregnant. Perhaps she was pregnant when they arrived. Anyway, he did not want his wife to work and he himself was quite busy taking care of her. Then one day, he said that a particular person in one of our servant's quarters was not behaving properly with his wife and so he wanted to leave. We released him from our bondage with alacrity.

A particular person, who had done some civil work in our official residence, had become quite friendly with us and had brought his daughter to us for academic advice from my wife. Seeing our plight, he took pity on us, especially since my date of retirement and the consequent shifting away from Delhi were fast approaching. He too brought a couple with a young child. The husband was working as an electrician and his wife had been working as an assistant in a jewellery showroom. He was quite confident that he would be able to manage a job at our new location, post retirement. His wife was to work with us. We promised to bear the cost of his child's education. Things appeared to be working out fine. In a couple months, we got their Aadhaar Cards and Ration Card made. We also paid for the man to learn driving so that he could be of help in an emergency. His wife, of course, used to come decked up for work as if she was going to a jewellery showroom. In due course, after all the cards etc. had been made, she was able to convince her husband that it would not be in their interest to shift from Delhi. The husband then, one day, came and told us that he was not certain whether he would get employment at our new location. He could continue with us till we were in Delhi. We were once again left with no option but to tell him to withdraw.

With only about three months left for us to shift, we became desperate and were willingly enticed into the murky word of Placement Agencies. A reference was helpfully provided by a relative, who had had good experience with one of the agencies. The agent came to negotiate and returned with a maid a couple of days later to seal the deal. I had a dinner engagement that day at a senior police officer's residence nearby. Since the agent was delayed, I asked my driver to bring him over as I left home. He was brought to my dinner destination. We interviewed the maid under a street lamp outside the house, which was surrounded by a fair posse of police force on duty. We found the maid (her name was Saraswati, we were informed) OK and told the agent to bring her home the next morning, which was a Sunday. Next day morning, he was prompt. I paid him the agreed retention fee and obtained the necessary papers for police verification. While leaving, he said that the maid had not brought a change of clothes, toothpaste etc., so he would like to take her to a nearby market with him and get her the necessary accessories. My wife said that she had a spare dress and we could provide toothpaste etc. too. He then left. The maid watched the daily chores, which were being performed by the current house maids, had her lunch and dinner, and was given a bedroll to sleep in our guestroom. The only other thing I could do during the day was to get a few passport size photos of the maid made in order to paste one of them on the Servant Verification Form. As a matter of abundant precaution, my wife latched the connecting door, separating the guestroom from the rest of the house.

Next morning, she was gone! She had left by the back gate meant for the helps staying in the servants' quarters, because the front gate was secured by a lock as well as a guard on duty.

That was the day, when as Secretary-General Rajya Sabha, I had to receive the nominations for the post of the President of India as the returning officer. Most of the early morning I spent drafting a police complaint. Several days later, a few newspapers splashed the news about my being cheated by a placement agency: "Agency dupes Rajya Sabha Secy-General", "RS officer cheated by placement agency", the headlines screamed. Several weeks later, the agent was caught by the police from his hide out even though the office details in his letter-head were found to be fake. I received a few emails from others who had been similarly cheated, with photographs of the maids who had similarly run away.

A case was filed in the court and I had to appear a few times, even after I had shifted to my new abode about 40 kilometers away. The case was finally compromised and I received back a part of the money I had given to the agent. The maid turned up for the final hearing in the court, carrying in her arms a small child, who was permitted to be born in jail, as a matter of custodial courtesy.

Going back in time, a little after the previous maid had run away, I received some good news from one of our contacts in Mussoorie that a young and newly married couple was interested to work with us. We were delighted. Some silver lining had appeared amidst the gathering dark clouds. The couple came and moved in with us to Greater Noida, when we shifted. The man was a bit aloof (he rarely smiled) and the wife perhaps, we thought, did not quite understand our instructions because of the dialect-gap. The man took ill soon after we had moved. During the first week of our stay, instead of devoting our full time to settling down in the new house, we were busy taking care of him (getting various tests done, admitting him in a hospital, carrying food and fruits for him to the hospital and taking his wife to visit him from time to time). We footed all the extortionist bills. I used to do all their outdoor work like paying premia of insurance policy, sending money, through electronic transfer to his bank account in Mussoorie etc. We also got their ration card, voter ID cards and Aadhaar cards made.

After they had worked with us for about 9 months, one day the wife's sister's husband, who was staying in Noida, came to visit them on a motor bike. May be connection was fortuitous, but the fact was that a few days after that our live-in couple said that they wanted to visit their village for a fortnight; and we agreed. When they were leaving, we saw they were carrying a lot of baggage, which was not quite necessary for the short visit and the month being April. We waited with bated breath; they returned, but minus most of the baggage. We asked the question whether they would continue to work, to which they replied in the affirmative. The next question was: Then where was the rest of the baggage? It mostly comprised warm clothing, which they said would be brought back before the next winter. We were skeptical, but could not really do much about it. They completed a year of their stay with us and we celebrated it with an annual bonus and an increase in the salary for them. Given their background of cooler climes, we also got an air cooler fitted in their room in view of the summer. We had also provided a TV connection in their room.

There was, however, a marked change in their behaviour, which was not quite as amiable as before. We thought it could be home sickness and ignored it. One day, my wife casually asked the man regarding his wife not being able to follow our instructions. He told us that she had a hearing problem from birth. We took her to a doctor, who advised an operation. For about a fortnight, both husband and wife stayed in the hospital. The operation was successful, but we were not. Within a week of their returning home, the husband said that they wanted to go home. I said that on the understanding that they were going to stay, I had given them a bonus and an increment, bought a cooler for them and also borne the cost of the wife's operation. The husband's curt reply was that so what, it was our duty. The day they were leaving, the man said that since he had packed his ATM card, he wanted me to loan him rupees two thousand, which he would electronically transfer to my bank account on reaching home. I gave him the money, but it never came back. When they came to us, the man had five hundred rupees in his account. Over a period of about 15 months they were with us, he had saved about Rs. 60,000.

But we had the last laugh. In their hurry to leave, they forgot to take with them their ration card, voter ID cards and the Aadhaar cards. Two years later, a call came from the man stating that he had gone to get Aadhaar cards made, but was told that he already had one. I asked for refund of the money that he had borrowed in return for the Aadhaar cards; he never rang back. In the assembly elections that were held in 2017 they would have realized that the voter IDs they hold are also old and were cancelled when we got their new cards made. I'm sure they would have obtained duplicates or got new ones made by now.

The departure of the 'hill couple' was followed by a tortuous saga of comings and goings: some amusing others downright farcical. The sum and substance of most of them was that while the working husbands were attracted by the furnished accommodation, the wives were not too keen to put in an honest day's work in return, in spite of a sizeable monetary compensation. With God's grace, a couple of years later, we found another 'Ram', and he has continued.

Part II

Learning Episodes

27 Learning English

The journey from being a child, who got tongue-tied when he heard a simple query in English [e.g. "May I speak to Mr. Agnihotri (i.e. my father)?"] on telephone, to becoming a lecturer in the Department of English, University of Allahabad, was quite arduous. My gradual and laborious progression on the learning curve (as far as the English language is concerned) will be somewhat obvious as you go through this article.

Let us begin at the beginning. My father was an engineer and my mother had mostly done home schooling, as was quite common for girls of middle class families in her time. (It is back in fashion today in some quarters.) She had a professional diploma in Hindi language. Having dumped the British rule in 1947, just after I came into existence, imitation of western culture was frowned upon in our family circle. Education in the so-called Convents and Public schools was a big no-no. *Git pit* (small talk) in English, as she called it, was looked down upon by my mother for obvious reasons. There were no daddy and mummy for us; we had babuji and ma. Birthdays were not celebrated in our family. I fortuitously know the year of birth of my parents, but not the date and the month.

Accordingly, and for obvious reasons again, I had my education in/through Hindi medium from 6th to 12th standard/class at BNSD (Bishambhar Nath Sanatan Dharma) boy's college in Kanpur. I remember the names of some of my close classmates there and am in touch with only a few of them. I shall always remember my teacher of English and Mathematics in 9th and 10th, who was popularly known as 'Gandhiji' because of his penchant to slap himself on his cheeks if a student came to the class without doing his home work. I also remember my mathematics teacher in the 11th-12th class, who had a very funny way of dealing with everything, ranging from the absence of students from the class to the complex mathematical formulae. My subjects in the intermediate (apart from English and Hindi) were Mathematics, Sanskrit, and Logic. I do not think any institution today offers a course in Logic at the intermediate or any other level in India. With this combination of subjects, my father had ensured that I shall do well. As it happened, I topped the intermediate board examination in the arts stream.

During this period, I, as well as my siblings, used to write out the spellings and Hindi meanings of English words with chalk on the floor of our house, again and again, in order to memorise them.

Next step was, of course, the bachelor's degree. I joined the DAV (Dayanand Anglo-Vedic) College in Kanpur, again with a very unusual combination of subjects, namely English, Sanskrit, and Philosophy, on the advice of one of my uncles, who was the only one to qualify for the civil services from my extended family. The choice of subjects as well as switch over to English medium, given the fact that the medium of appearing for the IAS etc. examination was only English, was 'orchestrated' by my uncle. However, the DAV college was primarily a Hindi medium college and the switch over was quite traumatic. For subjects other than English, even though books prescribed were in English, the classroom instructions were largely in Hindi. So I had instructions and did assignments for English Literature in English medium, and for Philosophy in a combination of Hindi and English. As far as Sanskrit was concerned, the instructions were in Sanskrit and Hindi, and I had to find my own way of converting them into English for the sake of the IAS examination.

I got the Bachelor's degree too in the so-called flying colours, topping in the arts stream once again in the Agra University (the only university in Uttar Pradesh at that time, which had an affiliation arrangement for all the colleges spread across the State). But I had not got very far as far as my preparation for the IAS through the English medium was concerned. I was still struggling with the English language and conversation. A very suave private tutor from the Christ Church College was engaged during the summer vacation to make me take the leap. He introduced me to the beauty of English language by making me read literary masterpieces, including works of Oscar Wilde and Dickens. That really took me off, given my liking of yore for Hindi fiction.

Then came a mid-course correction. According to the advice of my uncle, I should have done Masters either in Philosophy or Economics (which was his subject; but which I hated because it got me nowhere during my High School). But, taking note of the advice of my tutor from the Christ Church College, it was decided that I shall do my masters in English literature. So be it.

I joined the University of Allahabad for my Masters and duly acquired a degree in English literature, getting a First Division with second rank, in the process. The Head of the Department was a close friend of my uncle, who was a member of the university Senate. He let me use his personal library, which immensely benefitted me in my preparations. There was another course correction because of coming in touch with a large number of students in the Amarnath Jha (erstwhile Muir) hostel, where I was accommodated. Practically everyone preparing for the IAS there had done or was doing MA in Political Science. This was so because according to the then scheme of examination, a candidate had to offer five papers; and Political Science course of the University of Allahabad was tailor made for the purpose. After completing my MA in political Science, while I was preparing for the IAS examination, the Head of the English Department invited me to join the faculty, which I did.

But when the choice of subjects had to be made for the IAS examination, it was not English, but most of the subjects from the Political Science post-graduate syllabus that came to my rescue. Actually, I spent more time and effort in brushing up my knowledge of Sanskrit. It was not only an optional paper for the examination, but, I am pretty sure, I got into the IAS because I scored 75% marks in it. Knowledge of English helped, but Sanskrit put me in the list of successful candidates.

Having not had the facility in the English language from childhood, I was never very comfortable with it. It took the chief of the British Council in Allahabad to point out some mistakes in my pronunciation, particularly the word 'tuition', which I used to pronounce as 'tution'. But it does not matter. You may have heard a popular actress of yesteryears pronounce the word 'biscuit' as 'biscoot', while advertising a particular brand of that commodity. You know what I mean.

Untitled Poems*

I

it's
absurd
to imagine
one can eat
the clouds
like the icing
of a cake
and pour
the heavens out
of a teaspoon
while
a young dog
barks
at a pig
in a strange lane
smelling
of
overnight garbage
in the drain

* Originally published in McCord, Howard (Ed.) (1972) *Measure 3: Young Poets of India*. Iowa City (USA): The Tribal Press.

II

mumtaj mahal
the woman
who
inspired shah jahan
into building
a glorious monument
dedicated
to her memory

mumtaj mahal
the dream girl
of
so many an
idle
young man

mumtaj mahal
the breathless ideal
of
many a wife

mumtaj mahal
the mother
of fourteen children

mumtaj mahal
who died
fourteen years
after
her marriage
of child birth.............

and taj mahal
in all its syphilitic
whiteness
stands

by the yamuna
like
a leper
on the brink
of a black desert
its
four minarets
erections
of
brutally oversexed
shah jahan
still
hope
to explore
the yonder
fountain tanks
fringed
with
nicely mown grass
and
(queerly symbolic)
red rock sand....

Or is it the yamuna?

28 Driving Lessons

I have heard a parent boast that his son, though only about 15 years in age, can drive a car. It is also not uncommon for a father or a mother to gift a motorcycle/scooter or even a car to his/her son/daughter on 18th birthday. Often, in such endowments, the parents regret their decision when they outlive the beneficiary. My father sent me to a driving school only when he was sure that I shall be able to afford a car, i.e. when I had been selected to the Indian Administrative Service.

The driving school routine was tough; but in retrospect, it was value for money. During those fifteen days, I was made to drive all kinds of vehicles, including a bus and a truck. I got the driving license too, after a proper test. It was all a very professional exercise. No favours were asked, no quarters given. The driving license test was really tough. But I did not make the grade when it came to driving my father's car (a Standard, bearing registration number UPA 1123), which was a bit of a luxury model he had acquired on resale. He was extremely possessive about his car, and a very careful driver. The joke about my father's cautious driving was that once he gave a pass, with a phlegmatic wave of hand, to a bullock cart.

My first automotive acquisition (perhaps naturally, in retrospect) was a Standard Super 10 (1956 model) bought in 1972 on my first posting as Assistant Collector, Hyderabad. The primary reason being that in a big city I needed transport to commute for private purposes. But I had by that time, forgotten the driving lessons I had taken more than 3 years ago. The driver of my official jeep used to sit with me to guide me and make me pick up driving skills once again. One day, on a holiday, with my driver in the companion seat and my wife and a one year old son in the back seat, I drove out of my flat in a government colony. In a copy book fashion, strictly according to the driving manual, I looked left and right and then again left before crossing the road.

While I was thus crossing to the left side of the road, a VIP car (a white ambassador, of course, in those days) suddenly came from the left and it was being driven at a considerable speed. I was a bit nervous and could not check my movement. The left mud guard of my car bumped into the right mud guard of the ambassador car. Both cars stopped on the left edge of the road; the VIP car a little ahead of my car. Since I was in the driver's seat, I asked my driver to go and enquire about the future course of action. He went up and spoke to the occupants. After a little while I saw an arm, clad in a white kurta, come out of the back seat of the car, and wave vigorously. That car then moved away. When the driver returned, I asked him what had happened. He informed me that a Minister of the State Government was travelling in that car. When he was informed who I was, the Minister said that he did not want to take any action and told his driver to move on. The damage to my car was a bit of paint coming off its mud guard; but the impact left a big dent on the ambassador car's mud guard as well as my confidence as a driver.

My sturdy car remained with me for about 6 years. Being an old model, it was often in trouble. On one occasion, one of the back seat doors flew open. It was closed shut by a Good Samaritan bicyclist, who happened to be passing by. On another occasion, when I was travelling in it with some of my friends, it stopped on the middle of the road. The friends had to push it quite some distance before we reached a roadside repair shop. It moved with me to Khammam district and from there to Delhi, in right royal style, in an EVK wagon. One day, when we came down from our flat to go for shopping, it would not start. Someone had opened the door, cut out and stolen the battery meter, which had been separately installed. As I had to leave for a foreign training abroad for about three months,

I said enough is enough and sold it off. I got a princely sum of Rs. 2500, added another Rs. 2000/- to it from my personal savings and bought a black and white EC TV to watch Doordarshan programmes for a few hours every day. The year was 1978.

In 1981, more than a year after I had returned to Hyderabad, I got a positing to Visakhapatnam as CDM. Again I had to contend with the proposition of acquiring a means of transport for my private trips in the district. This time too I bought a second hand Standard (Herald) from a colleague for Rs. 10,000/-. Once again I went through driving lessons with my official driver in toe, but, fortunately, without any mishaps. The posting was short lived and when, after my return to Hyderabad, I got an assignment with the Central Government in 1984, I disposed of the car before proceeding to Delhi.

My next car, accompanied with fresh driving lessons, came when I was about to complete my tenure in Delhi in 1989 and was due to proceed on a sabbatical to do Ph. D. from IIT Delhi. In such a scenario, a personal car was a necessity. This time I got a brand new Fiat (Premier Padmini: DNC 2921) and had to perforce learn driving not only because of the long gap of more than five years since I had driven last but also because the new car had a steering gear system, to which I was unused. This one remained with me for 23 year and was a faithful companion, except that during my fellowship abroad it remained with a relative along with my personal servant and, thereafter, during my posting in Mussoorie for over 6 years, it mostly sat in the garage. When I got a posting to Delhi in 1998, I had to go through the 'learning driving' routine once again; not only because I had not been driving for a long time, but also because the traffic in Delhi had become quite chaotic in the meanwhile. Towards the end, it was gradually becoming a rare sight to spot another Premier Padmini on the road. Occasionally, I used to greet and be greeted by others driving the same model on the road.

I disposed of the Fiat in 2012, just before I was to say bye-bye to my official career, as it had already undergone two re-registrations and was getting uneconomical. I bought a

Maruti Wagon R. Once again, I had a new car of a different model. It was also a shift from steering gear to the gear in-between the front seats. I learnt driving again. A little later, I got a private driver, when I moved to Greater Noida in late 2012 after saying goodbye to government assignments. Since I had a personal driver now, I was hardly required to drive. The forays were largely to a nearby shopping complex to buy fresh vegetables early in the morning, before the arrival of the driver. One day, when I was backing out the car from inside my bungalow, I rammed the back bumper of my car into the trunk of a tree outside my plot. The car was repaired, but that was the end of my driving career. The year was 2014. I have renewed my driving license thereafter for the sake of identification and a degree of confidence, but not driven my car. I have practically forgotten the various controls.

Talking of my romancing with cars, I shall fail the Narco test if I did not mention that on my selection for a one academic year fellowship at Queen Elizabeth House, Oxford, I applied for and got an international driving license in the fond hope of driving across the United Kingdom, if not Europe. About half a dozen fellows, including five from India, were allotted a table and a chair each in a hall for our academic work. A couple of months after joining the establishment, when, after a visit to the library, I returned to the hall, I found my leather pouch missing. It contained some stationery items, a little money in the shape of coins, but most importantly my international driving license. That was the end of my international driving dream.

But before I sign off, I must confess that my first foray into driving took place when I was a post graduate student in Allahabad University. A close friend let me drive his Vespa scooter with immunity on a couple of occasions, although I had no license to drive. I did not enjoy the experience as changing of gears drove me nuts since it made the scooter jump up due to my callowness.

29 Learning Telugu

I distinctly remember the day when the allotment of State cadres to IAS officers of my batch (1968) was posted on the Notice Board of LBSNAA (Academy for short). I, however, came to know about it from my colleagues who belonged to Andhra Pradesh and were allotted that State's cadre. It was the beginning of a *bon homie*, which continued and grew over time. Unfortunately, all good things have to come to an end. At that instant, no doubt, I found that I had joined a newly formed group: the AP Cadre (1968), a tag which continued with me during my entire career and thereafter, till the formation of Telangana State. I am yet to be told whether I belong to Telangana or Andhra Pradesh cadre of IAS, post retirement.

There were ten of us to begin with (including an ex-army officer, who was allotted to a senior batch later). Some, of course, were very happy with the way the dice had rolled for them; others rued the turn of events but bore their 'misfortune' stoically. Being fairly low on the merit list, I did not expect to be allotted my home cadre, namely Uttar Pradesh. My first reaction on learning about my cadre was: 'Oh! now I would get to see entirely new places', which I had not seen in the past. Having been born and brought up in UP, I had rarely stepped out of it; and, geographically speaking, had never gone beyond Nagpur, in the southern direction. Later, of course, I had a sense of relief. Had my rank been one notch lower, I would have been allotted Assam; a rank higher, and I may have gone to West Bengal. It was indeed a lucky roll of dice for my, in comparison to the Hobson's choice between Scylla and Charybdis.

I was taught Telugu language for about a year as a probationer (now called Officer Trainee or OTs, for short), before I stepped into AP. The teacher was a Tamilian, who taught the language 'as spoken' in the Ralayseema region of the then AP. This, of course, I came to know much later, e.g. 'Vachuchunnamu' (I am coming). I passed the examination in Mussoorie in first go; although some of my friends, who were from North India like me, did suggest that I should have failed, because that would have given me an opportunity to visit Mussoorie again to reappear in the exam; a nice break after a prolonged stay in south of India.

The Telugu I learned at LBSNAA during my training, understandably, the formal Rayalseema Telugu, was of little use when I landed in AP and joined duty as a trainee in Nizamabad (which is and was part of the Telangana). Thereafter, my first posting was in Hyderabad (where Urdu was the prevailing mode of conversation most of the time) as Sub-Divisional Magistrate (called Sub-Collector). The situation then became worse. Whenever I tried to a make laboured conversation with the local officials in Telugu, which was by now, a mix of Rayalseema and approaching Andhra Region (on account of Andhra settlers in Nizamabad), I was helpfully prompted by them, not very soothing to my ego, with expressions like: "*Sab, aap bahut achhi Urdu* (meaning Hindi, of course) *bolte hain; hamko samajh aati hai. Kaikoon pareshan hote hain*" (sir, you speak very good Urdu, we understand it. Why do you bother?)

Irrespective of the helpful discouragements, I persisted. I bought two voluminous volumes of English to Telugu and Telugu to English dictionaries, which I lugged along for about 20 years through my various postings and transfers/trials and tribulations. The only satisfaction I got during that period, was that I passed the written and oral Telugu examinations (lower and higher) in first attempts. One of my colleagues had to pursue some other route to achieve that objective. But I didn't really get an opportunity to rough it out, as they say, and learn Telugu the hard way, at the deep end.

I had a brief lucid Telugu moment, when I was posted as Collector of Visakhapatnam. I really worked hard to make the best of it in terms of my knowledge and spoken acumen of pan-Andhra Telugu. I started speaking extempore to rural population [*'raitulara'* (dear farmers)] as well as to mixed audiences (*anna, akkulu*) during informal cultural and other functions. I read out formal speeches in Telugu (written in Telugu script, I swear), without resorting to any sleight of hand by way of the text being written out in (royal) Roman script. This romance with Telugu was short lived because I was shunted out of Vizag for obvious political reasons, and I refused to become a pawn in a very high powered chess game.

Several years later, during my prolonged stay at the Academy, Mussoorie as Joint Director, to my great relief I found that there was a qualified teacher to teach Telugu to Officer Trainees. Therefore, I and my wife were not called upon, severally or jointly, to teach Telugu to unsuspecting trainees. I thank God for that, because I do not know what kind of Telugu I would have taught with my *'raitulara'* accent and vocabulary. Being the only officer from Andhra Pradesh Cadre for most of my stay there, I was assigned the responsibility of counseling the trainees allotted to Andhra Pradesh Cadre in the course of long and dreary winter of Mussoorie. I was very glad to meet my colleagues, seniors and younger officers; and I renewed or formed new friendships. I also enjoyed the long forgotten perks of district life, such as an escort vehicle accompanying me during my travel in the district. It is, of course, another matter that during one of these month-long winter sojourns, thoughtfully organized year after year, I met with a serious accident, which permanently damaged some of my otherwise beautiful teeth, as mentioned elsewhere.

Gradually, largely due to my postings in Delhi and Mussoorie Academy (1984-1998), I lost touch with dear Telugu. But after that 14 year spell out of AP, I was expecting a posting back to Andhra Pradesh. A couple of years earlier I started brushing up my Telugu knowledge, skills and attitude (KSA, as they say in the training lingo). I bought cassettes, accompanied by a Handbook on Telugu, published by the Central Institute of Indian Languages, Manasgangotri, Mysore 570006. I also bought a copy of Rapidex book of Hindi-Telugu Learning

Course and worked hard on them for about one year. But then I was advised that I should not look for a future in Andhra Pradesh, because the only post available there for my seniority was not available to me. I still carry these cassettes (of little use now, unless I get them converted into CDs) and books with me, in a fond hope (because as Alexander Pope said: "Hope springs eternal in the human breast").

The fond hope has now turned into a practical proposition. Telugu is now a shibboleth, shared by me, my wife and my older son, who was not only born in Hyderabad but was with us during my postings in Khammam and Visakhapatnam, where he had to learn to express himself in Telugu. Much later, as an army officer too, he did a stint in Hyderabad. Whenever we want to have a private conversation among us in the presence of helps or visitors (in which case the volume of our speech is inaudible, or so at least we think), the language is Telugu.

But a disaster is waiting round the corner to happen. Just imagine our using this stratagem in the presence of a person, who later turns out to be, like me, a north Indian colleague from Andhra Pradesh cadre. God help us!

30 Learning Computer

My first encounter with a computer took place in 1970; but it was a man not a machine. At that time I was undergoing training as a newly recruited IAS officer in Nizamabad district of Andhra Pradesh (now part of Telangana). I was undergoing training on the post of a Block Development Officer (BDO). When I went around my office to meet various employees in their work environment, I was introduced to a functionary called 'Computer'. He was an unassuming young man with an intelligent look, but, obviously, he did not possess a computer as we know it today. His job was to keep (compute) data. He was part of the standard manpower package at the Block level, and was perhaps a nationally unifying factor, since all over the country the nomenclature was the same, albeit with some local variants as far as pronunciation of the word was concerned.

I continued to visualise a computer largely as a person, till in 1985, at the ripe age of 40 years, I was shown the machine version during a 5-day orientation programme for senior executives on information technology. During those five days at ASCI, Hyderabad, we were given long lectures on the use of information technology in various fields, but were shown the computer only once and that too in a glass case from a safe distance, lest we spoilt it with our dirty hands or looks.

The next step was a great jump, which made computer a part of my daily life, and it continues to be till date. It was a Level Two course, entitled 'MIS and Computer Applications in Government', organised by the CMC Limited in November 1987. The programme design had a clever ploy. A retired civil servant, who had learnt computer post retirement as part of a bet he took with his son, was enrolled as the training programme's *sutradhar* (master of ceremonies). The programme itself was largely hands on. The 'old man' flitted around throughout the course and would not only intervene during the lectures but also help us during the practical sessions. We were familiarized with three types of software/ applications, viz. word processing (WORD), spreadsheet (LOTUS 123) and database management (dBase). That got me hooked on and, on return to duty, I used to spend a lot of time, almost daily, at a recently set up computer lab in an institution under my charge.

Soon thereafter I acquired the first computer for my office, that is, the office of Development Commissioner (Handloom), for some obvious applications. The computer was primarily used for maintaining data, which was required to be periodically updated at short notice in order to ensure that the latest information on the subject was made available for official use. For example, one of the routine tasks we were involved in was putting together 'Notes for Pad' to assist the Minister with his preparation for replying to oral (starred) questions in the Parliament. We developed about a dozen standard notes to cover practically all major areas of over operations. These were then fed into the computer and were updated just before the beginning of each parliament session. This made our task immensely easy. Earlier, as and when a notice informing the admission of a starred question was received, a note based on data available in various files used to be typed out afresh manually by burning mid-night oil, so to speak.

This background helped me immensely when a couple of years later I enrolled for my Ph. D. in IIT Delhi. Familiarity with three basic office related software was a blessing in disguise. A few other applications were added to my repertoire for preparation of graphs and charts. But there were two huge problems. Firstly, the departments I was in touch with did not have a complete set of legal files of the software I needed, particularly Word. I had to move around with my floppies from student to student as well as scan the computers available in different departments to constantly add to and improve my basic set of files. After a few months I had put together a reasonably good set of files for various usages. When I inquired from one of my supervisors the reason for the absence of a complete and legal set, his answer floored me. He was of the opinion that the students of IITs were such a big hit abroad because things were not offered to them on a platter in the institutions; they had to struggle and get hold of required material the hard way. But another supervisor did get me a legal software (VP-EXPERT) for developing an expert system relating to handloom technology, which, in due course, led to the development of the final chapter of my thesis.

The other problem was really scary. The institute had a computer centre with a large number of machines for general use. But very few students really went there, because most of the machines were infected with various types of viruses, which could easily wipe out your data. Be that as it may, my struggled yielded good results and I was able to punch in my thesis with little difficulty. I was particularly lucky to get an application relating to Interpretive Structural Modelling (ISM) developed by the Tata Consultancy Services (TCS), from a Ph.D. scholar, who was an employee of TCS. This greatly helped me in conducting a data collection workshop to support the main hypothesis of my thesis.

The expert system I had started to develop with preliminary software acquired by one of the departments I was working with, really took off when I went to Queen Elizabeth House, Oxford on a fellowship. There I had access to a more advanced software (KES PS) for expert system development, leading to assembly of the application which finally became part of my thesis. The computer centre at Oxford was such a change from the one I had seen at IIT Delhi! It was like a breath of fresh, as compared to the ghettoish environment in the other one.

I am an old man and have, by now, used them all: desk tops, lap tops, iPad *et al*. They are all very useful indeed. But there is nothing to beat the wholesomeness of experience in putting an ink pen to paper and the smell of ink and paper! And, of course, the interrelated encounter of buying a new book, opening it up in the middle and inhaling the smell of the printed pages! I can trade all comforts of information technology age for these, to my mind, divine experiences. These not only inspire creativity, but also, if I may be permitted to state, offer orgasmic delights.

Some time ago I met my uncle, a former civil servant, nearing his 90th birthday. The talk veered round to the advantages of internet and conveniences of the computer. A look of anguished loneliness crept over his face because he thought he had missed the bus. He looked eager to catch up on it now, if possible. In short, he felt computer challenged. I could understand his agony, since both his sons are living away and one of them is in California. Familiarity with emailing and Facetime or Skype would have really kept him cheered up. In retrospect, I have indeed been singularly lucky in this regard; otherwise I would have easily been a fellow traveller of my uncle and this book could not perhaps have seen the light of day.

Incidently, I had purchased a small typewriter, secondhand, in the seventies. I and my wife had used it to acquire facility with the QUERTY key-board, before I, unfortunately, disposed it of on being introduced to the computer.

31 Japanese Lessons

Japan is special. If a country with an area of just 377,930 sq. km (slightly bigger than Germany, but lesser than California) and a population of 127 million people (2010) (we Indians are 1.27 billion, ten times that figure), could rise from the ashes after the Second World War like the proverbial phoenix, to become the second largest economy in the world, at one time, it has to be different. In the context of various initiatives of the new government, particularly, for the success of 'Swachha Bharat Mission', we need to sit up and take note of Japanese culture and traditions.

According to Bradford A. Teasdale, much of the nation's past success has been attributed to various traditional practices and cultural beliefs. From *sumo* wrestling to *origami, bonsai* to *sushi,* traditional Japanese modes have reached us all. The philosophical study of Shinto (the Divine Way) is at the heart of historical Japanese tradition. Another unique maxim that established many traditions in its wake was the emphasis on the household. *Giri* (which has historically been the keystone of Shinto ethics, encompassing the idea of community responsibility) was and continues to be found at the heart of the Japanese social system. Conventional rules of interpersonal behaviour, such as bowing, handshaking, seat arrangement, and gift giving represent the idea of etiquette; but nowhere is a better example found than in the concept of *keigo* (honorific and humble language). Emphasis on daily aesthetics has combined with the other traditional Shinto practices, creating a culturally rich society full of respect, pride, honour and discipline. Furthermore, the unique isolation of Japan has lead to an "island mentality" where self sufficiency and internal cooperation are immensely valuable.

The etiquette, ethics, and aesthetics associated with Shinto have paved the way for the high level of national unity and respect displayed by the Japanese today. Shinto ethics introduced the idea of social obligation to traditional Japan. Etiquette and its system of hierarchy have added to these ethical obligations, creating a society full of respect and honour. The Japanese are proud of their nation and its many unique traditions. Over the ages, their pride has fostered high levels of national unity. Traditional Shinto rituals and festivals are re-born annually in *matsuri* throughout Japan. *Matsuri* are much more than simple festivals, they are a catharsis from the strain and stress derived from the strict Japanese lifestyle.

Zaibatsu, the business conglomerations of modern Japan, provide another example of the successful nature of traditional household organization. Much like a family, *zaibatsu* are composed of many interacting components united under a common goal. In the case of these *zaibatsu*, the father figure is represented by a central holding company. Like children, many sub-divisions and related companies branch out from the centre. Many of the world's most successful multinational corporations adopt Japanese *zaibatsu*. Tradition has been a huge factor in forming the successful modern Japanese society. Tradition continues to play an important role in the prideful heritage of the Land of the Rising Sun. These traditions have stood the tests of time, lending to Japan's success.

According to Kevin B. Bucknall some of the key elements of Japanese culture to be noted, particularly those who want to do business with them, are: *(1) Self-Awareness, the Group, and Conformity; (2) The Consciousness of Being Japanese is Part of a Strong Nationalism; (3) The Desire to Conform is Strongly Built into the National Psyche; (4) Harmony in Group Relations is Heavily Prized; (5) There is No Strong Class System in Japan; (6) Only The Best Is Good Enough; (6) Hard Work is Regarded as Normal; (7) Orders are Followed; and (8) People are Generally Optimistic and Look on the Bright Side.*

Against this backdrop, let us look at an Indo-Japanese venture in India. Close to three decades ago, a Japanese company decided to set up a large garment manufacturing complex as a joint venture in one of the prestigious Export Processing Zones (EPZ) of India. They were attracted by a generous offer of sizeable premises and cheap labour. In due course, they got into the business of recruiting the labour force for garment manufacturing. An advertisement was put out in the local dailies inviting CVs, with particular emphasis on detailing the relevant past experience. As it happens in India all the time (with 1000 or more applicants for each job of a government attender, called multi-tasker now), they were literally swamped with hundreds of thousand applications.

The Japanese company, with the concurrence of its Indian counterpart, devised a simple formula for the first, off line, screening. All those who claimed to have one year or more of garment manufacturing experience had to be separated from others. Almost everybody had. The next step suggested by the Japanese company surprised its Indian opposite number beyond belief.

They suggested that only those who had none or less than one year's experience should be called for a practical test. The Japanese logic was very simple: if they recruited persons who were used to the traditional Indian way of stitching clothes, the selected personnel would have to do a lot of unlearning before their training on the new machines could begin. It would be a waste of time and other resources. They were thus left with a small lot of applicants, who had, perhaps honestly or otherwise, stated that they had practically no experience. They were invited for a practical test. 'What is the need for a practical test?' the Indian equivalent understandably enquired. 'To find out whether they are actually telling the truth when they say that they are inexperienced and to ensure that only those who had no past experience at all in garment manufacturing are selected,' was the reply of the smiling Japanese CEO.

Forget Shinto, *giri, keigo, matsuri, zaibatsu et al*. Think simple and straight, and single-mindedly at that. That is why Arjun (one of the Pandavas of Mahabharata fame) succeeded;

because when asked by his guru Dronacharya to look at the bird he was supposed to aim at as an archer and tell him what he saw, he replied: "I can see only an eye of the bird".

That the Japanese have a knack of finding unique and ingenious solutions to their problems, was brought home to me during my stay in Oxford when I met a Japanese tourist, who was taking a photograph of Oxford University Press (OUP) building. Upon enquiry he told me that he was keen to take a photograph to show to his friends back home that he had seen the Oxford University; but had been unable to find a building with the words 'Oxford University' inscribed on it. He was, therefore, photographing the OUP, while excluding the word 'Press' from the frame. Eastern solutions to western problems, that is!

Bachcha Esee Main Khair Hai (Child, in it lies your well-being)

Once there was a peripatetic ascetic. During his sojourns, he set up his hut outside the precincts of a village. When the news spread, people from the village started visiting him to offer their respect to him. They gave him flowers, fruits and cooked food as per their convenience. Some of them used to come and tell him about their troubles. After hearing them out, his standard response used to be: 'bachcha esee main khair hai' (child, in it lies your well-being). They used to hear him, feel consoled and go away.

In the village, there was one particular person, who was going through a bad phase in his personal and work life and used to visit the ascetic often to narrate his saga of troubles. The ascetic's standard reply was, 'bachcha esee main khair hai', implying that it could have been worse. After some time, that man got very frustrated and said to himself: 'Here we offer him all sorts of goodies in the hope that he would get us out of our troubles, but all that he ever says is, 'bachcha esee main khair hai'. He is a big hoax.' The man got so angry that he decided to kill the ascetic.

The man was aware of the ascetic's daily routine. The ascetic used to get up early in the morning to go to the river to take his bath. One day, the man reached the hut early in the morning with an axe, stood in front of the door of the hut and waited for the ascetic to emerge. At the appointed time, the ascetic opened the door, but when he tried to step out, he stumbled on the doorsill and fell down. Seeing the ascetic fall, the man forgot about his intension to kill him. He put away his axe and bending down to pick him up said: "Baba, are you OK?"

The ascetic replied, "bachcha esee main khair hai".

Part III

Other Episodes

32 Astrology @ Work

Recently, that is some time in 2015, we watched this spectacle on an Indian TV news channel about a slug-fest between two *dharma gurus* (religious preachers). One of them happened to be an astrologer. They really went at each other. I would not like to go into the unsavory details because you must have already seen it being repeated endlessly or, alternatively, you may, if you want, download it from You Tube. In a sense, it was sad, but rising above current sensitivities, to me at least, it was hilarious.

It reminded me of my father's encounters with an assortment of their cohorts. One of them used to come once in a while to write out rolls upon rolls of horoscopes. He had to be fed six *pooris* (round bread of unleavened flour, deep fried in oil) with potato curry every two hours in order to keep him going. Then there was a differently abled numerologist with a glad eye. My father was quite fascinated by his profession (sleight of numbers) and, ultimately, lent him substantial amount of money, after which he disappeared, never to be seen again. My mother played the reluctant host to these unwelcome guests.

Astrology was my father's hobby. He was an electrical engineer by profession. As a matter of fact, several of my science-type friends and colleagues are astrologers of repute: 'hobbitual' as well as professional. And that makes me wonder whether there is any connection, at least in India, between astrology and science; which is different from the unending controversy whether astrology is a science or nothing at all and only a hoax to entice unsuspecting clients, spider-like. It is largely on account of fake astrologers; but that is what you would encounter in any professional discipline in India, thanks to the prevalence of illiteracy and poverty in the country.

There is another aspect to it. Since ancient times, inquisitive Indians were blessed with clear skies right round the year (at least 2500 years before Christ), which their unfortunate offspring today are most unlikely to encounter in cities now. Even as late as in 1950s, during my short-lived honeymoon with astrology described later in this article, my father started my induction into it, by telling me how to identify planets, stars and constellations. Once I told him to come out to see earth's sister planet Mars, which at that time happened to be clearly visible but not twinkling. I had identified a planet he had not told me about. I was inducted.

When and how did my father pick up his astronomical (sorry, astrological) hobby, I have no idea; because he was quite accomplished at it even before I had reached the age of reason. But he was greatly respected for his ability to predict. An Income Tax officer had great faith in him. He used to visit us regularly. The only remembrance I have of his visit to our first floor apartment in Sisamau of Kanpur is that his rowdy kids used to jump from one made-up bed to another, lined up in our so-called covered verandah, in the evening. By the time they left, we had to do them up all over again (some time with loose or broken cots strung with twine). On one occasion, my father told this ITC, as they are popularly called now, to be careful while driving because his horoscope indicated that he might meet with an accident. He went home and next day, very early in the morning, he backed up his car from his garage, closed the garage door and then banged his car into it, not very hard, of course. He was unhurt, but the bad omen had been averted. Those were the days, may be early 1950s. Actually, three years before his death; my father told us that he was living on borrowed time.

Of course, most of the friends and foes came to consult him, as was expected, for matching the horoscopes of their daughters with prospective sons-in-law and *vice versa*. Others came in desperation when their life situation was getting out of control. My father was always very diplomatic with the later types, a fact that I came to realize much later.

My father predicted that I shall get into IAS; and I did. But, astrologically speaking, he expected me to do well; which I didn't (77/100). His explanation was that perhaps I had been distracted by some external factors, which he didn't specify; but I knew what he meant.

I have only a vague recollection of my early brush with astrology during childhood. An acquaintance of my father had come to consult him about his personal problem, when he was in the washroom. I asked the gentleman to show me his horoscope, which he did unaware of the disaster that was to follow. I studied the horoscope as carefully as a 10 year old novice could do; and then I dropped a bombshell. I said: 'Sir, you would either not have any child or even if you have one, it will die'. Actually unknowingly I had solved his problem, but not at all to his liking. The gentleman was, understandably, aghast. So when my father walked in, stuttering incoherently the gentleman told him about my prediction. My father, I vaguely, of course, remember, looked at me very disapprovingly, but diplomatically gave his acquaintance some explanation about my incorrect reading of the horoscope. I got an oral hiding after the gentlemen left. I was debarred from looking at visitors' horoscopes, come what may.

The last straw (on the camel's back, as they say) was waiting round the corner to land. My father, in his desire to get a horoscopic companion or a latter-day part-time assistant, had made me memorise some Sanskrit *shlokas* from *bhrigusamhita* (the then *Gita* or *Ramayana*, of predictive astrology) *et al.* As it happens with all growing up children, especially in those days, I fell sick and was running high fever. My mother was attending on me with a cold pack placed on my forehead. She heard me incoherently and, perhaps, inaudibly muttering something, which she could not understand. It was late in the night. She called my father and he understood that I was reciting one of the astrological *shlokas* he had made me memorise recently. I do not know what really transpired thereafter. What I do remember is that I was deprived the astronomical apprenticeship of my astrological father. Thus, at the ripe old of ten years I lost all touch with astrology.

Of course, much later in my life (wind forward to 1980s) I toyed with the idea of writing a semi-biographical novel, the hero of which was called Herschel, a planet which was originally named after its discoverer but later came to be known as Uranus (the seventh planet from the Sun, which has the third-largest planetary radius and the fourth-largest planetary mass in the Solar System). After I had written about five chapters, inspired by the success of an acquaintance, a young boy into his first venture into publishing, I sent the manuscript to some friends and publishers. A few publishers were quite sympathetic and showed some interest in my manuscript; but one of my trusted literary friends told me that my proposed novel was a little too autographical for his liking. In any case, none of publishers offered a fat advance as one of their ilk had done for the young acquaintance. I lost interest, because, given my current government position (post 5th Central Pay Commission recommendations, the watershed in government pay and perks), I could never think of leaving my job to pursue my 'writing' passion (to which I had been addicted since the age of ten), especially since I had a family to support as well as no courage of my literary conviction.

Sorry for the apparent digression; but the eponymous novel *Herschel* was a mix of life of my father and me. I hope that I find a publisher for my 'novel', before it is too late.

33 A Whistleblower's Dilemma

Period: Early 1970s. Location: A district in erstwhile united AP.

I was posted as Additional District Magistrate (State designation: District Revenue Officer/Joint Collector). My primary duties related to revenue and civil supplies administration, including court work under the relevant laws. Those were the heydays of command and control style of governance. There were strict controls on movement of food grains, even from one district to another; night-long vigils had to be kept to catch vehicles transporting essential commodities, without permit, from surplus to deficit districts (even while in transit through one's district). Then there was a draconian law under the Essential Commodities Act, called the Andhra Pradesh Guest Control Order, 1972, which had recently been promulgated and placed a numerical limit (25) on the number of guest who could be invited to a meal.

One day, when I was holding my court to hear cases under the Essential Commodities Act, a couple of advocates came up to me and presented an application on behalf of the District Bar Association for release of a quintal of levy (read ration/ subsidised) sugar to host a dinner in honour of the visit of the Chief Justice of Andhra Pradesh High Court (CJAPHC). One quintal of sugar meant that the number of guests was definitely going to be more than the permissible limit. I pointed this out to the applicants; but they were adamant and I did not relent. The application was not entertained.

In due course of time, I received an invitation to the dinner. Since I apprehended a violation of the Guest Control Order, I decided to abstain. As it would have been discourteous to be in station and not be present at the dinner, I made a programme to travel out of the district headquarters. However, I instructed my Tahsildar to attend the dinner and give me a detailed report on my return.

Next day when I returned from tour, the Tahsildar gave me a report enclosing a list of about 40 persons, who had attended the dinner. The list included the District Magistrate, the District & Sessions Judge, and the Superintendent of Police, among others. Of course, the CJAPHC was the Chief Guest. Since the Tahsildar did not partake in the dinner, he did not include his own name. The report of the Tahsildar stated that the dinner was hosted on two tables, which were placed on two different locations, across the road, in the District Court premises. One of them was for vegetarians and the other for non-vegetarians. The number of guests on each table was within the permissible limit. However, the food had been cooked in a single room. In my opinion, therefore, there had been a violation of the Guest Control Order.

For a couple of days I wondered what I should do. My doubts started to melt away when I thought of the two very strict and upright officers, who were at that time posted at the State Headquarters as the Commissioner and the Director of Civil Supplies, respectively. If the news about the dinner had reached them from some informal source, I would have had no place to hide. I, therefore, sent a formal proposal, enclosing the report of the Tahsildar, to the Director of Civil Supplies seeking his advice regarding filing of the case in an appropriate court. I argued that since the President of the District Bar Association was the accused and the District and Sessions Judge participated in the offence, the case could not be filed in a local District Court. I further stated that since the CJAPHC was also present at the dinner, in which the violation of the Guest Control Order took place, it would perhaps be advisable to file the case in a court of a neighbouring State.

After a long and agonising wait of about two months, I got a reply from the Director of Civil Supplies which *inter alia* stated:

"We have had the matter very carefully examined and we have also consulted the Government Pleader appearing in the

High Court. We have been advised that we will not be able to sustain the prosecution as technically, there has been no violation of the Andhra Pradesh Guest Control Order, 1972 even though the spirit of the Order has been violated."

So far so good! But what the letter went on to state in the next 14 lines was devastating. The matter had been brought to the notice of the CJAPHC for appropriate action. Displeasure of the Government had also been conveyed to the District Collector; and, through him, to the SP as well. The letter helpfully ended with a note of appreciation for me.

What followed was not, of course, mayhem; but could have been. Luckily, the Government changed soon thereafter, and the Collector and the SP were transferred. The letter addressed to the Collector was opened by the new incumbent. I survived to work with two more collectors. There were, however, rumours that some advocates had planned to file a false case of assault against me, but better sense had prevailed. But something else did happen. There were some reprisals, which led to several days of frenzied activity and sleepless nights; but they had better be left unsaid. The prosecution rests, Your Honour.

But the story was not, by any means, over. The spirit of the Guest Control Order has been alive and kicking. Years ago, before the beginning of militancy, the Jammu and Kashmir government had put a cap on the number of guests and pruned the wedding spread, but the restrictions had petered out after a while. In 2017, an attempt was made again to put a ceiling on the number of guests to be invited to marriages and other functions. The Karnataka government in 2014 planned to tax extravagant weddings, where the expenses crossed Rs 5 lakh, so that the money collected through such levies can fund marriages of those not so privileged. At the Centre, in 2012, late Dr. Akhilesh Das Gupta introduced a private member's Bill in the Rajya Sabha entitled 'The Marriages (Simple Solemnisation, Compulsory Registration and Prevention of Wastage of Food Items) Bill, 2011'; but it died a natural death. The extravagant expenditure during the wedding of G. Janardhan Reddy's daughter in November 2016, inspired Ms. Ranjeet Ranjan to introduce a similar Bill in the Lok Sabha. We shall have to wait to see the fate of this one.

34 Family Values

Call it cronyism or nepotism or by any other name, it is ingrained in the Indian psyche as 'family value'. If a member of the family cannot go an extra mile (legally or illegally) to help his/her relative, he is not worth his salt. I am reminded of a person in the armed forces boasting as to how he told his nephew in advance the set of questions, he was going to be asked during the impending interview. "It is a done thing, you know", he said. But his enduring regret was voiced thus: "The b****r still couldn't get through."

Against this backdrop, I would like to recount an episode from my official experience, when I took an unusual step to get over this problem during a recruitment exercise in my organization. I was posted as Vice-Chairman and Managing Director of Andhra Pradesh State Agro-industries Development Corporation (AP AGROS) for a few months in early 1990s.

The AP AGROS was established on 05.03.1968 with an equity participation of Government of India and Government of Andhra Pradesh. Its basic objective is to serve the farming community and effectively contribute to the development of agricultural sector in the State. In the prevalent agricultural scenario, where making agriculture a viable and sustainable economic activity for the farmer was a massive challenge, it was expected that the critical interventions of AP AGROS by way of farm mechanisation, supply of quality agri-inputs, and land development, among others, would assist the farmer in achieving improved yields and income and contribute eventually to promoting the food security of Andhra Pradesh.

In the short period of my stay there, one of the tasks I accomplished was to recruit about a dozen field officers. The past practice was to advertise the post and make the selection based on an interview. In my opinion, making selection simply on the basis of an interview was not a very professional approach and was open to malpractices. I, therefore, decided to have a UPSC type selection based on a written examination (80% weightage), followed by an interview (20% weightage).

The posts were advertised and, as expected, a large number of applications were received. It was decided to outsource the initial screening up to the stage of interview in order to maintain objectivity and fairness in the process. A confidential procedure was adopted for the selection of the agency to do the job for obvious reasons.

It is again common experience, when a position in government, and perhaps elsewhere too, is advertised, that a large number of persons apply without bothering to check whether they meet the basic qualifications for the job mentioned in the advertisement. The agency, after initial scrutiny of the applications received, told us that only a couple of thousands of applicants met the basic criteria out of several thousands who had applied. I am sure that had the post been advertised today, the numbers would have been in lakhs rather than thousands.

The agency, through a confidential process, about which only a couple of us in the organization were aware, got an objective-type question paper set. A large public hall was selected for the conduct of the examination, which went on quite peacefully. The agency was asked to short list and recommend about 100 candidates for interview, since we needed to appoint only about a dozen officers.

The interview dates were fixed and the short-listed candidates were informed; this procedure was spread over about five days, because, for the sake of uniformity in the assessment, we appointed only one interview board, which had a mix of insiders and outsiders; with outsiders predominating.

It is when the candidates started receiving the interview letters that the family values made their presence felt. I had, of course, started receiving phone calls recommending the candidates as soon as the posts were advertised, but they came thick and fast, from a wide spectrum, after the written test was announced.

I knew that the calls were inevitable. So I decided to maintain a log book of the calls received. In retrospect, an analysis of the data made an interesting reading. In all I received recommendatory calls in respect of 24 candidates. Most of them were in the nature of a single call; but one state Minister recommended three candidates and two senior state government officers persisted with the request for their candidates and rang up three times each to enquire about the status of selection. One Minister rang up twice to recommend the case of the same candidate. Two Ministers rang up to plead the case of the same candidate.

Among the calls received, one was on behalf of a Union Minister, six from the Ministers of the State Government, nine from civil servants, two from politicians and others from private persons. Even though in the selection process, provision was made for appointing scheduled caste and scheduled tribe candidates, none of the call sought to importune such candidates. Most of the calls were received immediately after the written test was announced, but seven calls came even after the interviews had been completed. Out of the candidates finally selected, there were three about whom calls had been received. I informed the callers in respect of two of them, since I knew their telephone numbers; but I took care to tell them also that the candidates had been selected on merit.

The nature of the calls varied. Some were straight forward and crisp. Some mentioned the good qualities of the candidate being recommended. Some others pointed out the indigent condition of the candidate's family. Most of the calls were in the form of mild requests; but some were predatory in nature and there was name dropping too. Some were ingenious. Thus, in one particular case the caller said: "I am sitting in my office. In front of me is the photo of Sai Baba. The name of the candidate I am recommending is also Sai Baba."

In my induction talk to the field officers after their recruitment I told them that even though a large number of calls recommending candidates had been received, the selected candidates could rest assured that all of them had been selected on merit and not on the basis of any recommendation. I exhorted them to remember this, at all times, in the course of performance of their duties during their career with the AP AGROS.

It must be said to the credit of the Chairman of the organization that he did not interfere in the entire process.

35 Doing Ph.D.

From my childhood, I was always an introvert, who was fond of reading, and, perhaps with a thick-lensed pair of glasses, had a studious look too; but I was not really a scholar, in today's academic sense. Actually, I had literary leanings and was fond of reading novels from a very early stage in my life. But the seed must have been there somewhere, which sprouted when it found a propitious eco-system.

I was posted as Development Commissioner (Handlooms) and was about to complete my five year tenure with the Government of India. My two children were in the 10th and 12th standards. I was, therefore, looking for ways and means to extend my stay in Delhi for, at least, a couple of years so that they could complete their schooling undisturbed by the trauma called transfer and also take the next step of getting launched into their future careers, before I reverted to my pills and plaster in Andhra Pradesh. I took to applying for assignments with an academic flavour, entitling me to get a sabbatical known as the study leave (with pay) in bureaucratic circles. There was one hitch or the other, including expected rejections, before I found the best fit in the Textile Technology Department of IIT Delhi, with encouragement from the concerned faculty. I had just completed 7 years of working in the field of textiles, in the state and the central government put together, and the Head of the Department thought that my doing Ph. D. from his Department would provide an opportunity to the fresh graduates to learn something about public policy issues in textiles. It suited me to get a direct admission to a Ph.D. programme, without having to take the M. Phil. route, which would have enabled me to get leave only for one year to begin with and with no guarantee of my admission to the Ph.D. programme thereafter. My initial attempt was to get the leave by showing some academic assignment and write some sort of a report at the end of the two-year leave to satisfy the authorities. But if I got direct admission in the IIT for a Ph.D. through an understanding with the Head of the Department, I could possibly disappear after 2 years, leaving my benefactor in the lurch. But there was a catch; I had to apply and get through an interview.

I still remember two questions that were put to me during my grueling interview. The first one was obvious: 'With no science background at all, why did I think I could be admitted to an IIT?' I had no straight answer. I mumbled something on the basis of my mutually beneficial understanding with the Head of the Department, who kept quiet, but nodded his head. The next question stumped me altogether. Another member of the interview board, who later became my first supervisor, said: 'What is R^2 (pronounced R-squared)?' I did not have a clue and said as much. In the course of the interview, however, I was able to impress upon the Interview Board that given my general academic credentials and the experience in the chosen field, I would be able to do well, with adequate guidance from the faculty. This proposition led to another complication, because it was decided that I shall do my mandatory four courses (in order to earn 12 Credits) in the subjects chosen by my supervisor, in order to prove my credentials as an IIT alumnus.

Along with the Director of IIT, who happened to be a former Professor of Textile Technology Department, my real supervisor was the faculty member, who had stumped me with his question on R^2 during the interview. The courses he chose for me to do in the next two semesters were: Operations Research (OR) and Decision Theory, Computer Applications, Social Research Methods and Introduction to Management and Systems. As luck would have it, the course on Computer Applications did not take off because the requisite number (ten) of students did not register for it. I was, therefore, asked to do a course on Management of Human Resources, which was a great relief, because each and every word of its title, I knew the meaning of. In addition, my supernumerary supervisor, the Director, asked me to write a dissertation on the History of Textile Technology with him (you know what it means) for publication in a forthcoming book on the History of Technology in India, being put together by the Indian National Science Academy in Delhi. It was all slog with no 'credits'.

The scene was thus set and I had been fixed nice and proper, but had not managed any 'setting'. One topic of which I did not know head or tail of and which gave me sleepless nights was 'Operations Research'. If the suggestion to write a dissertation had been made by the Director a little earlier, the assignment would have qualified for a proper course to earn three credits and I would have found a valid excuse to dump OR; but it was too late and too much. After I had registered for the three courses from the original list, I straightaway proceeded to a bookshop to get a book on Operations Research; I found several but bought the one that was written by an Indian author and was also the cheapest. My next stop was the railway station, not to commit suicide (an idea that came to my mind after I had reached the station and had had an opportunity to flip through the pages of the book that I had just bought) but to receive my son, who was on his first vacation back from NDA, which he had since joined. As I waited for the arrival of my son's delayed train, my (Agni's) agony increased. The book made no sense to me at all! I was used to reading books, with pages and pages of text. Here was a book with all kinds of esoteric mathematical formulae and equations. I was profusely perspiring not only because it was summer but also on account of intimations of failure that were looming large in front of my mind's eye. Fortunately, the train arrived and drove away my blues, at least temporarily.

The fact that my tormentor left on a long term foreign assignment, did not bring any relief because the dye had been cast. My new 'working' supervisor (I had three of them, the other two being the Director of IIT and the Head of the Textile Technology Department) was one of the nicest persons

I had ever met. In my first meeting, he told me that he had recently supervised another IAS officer (who happened to be a colleague I knew well) and, therefore, I need not worry. This, of course, was a great relief and boosted my confidence a lot to face up to the academic challenges of IIT and beyond.

I must mention that I had a hard time getting access to basic software [called Word Star (for word processing), Lotus 123 (spreadsheet) and dBase (database management)] in IIT Delhi. The computer Centre there was called an 'AIDS colony', because if you took your floppy (yes, that is what we used those days, with a few kilobytes of memory) for any purpose there, it was bound to get infected with a multitude of viruses. I put together an optimal set of files to build up at least my Word Star software for punching in my thesis, by using my good contacts with various students. I also had a taste of student life when, for organizing data collection workshops, I had to obtain funding from my previous organization and do everything, from arranging the tables and chairs, dusting them and placing the note pads and balls pens on the table as well as arranging the computer and projection system for the purpose. Coming down to earth helped me building contacts with all and sundry. I got a unique TCS software [for Interpretive Structural Modelling (ISM)] and was also able to purchase an Expert System with the funding I had arranged.

The rest (if there was any) was smooth sailing over a period of next 2 years, one of which (about nine months) I spent in the QEH, Oxford, after which I got a posting in LBSNAA Mussoorie. It was a posting imposed on me, but suited me fine. The Government of India had issued a direction that anyone who went for a long term training abroad should be available for serving a term in a training institution in India, if required. A senior colleague, whom I knew, placed the 'requirement' and I landed up in Mussoorie. It helped me a lot in concluding stages of writing my thesis, the final chapters of which had been fine tuned in the academic environs of Oxford.

I had already put in a lot of effort in learning the use of basic computer software/applications, in anticipation of joining the IIT; I was able to work on it further in Oxford (especially Artificial Intelligence and Expert Systems) and finally in LBSNAA (for computer graphics on Mac). This was particularly so because my lovable second supervisor drilled into me that I had to prove to the IITians that I was worthy of the IIT. He wanted me to develop an expert system on Handloom Technology as an icing on the cake of my thesis, and I did. For want of resources, I also punched in my thesis all by myself.

I submitted four hard bound copies of my thesis to IIT Delhi in 1993 and was expecting to get the degree in 1994. But after about a year or so, I was informed, in Mussoorie, that the external (foreign) examiner had misplaced his copy of the thesis and, therefore, I had to submit another copy of the thesis, which I did. The comments from the examiner received some time later were largely in praise of my command over the English language. It is, perhaps, a sad commentary on the control group in IIT. I finally got the degree in 1995, a few days before my 50th birthday. There were a couple of VIPs on the stage, one of them later became the President of India and the other, the Prime Minister. But the degree was handed over to me by the Director of IIT. (The photograph says it all, since it shows only the Director and me.)

Doing Ph.D. gave me a lot of academic self-esteem and also brought me closer to my family. I was a student attending IIT part time. At that point of time, my wife was teaching and my two sons (who were studying in the same school) and I, were all students. A teacher student ratio of 1:3, bloody good indeed! I used to leave home around the same time as my wife and the two kids left for school and used to be back around the same time.

And there was a familial serendipity in the offing. My father was an engineer from Banaras Hindu University (BHU). And out of four siblings, my elder brother was a graduate from Roorkee University. My younger brother was a graduate from IIT Kanpur; by then the IITs had been established. In the meanwhile, my sister had got married to a Professor in the IIT, Kanpur. I was the only odd one out. Then I got Ph. D. from IIT Delhi and made an engineering connection; the seed had sprouted. Not only that, much later, BHU and Roorkee too were christened as IITs; so all of us could claim to be IITians. My father (may his soul rest in peace) and the elder brother may scoff at it.

And in case you want to know what is 'R-squared', it is a statistical measure of how close the data are to the fitted regression line. It is also known as the co-efficient of determination or the co-efficient of multiple determinations for multiple regressions.

36 An Investment in Character Building

This is an example of how initial experiences of newly recruited officers, to some extent, may be responsible for their future conduct. It is also about the different administrative milieu prevailing in different states of our one country, which has a somewhat uniform culture. I am going to provide a snapshot of what happened during one presentation session of IAS trainees who, after their one year training in the districts of their allotted states, had come back to the LBSNAA (Academy, for short) for their final rounding up Phase-II training. I must admit that I cannot vouch for how deep and lasting impression their initial experiences made on them, and whether those experiences actually informed their future conduct.

But the range of experiences, for an observer, is mind-boggling. But before I begin, let me put in a disclaimer. This business about Phase-II training was new to me as the Joint Director of Academy (1992-98). My batch (1968) was actually the last one to have only one phase of training in the Academy, before we went into outer space (read State) with a one way ticket.

Against this backdrop, I must make another confession. During my first year as Joint Director (1992-93), I thought of trainees at the Academy as persons who were on a normal learning curve. Being the Joint Director I had to prove my acceptability to the existing faculty. As a matter of fact, during my first meeting with the faculty, a couple of days after joining the Academy, one of them asked: 'Which subject(s) would you like to give lecture(s) on during the forthcoming Foundation Course?' Foundation Course (or FC in common parlance) had a mix of trainees from various services and was only a couple of weeks away. I had to think hard, because my Ph. D. was in Public Policy. It was of no use to new trainees, who wanted to know the tips and tricks to deal with situations that would come their way during the first 4-5 years of their career. Policy formulation comes a little later (if I am permitted to make an understatement). I chose Panchayati Raj, because I had not only served in that department in the State of Andhra Pradesh, but also coordinated the elections to the Panchayati Raj bodies held in the State after a gap of 11 years and, additionally, put together a long pending report on reforming the system, as Secretary of a High-Powered Committee. It was also very much in the news due to the 73rd and the 74th Constitutional Amendment Acts. So be it. But I am digressing and according to my spouse I have crossed the *Laxman Rekha*.

Going back (before I go forth), despite my wife's warning, I failed miserably in helping the coordinating faculty in getting a guest speaker to lecture on Ethics in Public Administration during the ensuing Phase-II. But I must admit that I am a quick learner, maybe I am wrong, because you have to learn at the end of each conversation and demonstrate that learning at the next encounter. But I learnt, at least on this 'first' occasion. I became wiser, the second time round, about the sea (in high tide) change in the learning curve of the trainees, when they came back to the Academy after their 'exposure' in the districts. They had undergone an attitudinal change. In classic training terminology, training is about KSA (Knowledge, Skills and Attitude). The trainees had all of these attributes much above mine. If I may put it on the currently acceptable scale of one to five, I was at 3 at best, while they were approaching five on all parameters, except attitude. But their attitude was dictated by their age (primarily), knowledge and experience, in that order.

Our job during Phase-II, I was advised by the old hands, was to 'soften the edges' of trainees' angular experiences in districts. Accordingly, several experience sharing sessions formed the core input of Phase-II of training at the Academy.

Now I shall come to the core issue (I shall not use the expression 'meat of the menu' for obvious reasons). We had an experience sharing session for the trainees of Phase-II on 'Touring', because that is one of the basic responsibility of a field officer during early part of his career, particularly as sub-divisional and district magistrates. There were three trainees who had volunteered to present their experiences on that subject. After they had made their presentations highlighting the duties and responsibilities of a district officers on the topic, based, of course, on their specific (read 'angular') experience of just one year in one district, there was a question and answer session, during which God's own truths were revealed. And that really is the meat or vegetable of the matter; the choice is yours. I am again digressing at my peril.

The question was "How do you 'look after' the VIPs" (meaning mostly the senior officers and, occasionally the Ministers etc.) "during their visits to the district?" First presentation was by a trainee who had spent his one year in a northern state. The gist of his presentation gave the impression that there was no problem at all. It was the job of the Tehsildar (concerned), with the excise officials in toe, to look after them, in whichever way they could. As a matter of fact, he said that he stayed in the State Guest House and was not required to pay anything for the rent or the food and other services for one full year because his collector told him that they were all on the house.

The second presentation was from a State in south India, ruled (if I may say so) by a left coalition. That trainee too said that he had no problem. All VIPs, including Ministers, used to demand the actual (not notional) bill and pay it without any demur. The third presentation was a real revelation. This was by a trainee from a north-eastern state. He had a very different type of problem. Let me give you the background at the cost of an umpteenth digression. He was holding independent charge of the post of the Tehsildar, to boot, when his Collector/ District Magistrate/Deputy Commissioner decided to inspect his office. As first impressions count, our new recruit sought advice of the old guard on the ticklish issue of 'making necessary arrangements' for the VIP visit. He was provided full information (including the brand of whiskey, and the meat preparations) on the arrangements that had been made in the past on such occasions in order to earn an 'excellent' report from the boss. My friend enquired about the amount of money that would be needed to get the crucial items. He was told that it would cost about rupees one thousand, which was almost one-fourth of his salary in those days (1992-93). He withdrew the money from his bank account and gave it to the Tehsildar-in-waiting. When the trainee had finished, there was pin-drop silence. One of the members of the faculty started clapping slowly and the house picked it up. While summing up the three presentations, a faculty member told the trainee from the north-east that he should not worry too much for the monetary loss, because it was investment in character building!

Now I can digress, not really. As an Additional District Magistrate, I had found myself in a similar situation. A Member of the Board of Revenue had come to inspect the Collectorate. I was made the officer-in-charge to look after him. Actually, he did not need any 'looking after' because he had no special needs. After the inspection was over, I sheepishly asked him as to how had it gone and was he satisfied with our work. He laughed and said: "That would depend on the quality of your fish". I had invited him for dinner at my place that night, and he was a Bengali gentleman. Luckily, we had a good cook. But those days were different or were they? Perhaps I got the lucky number.

37 Bachua Tewari: Voting Day Tamasha

I first met him in the chamber of the District Magistrate, when I was deputed as an election observer to Bihar in the mid 1990s. He introduced himself as a worker of a political party which had decided not to contest a seat from the constituency. He added that even though he was about 60 years old, people said that he had retained the ways of a child on account of his name.

I next met him a few days later when he came to cast his vote at the Polling Station of his village, where I happened to be present. We immediately recognised each other. He cast his vote while we exchanged pleasantries. Suddenly he turned to one of the Polling Officers to remind him that he had forgotten to put the indelible ink mark on the index finger of his right hand before handing over the ballot paper to him. He made the Polling Officer put the mark on his finger although he could have walked out of the Polling Station without that crucial formality having been completed. Later in the day I came across instances where it was complained that some persons were voting again and again even after the indelible mark had been put on their fingers, either by wiping off the mark or by threatening the polling personnel when they objected. Bachua Tewari was indeed an exception.

Later he narrated an incident recounted to him by one of the Presiding Officers (I shall, for the sake of expediency, call him Ram Naresh) of a Polling Station. While Ram Naresh was on polling duty at a Polling Station in an earlier election, the workers of the ruling party came and snatched away the ballot papers, unlawfully stamped them and inserted them into the ballot box. Ram Naresh watched the proceeding helplessly as the political workers were in a large number and they were also armed. There was no force provided to safeguard the Polling Station. After the miscreants went away, workers of the main opposition party (apparently having been informed of what the other party's workers had done) came to the same Polling Station and snatched away the ballot box itself. A little later, the men of another party arrived and started looking for the ballot box, which had already been taken away. Ram Naresh told them that the ballot box had been taken away by the second party, but they did not appear to be convinced. He then offered them a solution to their problem. Ram Naresh told them that since the ballot box with the unlawfully stamped ballot paper stuffed into it had already been taken away, all he could offer to the men of the third party were a host of documents and the corresponding envelops which were still with him. Several of these required meticulous filling up of the details by the Presiding Officer at the end of the day. He told the workers of the third party to take away those papers so that *they* would have the satisfaction of showing something to their bosses for their labour and, at the same time, save *him* the bother of having to fill them up.

After this narration, Bachua Tewari asked: "Have you had your breakfast?" "No", I said, "on a solemn occasion like this, I prefer to observe fast."

The methods of retaliation by political parties to booth capturing were refined over time. If one party snatched, stamped and stuffed ballot papers, the other party did not necessarily *have* to lug it with the ballot box and the election documents any more. During my stay as an election observer, I came across instances where the second party had poured water (helpfully arranged by the authorities on account of the scorching summer heat) into the ballot box; and the members of the third party arriving on the scene thereafter had poured acid or ink or even naturally relieved themselves into it.

The hapless and terrorised local Presiding Officers at the concerned Polling Stations, faced with such onslaughts, in most cases, preferred to keep mum. In some cases they reported the event without mentioning any names, to save their skin. In other cases, they adopted ingenious ways of reporting the crime: a few returned with unsealed ballot boxes, and others indicated insertion of unsigned ballot papers in the ballot paper account.

The situation has somewhat changed after the introduction of the Electronic Voting Machines. But more ingenious ways of beating the system have emerged with equal effect. Local solutions to global problems, that is. The technology has radically changed, but not the intentions. However (and there is always a however in the end), the scope and scale of mal-practices, from all accounts, has perhaps been considerably reduced; or has it really?

The Last Slap

A young man of about 30 was to be hanged for a brutal murder. The jail warden asked him for his last wish. He said that he wanted to meet his mother. The mother was summoned. When they were face to face, the young gave her a tight slap and said: "If you had slapped me for my mistakes when I was a child, I wouldn't be here today."

38 Taking the Road Less Travelled by

During a career in civil services there are Opportunities and Threats based on your 'recognized' Strengths and Weaknesses. (Sorry, if it does not generate a mnemonically memorable acronym like SWOT). But on the day of reckoning, it is just a matter of perception or, as they say, 'a state of mind'. Again, the numbers do lend significance to them. There are stories in the media, from time to time, about officers who have been transferred 40 times in 20 years (actually the officer concerned was my trainee at LBSNAA) and another who was transferred 60 times in 30 years. The average, however, is the same: two postings every year. Then, according to a study done quite some time back, in a particular State of India, the average tenure of a District Collector/Magistrate was about 6 months. By those high standards, I am a below par transferee. My average works out to a miserable three long years on every post; and that too because of a few (about four) bad-fish postings/scores. If you take them out, the average shoots up (like blood pressure) to four years. Actually, I have fought and won against an attempt to transfer me. More about it a little later.

The purpose of this episodal interlude is to focus on a few occasions/situations when either I refused or resisted or prevented a posting. Whether I won the battle hands up or down, I shall leave it to the reader to decide.

It all began with a request, early in my career, for cancellation of my first posting as a CDM, Mahboobnagar (in Andhra Pradesh) because I was, at that point of time, giving final shape to my house under construction in Hyderabad. Selfish motive, I, unabashedly, admit; but in those good old days (early 1980s) the authorities in Andhra Pradesh, at least, used to be much more responsive to officer's problems than they are today. And it worked.

I won laurels in the alternate posting (getting the sobriquet 'Ordinance Agnihotri', for the number of ordinances I piloted with the support of the then Chief Minister) for making the Panchayati Raj Act of the State operational for the ensuing elections to Panchayati Raj bodies, which were being held after a gap of 11 years. It, unexpectedly, resulted in a so-called prized posting (CDM, Visakhapatnam), which I gladly accepted, though it did not last very long.

On two other occasions it was not as simple as that. I really faced a dilemma. Actually, I was not quite sure whether I did the right thing in not choosing the obvious course of action by refusing or subverting the posting. Perhaps my career would have taken a very different course, had I not chosen a road less travelled by. This had, of course, happened to me very early in my life too when I took the IAS examination rather than continue as a member of the teaching faculty in the Department of English Studies of Allahabad University.

First *dharma-sankat* (dilemma) came my way when I was Additional Development Commissioner, in the Office of the Development Commissioner (Handlooms). It was a Director level post, in between the more familiar designations of Deputy Secretary and Joint Secretary. In due course, after about two years of my joining the post, I was 'empanelled' (so to speak) to be promoted. In such a situation, firstly, the officer has no choice. Secondly, in the normal course, the officer is promoted in the same organization where he happens to be working, if a vacancy is available there. As it transpired, there was a problem of plenty. My boss (Secretary, Ministry of Textiles) told me that there were 4 posts available in the Ministry; and very graciously offered that I could choose any one of them. The Posts were: Development Commissioner (Handlooms), which my immediate boss had just vacated on promotion; Development Commissioner (Handicrafts); Joint

Secretary (Exports) in the Ministry of Textiles; and the Director General, Apparel Export Promotion Council (DG, AEPC). Of these four, the last two were considered 'prized postings' (in that order) in the Ministry because they offered plenty of opportunities to travel abroad. While the post of DG, AEPC scored over the other in this regard, the post of JS (Exports) offered the real possibility of a posting abroad, in due course. I, therefore, intuitively thought that the Secretary would expect me to plumb for it. In any case, out of the four, in his heart of hearts (as they say) he would have liked me to opt for the post of DC (Handicrafts), because he had occupied it before becoming Secretary, Ministry of Textiles. He was taken aback when I preferred to take my promotion as Development Commissioner (Handlooms). I chose it for two, to me obvious, reasons. It would be a smooth transition for me and I would not have to start 'learning on the job' all over again. Secondly, because, thanks to the handloom Diva (late Mrs. Pupul Jayakar) I had developed a liking for the sector and was in a position to push through certain reforms on which I had been working for the past two years (they call it job satisfaction). I had been a party to setting up of two institutions (NHDC and NIFT) and I wanted to see them take shape. I had also conceptualized a composite handloom marketing complex to be set up in different cities for the marketing of handloom products of different States of India. I had also worked on two hard measures, namely abolition of the much touted handloom rebate scheme and the leaky Janata Cloth scheme, which had been the sources of a variety of corrupt mal-practices.

The Second dilemma arose about 18 years later. Before my turn for promotion as Secretary to Government of India could arrive, I had completed my extended 7 year tenure with the Central Government and was due to revert back to my State. A helpful Cabinet Secretary arranged a temporary assignment for me as OSD to the Twelfth Finance Commission to keep me off the regular channel and, thus, allow me to continue in Delhi to bridge the gap of a few months when the need to revert would recede permanently. I was shifted to the post of Chairman, Tariff Commission after a few months on promotion. But before I could settle down there, I received an order to take over as Secretary, Ministry of Parliamentary Affairs. These two short postings, in succession, were *inter alia* responsible for bringing down my average tenure of postings from four years to three years.

Be that as it may, I settled down in the new post and was coming to like the new assignment. It used to give me a heady feeling when Ministers would talk to me about scheduling or re-scheduling their item in the government's List of Business in the two Houses of Parliament. My reach extended to all ministries and Departments. I used to have quarterly meetings with their representatives to review pending items of Parliamentary Committees etc. After about a year, the Government changed. The NDA went out of power and the UPA moved in. It was June of 2004 and the new Lok Sabha had just had its first session to perform the ritual of swearing in the newly elected Member of the Lok Sabha. We were busy preparing for the first proper session of Parliament after the change of guard. The session was to begin in the first week of July and, as had been the practice during the General Election years, it was the Monsoon Session and the Budget Session rolled into one.

On a hot summer afternoon an officious looking retired senior bureaucrat, with whom I had a nodding acquaintance, walked into my room with a sheaf of papers in his hand. He started reading out my service record from one of the sheets. At the end of it, he looked inquisitively at me and observed: "You have a Ph. D. in textiles; you should be Secretary in the Ministry of Textiles". All this time, while I remained seated in my official chair, he stood his 'officious' ground. To say the least, I was a bit amused by his dramatic entry and the pompous announcement. But I kept quiet and waited for his next move. He turned around and walked away. I thought, he had surely gone wonky. I put the interlude away from my mind and got busy with making preparations for first regular Parliament session of the new government.

It was end of June. I had already made a detailed PowerPoint presentation on the working of my Ministry to my

Ministers (one Cabinet and the other two Ministers of State), which had been appreciated by them, including the fact I did it all by myself. A few days later, one of the Ministers of State, who was also the Minister for the Department of Personnel and Training (which deals with the postings and transfers of bureaucrats in the Central Government), came to my room and said: "Congratulations".

I was surprised and asked him: "Why, Sir"?

"You are being posted as Secretary in the Ministry of Textiles", he said, taking hold of my hands and shaking them vigorously. I was aghast. The details of the brief encounter with the retired bureaucrat I had had a few days ago flashed through my mind. 'What the hell?' While still allowing him to hold my hand, I composed myself and requested him to have a seat. We had some discussion on the arrangement for the ensuing Parliament session, while I tried to organize my thoughts on the news he had just broken.

After some time I said: "Sir, if you permit me I would like to say something about my transfer at this juncture."

The Minister had a puzzled look on his face but did not react.

I continued after a pause: "Sir, the first Parliament session of the new Government is less than a week away. All the Ministers have been newly appointed. In the Ministry of Parliamentary Affairs, the lone post of Joint Secretary has been lying vacant for quite some time. Even if a new Secretary is posted immediately, he may take a couple of days, to join and even then may not be able to assist you adequately. Would you like to deal with the three Deputy Secretaries in the Ministry directly during the forthcoming session of Parliament? The new Government is perfectly justified in making changes in the bureaucracy; but one post that need not undergo any change, at this point of time at least, is my post."

The Minister apparently understood the logic of my argument and left post haste. The next day, when we met he told me that he had been to the PM's office and got my impending posting nipped in the bud, as they say. I continued on the post for over a year thereafter till my retirement. I got a brief pat on my back by way of being posted as a Member of the Central Administrative Tribunal, about eight months after my retirement. A year or so later. I got a big hug when the Minister for Personnel asked me to call on the newly elected Vice President of India and Chairman of the Rajya Sabha. The rest, as they say, is history.

Several years later, when, after my retirement from the post of Secretary-General, Rajya Sabha I met (now former) Minister of State for Personnel at a function, he introduced me to a third person as 'the man who wouldn't be Secretary, Textiles'.

It is a different matter that had I chosen, on either of the occasions, to take the 'textile' route [Joint Secretary (Exports) or Secretary (Textiles)], I would have had a very different career progression. I have no regrets though.

39 Make In India: What an Idea!

Of late, a lot of excitement has been generated by the Modi Mantra of 'Make in India'. As a matter of fact, as one of the Union Ministers has put it, there are four of them going by the acronym MISIDICI, which stands for Make in India, Skilled India, Digital India and Clean India. Bharat Ratna Atal Bihari Vajpayee has been credited with initiating quite a few of the initiatives of the present Government. Let us, therefore, begin at the beginning.

The year was 1999. The National Democratic Alliance, led by Atalji, had formed a stable government, which completed its full term in 2004. I was then Additional Secretary, Department of Administrative Reforms and Public Grievances (DARPG). The Minister in-charge was Mr. Arun Shourie. He took to his assignment like duck to water. He was full of ideas and, under his guidance, several administrative reform proposals were conceptualized and executed.

One day, in the course of our conversation, he mentioned about the prevalent mis-conception that nothing works in India, because of various hurdles, including inspector raj, restrictive laws and procedures, corruption and so on. At the same time, there were many success stories of Indian civil servants, scientist, entrepreneurs, NGOs *et al* having achieved national as well as international acclaim.

Thus the IDEA was born to organize a series of lectures show-casing indigenous Indian success stories to motivate civil servants and students and inform the media as well as international community. It was aptly named 'Ideas that have worked'. I was required to work out the modalities of implementing the idea. *Inter alia* it required identification of speakers, identification of invitees, a venue which could accommodate 400+ guests/invitees, and arrangements for refreshment and logistics, in general.

I put my thinking cap on, to find my partners in crime. And as an old parable states, one tries to searches for a solution under a lamp post where the light is, and not where it ought to be. I found two partners in the joint venture. One was the recently set up Civil Services Officers' Institute (CSOI) at Kasturba Gandhi Marg, of which I happened to be the Vice-President and ex-officio Chairman of the Executive Committee. It helped rope in members to attend the events. The other was the Andhra Pradesh Bhavan, which had a very big auditorium, located in close proximity to CSOI; since I belonged to the then united cadre of Andhra Pradesh. AP Bhawan arranged not only for the auditorium but also their caterer, who served authentic South Indian cuisine. Depending on the timing of the lecture the catering was for lunch or high tea, mostly lunch.

The speakers were decided, mostly, by Mr. Arun Shourie and, occasionally, based on some of my suggestions/ recommendations. The speakers were the pick of the lot. The first Guest Speaker on 11 March, 2000 was Dr. A.P.J. Abdul Kalam, who was then Principal Scientific Adviser to the GOI and later became the President of India. The title of his talk was *When Can I Sing a Song of India*. The other speakers included dignitaries such as Dr. Varghese Kurien, Ratan Nawal Tata, Mukesh Ambani, Jayant Narlikar, Ms. Ela Bhatt, Dr. Bindeshwar Pathak, N.R. Narayana Murthy, R.A. Mashelkar, late Dr. S. Dabholkar and Vilasrao Salunkhe, among others. Twenty lectures were organized over a period of 19 months between March, 2000 and September, 2001.

The invitees were primarily civil servants, trainees and faculty of civil services training institutes, diplomats, media, students and faculty of universities, among others (not excluding some personal friends and relatives, who made a request depending on the speaker of the day). The number of invitations went up from about six-seven hundred to over fifteen hundred at a time. The attendance used to vary from about two hundred to four hundred. But then, Shri Chandra Babu Naidu, the present Chief Minister of the divided Andhra Pradesh, who was then the Chief Minister of united Andhra Pradesh, came to speak at A.P. Bhawan. More than 600 persons turned up to hear him. But we were prepared. A big TV screen had been fitted in the lobby of the AP Bhawan auditorium, with adequate seating arrangements for guests to watch the proceeding live.

All good things have to come to an end, as they say. So the *Ideas* series also concluded and left with us a lot of issues to ponder over. In the year 2004, the Department of Administrative Reforms & Public Grievances brought out a publication entitled *Ideas that have Worked*, published by Penguin, Viking. And that was perhaps, inadvertently, the precursor of Make in India.

40 The Ideas that did not Work

As mentioned earlier, during my tenure as Additional Secretary, DARPG, under the guidance of my minister Mr. Arun Shourie, a series of 20 lectures, entitled 'Ideas That Have Worked', was organised over a period of 19 months between March 2000 and September 2001. The lectures showcased the success stories of Indian civil servants, scientist, entrepreneurs, NGOs *et al* who had received national as well as international acclaim for their outstanding work.

However, during that tenure, I got an opportunity to work on a few other ideas that did not work. The first one of these related to downsizing the bureaucracy. The Minister, being in charge of the Department of Administrative Reforms, was, naturally, very keen on bringing about administrative reforms. Having been otherwise, as a reputed journalist, in touch with what ailed government, one of his priorities was to streamline the administration of the central government. I was required to prepare a Cabinet Note on downsizing the bureaucracy. I did a bit of research and consulted all possible documents, including the Report of the Administrative Reforms Commission (ARC) set up in 1966, which submitted its reports in 1970s. At the time of preparing the Cabinet Note we had close to fifty Ministries/ Department in Government of India. The ARC, 1966 had suggested reducing the then number of Ministries from about 32 to 16. Our Cabinet Note was more modest, taking into account the current realities. The Minister was very keen to push it through. After about two months I enquired from him about the fate of the proposal. He checked with the Prime

Minister's office and was told that it had not found favour with the highest authorities. The matter was allowed to rest at that. The Minister too lost interest and moved on to pastures more up his street.

The new Minister for Personnel (including Administrative Reforms) was Vasundhara Raje, who too took a lot of interest in streamlining administrative system of the central government. Under her leadership two very landmark decisions were taken. One of them related to restructuring of the lower bureaucracy, which resulted in abolition of the posts of lower and upper division clerks, coupled with creation of additional posts of assistants. The other one, in due course, led to introduction of the New Pension Scheme, which held promise of reducing the pension liability of the Central Government in the long run.

However, the very first thing she felt concerned about was the dress code of the civil servants, men in particular. A little while after taking over charge, she made a trip to Chennai for some work. It was scorching summer time in May; but the local protocol officer had come to receive her at the airport in black woollen *bandgala* (closed collar) coat. On return, she told me to do something about it. I got in touch with the National Institute of Fashion Technology (NIFT), with which I had worked a decade earlier, and it agreed to provide consultancy at a hefty fee. Several alternative designs of men's formal dresses for summer and winter seasons of India were prepared and reworked several times on the basis of the suggestions given by the Minister. A fashion show was also arranged for the Minister to see and give her final approval. The project report of NIFT was put together in the shape of a brochure, which not only provided the specifications of various dresses but also sketches of dummy models wearing them. The proposal needed approval of the Ministry of Home Affairs. We duly sent it to the Secretary of the Ministry. We did not hear from him ever; apparently, he was not amused. But that did not prevent some civil servants as well as other gentlemen from getting dressed in comparable apparel over a period of time, thanks to the NIFT faculty and students, who were in touch with the garment industry.

But we went further ahead. It was proposed that in order to bring the government closure to the people, a 'Year of the Citizen' may be observed. The Concept Note prepared by me argued that while, on the one hand, the expectations of the citizens from the Government have been growing, the public service delivery has always fallen short of these expectations, the world over. The citizens not only require responsive services which are provided efficiently, but would also like to have a greater say in how these services are designed and delivered. Fortunately, the availability of new technology and vistas opened up by New Public Administration and Management (NPA&M) have made it possible to improve the quality of public services.

Citizen-centric governance with a human face is the professed aim of the third generation public administration according to the experts. The project for observance of the Year of the Citizen was to have the following main objectives:

(i) To make the working of the Government Organisations more citizen-centric and citizen friendly; and

(ii) To create awareness amongst citizens about their rights and obligations relating to public services.

In the course of the year, several events and activities were planned to be organised. Some of these were current or ongoing. It was also proposed to develop and implement a media plan to generate awareness among the citizens regarding various activities scheduled for the year and solicit their active participation in them.

Among other things, all Central Government Ministries/ Departments/Organisations with a large public interface were to draw up a programme to create awareness among the citizens, with particular focus on the weaker sections, about their rights and obligations. This campaign would have, *inter alia*, included wide publicity to the programmes and schemes, rules and regulations, citizen's charters, grievance redress mechanism, etc. of these organisations through radio, TV and web as well as print media. It would have also required organising a *Janta ki Adalat* type of programme on Doordarshan on a monthly basis for Central Government Ministries/ Departments/Organisations with a large public interface. In order to create awareness among the citizens about the citizen-centric initiatives of the government, a tableau was to be mounted during the Republic Day parade on 26 January, 2002.

In order to give shape to the proposal, a media agency was engaged as a partner to prepare the media plan for wide publicity. Several meetings with the agency were chaired by the minister, who took keen interest in fine tuning the proposals. Each and every detail was meticulously chalked out. Finally, the project was submitted to the Prime Minister's Office (PMO), and that was the last we heard of it. We could not get the approval for mounting the show. I left the Department on a somewhat unwanted promotion and moved on.

Much later I came to know that the Ministry of Information and Broadcasting had launched an 'India Shining' campaign on a massive scale to highlight the achievements of the government between 1999 and 2003. In some quarters, it was held responsible for the party's debacle in the elections that followed.

On both the earlier occasions, when my proposals relating to downsizing the bureaucracy and observing the Year of the Citizen, attempting to refurbish the image of the government, did not pass muster, I was told by the ministers concerned that they had been rejected by the PMO on account of the apprehension that they may hasten the downfall of the government.

Policy Implementation: The Wise Old Owl

In a village lived an old owl, who was much in demand among the diverse population of birds and animals in the village for his ability to solve their day to day problems.

Once a mouse came to him and said that the local cat was bothering him all the time.

"How can I get over this perpetual harassment?" he asked.

The wise owl pondered over the problem for some time and then pronounced: "You too should become a cat and your problem will be over."

The mouse was very happy that a solution to his perennial problem had been found, and merrily went home. However, when he later thought over it, he found that he did not have the wherewithal to become a cat. He went back to the owl.

"Sir! you told me to become a cat in order to escape harassment from the local cat. But how can I become a cat?" He asked.

The wise old owl smiled and told the mouse: "I give only policy decisions. Implementation is your problem."

41 Unexpected Administrative Reforms

There is a popular Aesop's fable about the Hare and the Tortoise, in which the lazy tortoise unexpectedly wins a race against the agile hare. It is sometimes applicable to reform initiatives of governments. While some ordinary ones hang fire, some big ticket reforms, which initially appear to be no runners, win the day. In this article, an expected-to-be tortoise transforms itself into a hare.

Then there is the doctrine of *nishkama karma* propounded in the Gita, according to which: "You have the right to work only but never to its fruits. Let not the fruits of action be your motive, nor let your attachment be to inaction" (Chap. 2, *shloka* 47). The civil services fraternity would heartily endorse this because of their relatively short tenures on specific jobs. For the so-called generalist services [which are at the receiving end, Left, Right and Centre (capital intended), after the report of the Seventh Central Pay Commission], it actually often amounts to a total break from the past and having to start afresh. So while you are at it, do your job, heart and soul, but do not look back and rue or regale in the outcome or impact of actions you initiated, because on them you have no control, and, in any case, you are simply not there on the scene of action. My apologies for breaking the rule or the doctrine. I do not care.

At this point you must be wondering what am I leading you up to or up what garden path? In other words, what is the symbiotic relationship, if any, between the tortoise or the hare, on the one hand, and *nishkama karma* or the generalist civil services, on the other? Have patience and let the story unfold itself, as they say.

Let us begin at the beginning. More or less in the same week in the second half of February, 2002, as far as I can remember, I submitted reports of two committees, namely the Committee on Cadre Restructuring of Central Secretariat Service, and the High Level Expert Group (HLEG), constituted under the chairmanship of Shri B.K. Bhattacharya (former Chief Secretary, Government of Karnataka), to the then Minister of State of Personnel, Public Grievances and Pension (who is now the Chief Minister of Rajasthan).

The first Committee (of which I was the chairperson) was assigned the task of recommending restructuring of the Central Secretariat Service (CSS), the long standing and time tested back-bone of the Central Government Secretariat. The Bhattacharya Group was required to recommend a New Pension Scheme (NPS) to replace the existing open-ended (bottomless pit) pension scheme, which, over the years, was exponentially increasing the pensionery liabilities of the Central Government, thanks to the increase in average life expectancy, especially of the civil servants (despite some relief when the age of their retirement was increased by 2 years around Y2K), and who (along with their family members) are looked after extremely well by the government.

I did not know which one was tougher in terms of getting the government's nod of approval. In terms of personnel, it was perhaps more difficult because it involved changing the terms and conditions of some of the existing employees; while the other was going to impact only on future employees. But you 'never can tell' the reaction of the employees unions. In terms of financial commitment, the second one took the cake by a huge margin. While the first one would have resulted in some savings, the second one would have required a progressively increasing financial commitment from the government over the next 30 years or so, according to some actuarial calculations.

The Committee on Cadre Restructuring of CSS, *inter alia*, recommended that recruitment of LDCs (Lower Division

Clerks) should be stopped and all the existing LDC vacancies be abolished with immediate effect. It further recommended discontinuation of direct recruitment to the grade of Section Officer through Civil Services Examination of UPSC as well as abolition of *in situ* upgradations in any of the grades of CSS; and all promotions, in future, were to be made on the basis of available vacancies. There were, of course, some sops thrown in by way of an increase in the posts of Under Secretaries (from the existing 768 to 1400) and of Deputy Secretaries (from 54 to 330). While implementing the recommendations, Government accepted all the hard ones listed above, but added a few more sops, in good measure. It took some time (close to two years) to decide, but was done quite quickly according to me, relative to time it normally takes government to decide and implement big ticket reforms.

As regards the report of the Group on pension reforms, it too took only about two years and got implemented with effect from 1 January, 2004. The HLEG had suggested a new hybrid scheme that combined 'defined contributions' from employees and the Union Government on a matching basis, on the one hand, while not committing to the employees a 'defined benefit' as pension. While government had to continue with its payout of pension to the existing employees, who joined service on or before 31 December, 2003 (the number of pensioners thus, increasing from year to year), it also required making budgetary provision, year after year, for government's matching contribution (up to 10%) to the future pensioners, namely, those who joined service on or after 1 January 2004, a number that would increase from year to year. Thus the cumulative liabilities on both these counts would have gone up for several years (30 years, according to one actuarial calculation), when the benefits of the NPS would gradually start becoming visible on government's balance sheet (if there is one).

Thus, as the scenarios panned out, the government decided to bite the bullet (notwithstanding the prolonged agitation of the employees unions, at least in the first case; and their still continuing agitation in the other). The recommendations of both the committees were accepted, in principle, within two *light* (*italics* intended) years, but after I had moved on in my career, in pursuit of my *nishkama karma* dharma. All the hurdles were crossed by the intelligent tortoise, who had transformed itself into a hare.

42 Beware of Dog: A Requiem

We were blessed with him as a six-week old puppy by a couple, we had known for a long time. They presented him to us as a gift, when they came to lunch with us one day. Later, I would recollect telling them that God had given me two sons and they had given me the puppy. It was quite an experience for my wife and me to keep track of the small entity pottering around in our two-room first floor apartment in a guesthouse. He had to be taken down for his jobs quite often and we were scared to leave him out in the open for fear of our old bones not being able to keep pace with his frolicking movements. Gradually, he grew up. We remember the first time, he made an honest attempt to climb up the stairs. Initially he got tired after a couple of steps; but soon enough he was able to climb a flight of more than twenty steps all on his own. We named him Lord Astor, for no particular reason except that I happened to be reading about one Lady Astor, when the decision to name him was to be taken.

Later, we moved into a flat in a government colony. As he grew up, he came to be attached to us, more than we were attached to him. He always wanted to be with us. He did not appreciate our leaving him alone in the house. Once my wife had to go out of station. When I returned after dropping her at the station, I found that he had messed up the whole place. He perhaps thought that we had left him for good. He could not express it, but he felt very insecure when we left him alone in the house. He developed the habit of eating his food only when someone, preferably one of us, was in the house. His sense of insecurity and loneliness grew when my wife took up a job, which kept her out from about 07:30 am to 01:30 pm. Thus, on the best of weekdays, he remained all by himself for about 4 to 5 hours. His eyes said it all.

He gradually adjusted to our routine and would go and sit at a specific place in the house, mostly his basket or a particular chair, when it was time for me to lock up and leave. But he did not like our going out without him during weekends. He would rush out on hearing the sound of the car being taken out of the garage. He would manoeuvre himself to get into the car. Once inside the car, he would look out of the windows with a great deal of concentration as if searching for someone or something. His love for the cars grew to an extent when we feared that any one could take him away by offering him a ride. In the house, he was fiercely possessive about us. He would not even let my daughter-in-law touch our feet or an outsider shake our hands, let alone kiss or hug us. He would closely observe the newcomers to the house, sometimes standing behind diaphanous curtains of the drawing room. We too were equally possessive about him, which often made us over-protective.

We always faced this dilemma of whether to let him sleep with us or to put him in his basket outside our closed bedroom door. We used to switch between the two depending on the season, our mood or the behaviour of Astor on that particular night. If we moved him out after he had been sleeping with us for a few days, he would make an eerie pleading sound outside our closed door, long into the night, which uncannily sounded like 'please'. During the peak of summer, we did pull his basket into our air-conditioned bedroom.

He did not like the usual dog food except the bone. His favourite dishes were the same as ours. He particularly liked to eat rice with lintel and a dry vegetable preparation of cauliflower and potato, hand-mashed by me. His other favourite dishes were chicken curry, *rogan josh* (a type of lamb curry), and dishes made with *paneer* (unprocessed cheese). He was also fond of sweets and loved the smell of *ghee*. He liked milk, but it did not suit him. He did not like fish, nor did I. Above all, he wanted to eat what we were eating on a particular occasion and would also like to eat his food in the same room where we were having our meal. Any other favourite dish served to him would evoke little or lukewarm response. Actually, his favourite dishes rotated from time to time. Being a small-sized Dachshund, he could not reach the top of the dining table with his paws, but would place them on our lap and raise his face up to catch the smell of the food on the table. But he never picked up any food item unless it was given to him. He was also fond of the strong perfumes of toilet soaps and talcum powder, which he fancied being rubbed on him. Confirming the findings of Pavlov, he would enter the bathroom after I had had my bath, inhale the smell of soap used a little while earlier, return and climb on the bed, and start rubbing his back on the bed-cover. He would perform a similar operation, if we sprinkled a little bit of talcum powder on his back. We called it his 'powder dance'.

We treated him like a full-fledged member of our family. We referred to him as our grand-dog. We celebrated his birthday, which was, of course, only an excuse for us to have a bash. Astor only got a piece of *rogan josh* as his share of the fun. We gave him *prasad* (god's offering) on all religious occasions as well as that which we brought or received from various shrines, and prayed for a better next-life for him. On his part, he smelled (we called it 'touching') the feet of all our friends and visitors with his snout. My wife started looking for a mate for him after about two years of his coming into existence. We found a couple, who had a female dog of the same breed, and left him with them for a few days for him make it up with her. But nothing happened. We teased him saying that he was perhaps a devotee of Hanuman (the Hindu bachelor god) and was, therefore, ordained to remain a *brahmachari* (bachelor).

Astor's greatest friend was a street pariah popularly known as Jamie in our colony. I never saw Astor as anxious to meet anyone (including us) as he used to be when Jamie stood on the other side of the door/gate of our house. Astor would whine and try impossibly to slink out from under the gate to be with him. Jamie, of course, was a dog of a golden hue with a silver smile. He was extra-ordinarily fond of me. He went long distances to sidle up to me all over the colony. Astor had a way with the monkeys too. Once we took him to the terrace. Suddenly, a hoard of monkeys trooped in. Even as we tried to rein him in, he ran after them. We were afraid for him, because we did not think he could single-handedly tackle them. But we had misjudged. He went up to one of the monkeys as it was walking on the parapet, and raised his snout, which brushed that of the monkey. In a few seconds, some communication took place between them and the monkeys quietly walked away.

He was playful, naïve, stoic and disciplinarian at the same time. He would pull out a slipper from my wife's foot and wait at a distance holding it in his mouth, expecting her to give him a chase. He was fiercely possessive of his toys and liked to display them to our first time visitors. If we threw a ball at him, he would go and pick it up but not give it back to us. Once I brought a shoehorn, which was shaped like a human figure. Astor assumed that it was a toy brought for him. The moment I put it down on the dressing table, he picked it up and ran. We had a hard time retrieving it.

He knew how to get his share of affection and love from us. When we sat down in the chair to watch the TV, he would quietly persuade my wife to arrange her legs to form a lap for him to leap on to; and once he had settled in her lap, he would put his head on my lap, if I was sitting next to her.

One day, my wife rang me up in my office to tell me that Astor had gone missing. I have never felt such panic in her voice as was there on that day. The only thing that had actually happened was that his coat had got entangled in the spiked wire webbing of the lawn in an obscure corner, and he sat there without making any fuss, resigned to his fate.

He would like us to go to bed immediately after we had finished our evening meal. If we sat before the TV for any length of time, he would pull at our clothes to let us know in no uncertain terms that it was time for us to go to sleep. Once in the bed, we had to lie down and my wife had to cuddle him up. If that did not happen, he would silently but doggedly pull at her clothes and body parts till she complied. On other occasions, he would sleep near our feet, till we pulled him up to lie along side us. He had perfected the art of sneaking into our bed through ever-so-small opening offered by the flap covers of the mosquito net. He was mighty scared of slippers and rolled newspapers, since we had used them to discipline him during his early childhood.

Above all, he was, most of the times, supremely obedient. He took half-yearly pokes in the pet clinic with great equanimity, even as he did his jobs on the doctor's table. He took all the medicines dutifully. He let his ears be cleaned with methyl alcohol and anointed with antiseptic cream in a meditative mood with utmost serenity. He enjoyed his weekly bath with shampoo. When he thought he was in our way, he would always back away. Whenever we talked to him, he would tilt his head to one side and pin his ears back, trying to listen very carefully in order to make sense of what we were saying. But he was nobody's fool. If he sensed any danger to his or our life and liberty, he would always fight back tooth and nail.

In the beginning, we used to go for the morning walk with him, but found his frequent stoppages hampering our objective of a brisk walk. We then switched to first taking our round and them taking him for a walk later. Initially, when we started leaving him behind while going for our walk, he resented. But later, he got reconciled to this routine too. He would lie in his basket when we got ready and went out for our walk. On return, however, we would find him waiting behind the entrance door ready to get his share of the morning walk.

On that particular day, when we returned from our morning walk, we found him waiting, as usual, behind the door, wagging his tail ever so slowly. As we moved towards our bedroom, he exhibited his customary impatience at not being taken out for a walk immediately on our return. While I was placing the flowers, which my wife had gathered during the walk, before the deities in the cupboard, I heard a couple of piercing shrieks. I turned around and saw Astor lying on the ground and writhing. By the time, I reached him and placed my hand on his body, his eyes had turned stony and I could sense the life ebbing away. Later, upon being told the symptoms, the doctor said that he had died of cardiac arrest, perhaps on account of the fact that he was a diabetic. We put a few drops of *gangajal* (water from the Ganges) in his mouth and prayed for peace to his soul.

He died a few minutes before 7 am, such that I had enough time to arrange for the disposal of his dead body before going to office. In a city, which cares little for human lives, we could think of no one whose morning chores we could choose to disturb to share our grief. We sat holding each other's hands, while Astor's body was taken away for burial by the municipal authorities. It would be to our everlasting regret that we could do nothing to help him when he lay there struggling for life.

We may have to live with several inevitable and lingering regrets. I regret the fact that had I known that he was experiencing a cardiac arrest, I could have tried to pump his chest or done something to revive him. My wife regrets the fact that she was in the toilet, just a couple of feet away from the place where Astor collapsed. May be, in a sense, it was good for her not to have seen his face contorted in pain. Was the deworming tablet that we gave him a few days before or the calcium tablets that we were regularly giving him on the doctor's advice, were the culprit? Was it our type of food that we shared with him that killed him, specially the sweets and the ghee? Or was it the loneliness and isolation, that he was subjected to on account of our lifestyle?

He passed away on a Tuesday (the day consecrated to lord Hanuman), a *brahmachari*, at a young age of four dog years. Till today, his memory is enshrined in the wooden signpost on our gate: 'Beware of Dog'.

P.S.: Dear God! please tell us why, of all the dogs in the world, our Astor had to have a cardiac arrest and die prematurely? Did our *prasad* and *gangajal* ensure a better after-life for him?

43 Fighting Demons of Demonetisation

"On this 9/11 (Indian style)", someone tweeted, "the USA (the oldest democracy in the world, according to some experts) and India (by far the largest democracy in the world) moved from black to white, overnight." In both cases the public came out on the streets; but, of course, for different reasons.

In the USA there was 'anger on the streets', with protestors displaying placards with the message 'Not My President'. More than a thousand CEOs urged Donald Trump (since nominated Time's Person of the Year) to 'stop divisive politics'. It was really 'shock and awe' and a news magazine had reportedly prepared its next issue in anticipation of Hillary's victory, some of which got into circulation. A Swede is reported to have helpfully offered himself on e-bay to marry any American woman who, dismayed by the electoral verdict, wanted to leave the USA and become a Swedish citizen.

In India the people were on the street, fretting and fuming about the delay in exchanging their old notes with new ones as well as on account of mal-functioning of or non-availability of cash in the ATMs ("ATMs run dry of cash and Delhi'ites of patience"). Even after several days, I found many ATMs closed or non-functional, while others had not even seen a cash delivery van since the demonetisation demon was unleashed. ATM came to be expanded as *'Ayega To Milega'* (if it comes, you'll get). Asking people to queue up twice a week or more to withdraw Rs. 24,000 (in actual practice the banks started doling out two to ten thousand rupees only per visit) through cheque, made the queues longer. I have some experience of standing in queues, the latest being having to wait for my turn to get the monthly quota of medicines from the Central Government Health Scheme (CGHS) dispensary (Wellness Centre, if you please), which is located across the corridor from a bank branch. But in my later visits to the dispensary, I found that the queue had shifted to the bank, leaving me a very happy Wellness Centre customer.

The cash crunch led to sporadic violence and ration shops in some places were allegedly looted. While there were some cases of dire distress, there were also others of philanthropic humanitarianism, where shopkeepers extended credit facility to their customers. Others helped out foreign tourists without the new Indian currency. During the honeymoon period, some RWAs served water, tea and snacks to people standing in queues to exchange or deposit their old notes; a band played music to entertain the 'queuers', wow! Iconic Indian 'jugad' was on display all around; local solutions to local problems, that is.

Nevertheless, there was a general public perception that the initiative, though laudable since it could have a positive domino effect on the economy in the long run, had been launched without adequate preparation and hence the arrangements for its implementation left much to be desired. For example, a large number of mobile banking vans (including micro-ATMs) could have been pressed into service. Again, the banks could have operated for the public at large in the forenoon, setting aside a few hours in the evening to attend to their genuine account holders' non-currency requirements. Separate queues for women, differently abled, senior citizens and account holders could have been arranged to begin with itself. Similarly, separate queues for exchange and deposit of old currency too could have been put in place. Some remedial measures, on these line, were, of course, introduced subsequently, including use of indelible ink on the right index finger to ensure that the same person did not queue up to exchange notes again and again; but, given the small size of the premises of most of the bank branches and the logistics of queue management, I wonder how many of them could effectively be implemented across all banks. One thing is, however, certain; everyone was made to fall in line, except, of course, a few privileged ones.

In the meanwhile, government introduced certain measures to relieve the distress: anticipated as well subsequently witnessed. Thus, use of old currency was permitted for purchase of petrol, diesel and CNG; railway, airlines and metro tickets; gas cylinders; medicines; grocery and milk products from cooperative or government stores; payment of electricity and water bill; house tax; and at government hospitals, and ASI monuments! This led to a rush for purchase of advance / waitlisted railway and air tickets in large numbers, in particular. People wiped out the shelves of cooperative stores, buying their quota of victuals for the next three to six months. Standing in a queue to buy groceries was considered a better option than in the one for exchange of old currency notes! There was also considerable last minute as well as back-dated purchase of white goods, gold and foreign currency. The government moved in to introduce some restriction and the authorities raided the premises of jewellers and foreign exchange dealers. But some of the concessions given were prematurely withdrawn. According to various estimates, over a 100 modifications to the original orders were issued from time to time. Some called them knee-jerk reactions while others described them as measures of responsive governance.

Normal shops had little business and contemplated closing business for a few days; the multiplexes wore a somewhat deserted look; but there were long queues in front of banks, and a couple of days later at ATMs, whenever they were open. During the following weekend, the lines got longer. A middle-aged woman in Mehbubabad of Warrangal District, Telangana State, panicked and committed suicide, when her stored cash of 54 lakh turned into waste paper overnight. Over 100 persons died, ostensibly while waiting in various queues or allegedly due to depression caused by non-availability of new currency on account of demonetisation. (More than 470 persons reportedly died grieving over Jayalalithaa's death.)

On the other hand, a sweeper in Pune found 52 thousand rupee notes in the garbage. In Mirzapur, currency notes were found floating in the Ganga. In Bareilly, shredded and burnt currency notes of high denomination were recovered. Migrant workers started returning to their homes.

The collectors of old coins and currency notes too were licking their lips in anticipation of a windfall in future. Banks were flushed with liquid cash; a large number of old electricity and municipal tax dues were cleared. Direct and indirect tax collections went up by 15% and 26% respectively. The monthly take home emoluments of the employees of currency printing presses showed a healthy appreciation, although the ATMs provided in their office premises continued to be as dry as others in the outside world. Further, for the cash-rich temples of India it did not matter. The old notes were still poring in and the government was unlikely to ask any questions because, in a sense, it amounted to payment of tax direct to God, the original source of the coffers of the Reserve Bank of India (RBI).

Cases of small thefts perceptibly declined; in one case, the snatched purse was returned with a slap. (In any case, with Government's drive to make people shift to digital mode of transactions, and, hopefully, with the literacy situation in India improving, the crooks are bound to migrate to cyber crimes.) The mobile wallets saw a god sent opportunity and started aggressively marketing their wares. Even the normal banks started taking various overt and covert measures to entice people to become their customers and open accounts with them. The Government too chipped in to launch a new TV Channel (DigiShala) to promote cashless economy. On the 50th day of the window provided by the Government to deposit demonetized currency notes, Prime Minister launched an Aadhar-based mobile application called BHIM (Bharat Interface for Money), ostensibly inspired by Bhimrao Ambedkar, to facilitate digital transactions even without internet connectivity.

Politicians had their own take on the event. The decision was variously described as 'Tuglaqi farman', an anti-poor measure and an undeclared financial emergency. It was alleged that having made arrangement for itself, the ruling party had attempted to stymie the opposition in the forthcoming elections. On a more sober note, it was also suggested that the withdrawal of the currency should have been preceded by an announcement a few days earlier. Several politicians, in addition to civil servants, and businessmen, however, started swearing by demonetisation in order to establish their honesty credentials.

Anyhow, it established the supremacy of small currency. People were found flaunting hundred rupee notes. Demonetisation became a great leveler!

At a personal level, I belong to that generation which has been witness to three demonetisations (1946, 1978 and 2016) so far; although I have no memory of the first one, being too young at that time. I actually felt nostalgic, since the realigned composition of my wallet reminded me of an era gone by, when it used to consist mostly of fivers and teners along with sundry coins, and an occasional hundred rupee note. (Of course, now it has more hundred rupee notes than those of lower denominations.)

But I did not have to rush to banks or ATMs. As a pensioner, my monthly pension gets credited into my bank account, a few days before the end of the month. I, therefore, make it a point to withdraw the money required for the next month, during the last couple of days of the previous month. I also ask my bank to give me the money in notes of different denominations, including at least one bundle of 100 rupee notes. When the bolt came from the blue, I had a considerable stock of 100 rupee notes to defray the daily milk and vegetable charges for a few months. But my plan was found wanting on one count. Since I had withdrawn currency notes of higher denominations too just a few days ago, I had to put them back in the bank.

For a variety of reasons, including demonetisation of currency in India and the unexpected result of the elections in the USA, some individuals wanted to drown their sorrows (also known as '*gam galat karana*' in Hindi parlance popularised by such icons as Devdas) in their favourite brand of the bubbly. But they were in for a shock on two counts. First, since the shops would not entertain the old high denomination notes;

and, second, if someone bought a small measure with lower currency and tried to down it in public in Delhi, he would have been fined rupees five thousand for the first offence. He also stood a fair chance of being arrested, even though, in the process, he might have gained some valuable experience of standing in a queue in preparation for the ordeal of negotiating interminable waiting lines in front of the banks. I, however, wonder whether the police was accepting the old high currency notes towards fine! Be that as it may, to rub salt on the festering wounds came the news, riding on the rumour wagon, that the price of salt had gone up many times. However, the level of pollution in Delhi reportedly came down, when a large number of cars stopped travelling beyond the nearest bank or ATM.

Ghalib said: *aur bhi gham hain zamane mein mohhabat ke siwa* (there are other woes in life apart from love). Under siege, since November 1 following clampdown by United Naga Council over the creation of new districts, the State of Manipur had bigger worries than demonetisation.

According to one expert, the use of Devanagari numerals in the newly released notes is in contravention of the Constitution of India. According to some legal eagles, of course, the entire demonetisation exercise is invalid for want of statutory authorization. Just before the last date fixed for returning the demonetized currency to the banks in the normal course, the President of India promulgated the Specified Bank Notes (Cessation of Liabilities) ordinance, 2016 in order to end the RBI's liability in respect of the notes withdrawn from circulation. According to some, this was a back door measure to legalise demonetisation.

At the end of the day, I was delighted to receive the mint-fresh crisp currency notes after a long time, having been routinely dished out senselessly vandalized and hopelessly frayed ones by the banks, with sickening regularity. The new 2000 rupee note, in the absence of its running mate the 500 rupee note, however, was, ironically, suitable only for buying high end liquor. Even the liquor vends gradually started using PoS (Point of Sale) machines, making the royal 2000 rupee note (the new pariah) quite irrelevant. As in the case of the discredited 1000 and 500 rupee notes, which were allowed to be used in certain establishments for some time, the shop keepers wanted you to make purchases as close to the denomination of the 2000 rupee note as possible, because they had no change. Given these factors, among others, the government's hopes of the new currency circulating through the banks were belied. The situation mimicked a human body syndrome: if it is not sure when it will get the next meal (read consignment of notes) it tends to store whatever it gets, for future use.

A good strategist, they say, is one who is willing to take one step back in order to move two steps ahead of others. Similarly, from being a predominantly cash economy, we receded into a barter economy temporarily in order to take a leap towards digital economy, I hope. In any case the 'shagun' (gift) at marriages started arriving in kind (including items available in medical shops) rather than in cash, as high denomination old notes were not acceptable. Some employers paid part of the salary to their employees in the form of groceries as well as old notes.

I made my own contribution to the 'cashless' economy by opening a Paytm account and putting into action my hitherto less-used credit/debit cards. I have stopped sniggering at young people who use credit/debit cards for small purchases, since I am doing it too. However, I use one of my credit cards more often, even at sundry establishments; but it belongs to a bank in which I have no account. A little later I opened an Ola account too. In due course I may have to add more e-wallets to my arsenal, such as Mobikwik, Buddy, Oxigen, JioMoney, freecharge, PhonePe, Pockets (ICICI Bank), Uber etc. in order to transact business in different establishments. It, however, not only requires opening several accounts, but managing them too. At present, we have three bank accounts and they are quite a handful. And again, if I have to e-transact everything, I cannot possibly afford the luxury of sending my Jeeves to make purchases or pay the Bills on my behalf. And no doubt I am going to miss the smell of cash as well as the sense of power that comes with handling currency.

Moreover, as cyber-crimes proliferate, I would need to guard my mobile more carefully since it is not only '*mera batua*' (my purse) that I stand to lose but also '*mera* mobile'. I realize the need to protect my (smart) mobile as I would my life, since already privy to a lot of my data, now it has access to my money too. And with my e-wallet gone with it, how would I ever buy a new mobile? There is further news that digital wallet can be a 'pickpocket', stealing data from your mobile. Venezuela, which like India, withdrew its highest currency notes from the market, has cautioned about cyber-crimes that target the digital economy. Pakistan, of course, cannot but mimic: its Senate has passed a resolution seeking withdrawal of high denomination Rs. 5,000 currency notes in a phased manner in order to curb the flow of black money.

There is, of course, the problem of PoS machines being in short supply. 'Digital India' initiative having been around for quite some time, what prevented the government (surely not the concern for privacy surrounding demonetisation) to promote and propagate PoS machines? The eleven point programme to encourage people to go for digital transaction announced by the Government a month after demonetisation, could have been put in place on day one.

Incidentally, the shock and awe of demonetisation reinforced the virtue of frugality and, post demonetisation, our monthly household expenditure went down. The reason, in retrospect, appears to be that the earlier disciplining of monthly expenses through keeping track of money withdrawn at the beginning of the month could not continue; and, at the same time, I was not quite used the unfettered freedom of expenditure that comes with the use of credit/debit cards, where, literally, sky is the limit. I, therefore, had to tread cautiously, till I could get into the groove of the new regime. Daily recording of money spent through different modes did help, though. But the number of pages of the notebook needed for writing down the expenditure details was reduced from three to two. Even according to banks' data, as credit card volumes went up, the value of transactions dropped. In any case, I am told that spending less is in national interest because, according to some experts, deferred consumption will spur growth.

Purchase of several goods and services requiring cash transaction has been curtailed, till such time as our newspaper man, vegetable vendors at the weekly *haat*, corner store owner, *kirana* merchant (who gives us hefty discounts on bulk purchases), house help/maid, gardener, electrician, plumber, carpenter, washer man, cobbler, drycleaner, manager of the car service station, old style taxi-wallah, car park attendant, the coolie at the railway station, local stationer *et al* start flaunting e-wallets or PoS. Some of them were not willing to accept a cheque, even though they ostensibly had bank accounts, because of the hassle of having to queue up to deposit it in their banks. But I found a silver lining in the gathering storm; my favourite sweet shop was willing to accept payment through Paytm, but it had downgraded its establishment and stopped accepting credit cards. My personal account book post-demonetisation showed that e-payments increased from about 5% to more than 40% over two months.

As a matter of fact, even though, as the readers can make out, I am a crisp currency aficionado, I have, as mentioned above, a modest stock of small denomination notes. I hate to present my corner store-wallah with a five hundred rupee note while purchasing three pouches of toned Amul milk costing sixty rupees; even as I watch, in disbelief, several young men giving him the opposite treatment. I had a chat with him in early December of 2016. He looked unconcerned; the business was as usual.

Whether demonetisation has been good for the country or not, perhaps only time will tell. But, in the short run, the official version is definitely at logger heads with the verdict of the economic pundits as well the ground realities. At face value, so to speak, the Government's expectation of a bonanza of old notes to the tune of three lakh crore of rupees not being surrendered, has been belied. According to some quick estimates, at the end of the grace period, 95% or more of the scrapped notes were back in the system, eliminating the possibility of the RBI or the Government harvesting a one-time windfall of a big dividend through the demonetisation exercise.

The Government has, however, consoled itself with the observation that the 'black money' which was lying in various secret hideouts and was, for all practical purposes, out of circulation all these years, has been mainstreamed. It is of the view that demonetisation has also paid off in terms of check on terrorist funding and circulation of counterfeit currency. It also seems to think that after 50 days of moratorium/patience it sought from the public, the hardships have tapered off and things have more or less returned to normal. Further, the move has got international approbation, with the result tourism industry has received a fillip and the number of foreign tourists has gone up by 7.43% on account of the image makeover. According to the Finance Minister, revenue collections have shown buoyancy. An upward trend is visible in green shoots in several sectors such as insurance, mutual funds, aviation and petroleum; and the business in those sectors is thriving. Overall crop sowing in the rabi season was up by 6.3% compared to previous year, and in spite of the hardship caused during the initial period, no unusual unrest was witnessed.

However, according to the foreign media, demonetisation has been a reckless bungle. As the days progressed, surprise and skepticism gave way to open criticism. The 'bold and decisive' move turned out to be 'poorly thought out and executed'. It was pointed out that the rich and corrupt would not suffer since their illegal fortunes had almost all been converted to shares, gold and real estate; however, the poor would be hit hard. *The Economist* has called it "cautionary tale of the reckless misuse of one of the most potent of policy tools: control over an economy's money".

Kenneth Rogoff, an economist and foremost champion of cashlessness (*The Curse of Cash*) declared that India's cash bonfire was poorly designed and was too much too soon. Steve Forbes has called the decision breathtaking in its immorality. "What India has done is commit a massive theft of people's property without even the pretense of due process – a shocking move for a democratically elected government." "Terrorists aren't about to quit their evil acts because of a currency change. As for the digitization of money, it will happen in its own good time if free markets are permitted."

On the other hand, according to Muhammad Yunus, founder of Grameen Bank in Bangladesh and winner of Nobel Peace Prize, 2006, demonetisation kills black money and increases liquidity. Most important is the fact that demonetisation has brought rural and organised sectors into the banking fold. Cashless economy is a boon. What is needed is to add incentives to the cashless model to make it successful. French economist and winner of Nobel Prize in Economics (2014), Jean Tirole, has said that it was not possible to catch corrupt money with demonetisation. It will, however, make future corruption more difficult. Cashless economy is a good thing. But it should be ensured that the poor, who are most dependent on cash, did not suffer. Prepaid debit cards could be given to the poor in order to mitigate the impact of cashless economy on them.

As regards ground realities, even after the grace period of 50 days, a majority of ATMs were not working full time and 500 rupee notes were not easily available in banks. Onions and tomatoes were going dirt cheap, farmers were shown destroying their crops in the field for want of a fair price and distributing their vegetables to the people free of cost.

As a reasoning person, I am massively confused. Is demonetisation then a meme or a post-truth?

When the hurly burly's done, when the battle is lost or won, it needs to be kept in mind that the problems of public policy are, most of the time, "messy", "wicked" and squishy" and public policy making process is highly polyarchal and diffused. (Demonetisation has impacted adversely on Nepal's economy.) As Charles Lindbolm has propounded, it is the science of "muddling through"; India's demonetisation experiment has panned out to be no different. But the least the Government could do is to amend the law to award life imprisonment/death penalty (*à la* certain countries), if possible, to persons involved in converting black into white post demonetisation, on a large scale.

If a referendum on demonetisation were to be taken in India today, would it go the Brexit and Trump way (the old guard over-ruling the aspirations of the young)? But since prohibition worked for Nitish Kumar, demonetisation might as well work for Modi, in the long run. If prohibition can turn into an instrument of social change why can't demonetisation?

Paper Weight at Chowpati

Once upon a time, several decades ago, in a small sleepy town in northern India, there lived an enterprising young man with a craving for travel. Being of modest means, he had often only dreamt of visiting the tinsel town of Bombay (now Mumbai). Once he had made enough money, he decided to go to Bombay to try his luck.

In small sleepy towns of yore news travelled thick and fast. The rumour spread that our friend, let us call him Mr. X, had got a call from Bollywood for a role in a film and was, therefore, proceeding to the city of dreams. People in the neighbourhood started visiting him in hoards to congratulate him as well as to find out whether he can bring them luck too. He was at pains to explain that he was just going for a short visit to see the city, in fulfillment of a childhood dream.

After a few days, just before his departure, he started getting streams of visitors. They came with a list of things they wanted him to buy for them from Mumbai. There were all kinds of lists, some short and others long; some real and others wishful; some of the applicants gave him money (mostly in loose change) in support of their requests, but a large number of them just gave the list and promised to pay him on return. Still others just handed over the lists, as neighbours often do in the hope that you may like to share your good fortune with them. The lists contained items such as fancy soap bars to razor blades to T-shirts to transistor radio and so on.

After about 15 days of excruciating wait for list-givers, Mr. X returned from Bombay to a reception reserved for our cricketing and Olympic heroes (albeit on a small scale, given the size of the town). Some of them went to receive him at the railway station, others made discreet enquiries from his family members; but Mr. X kept his

(*Contd.*)

(*Contd.*)

council for the time being. After a day or two he sent out the word to the list-givers to find out the fate of their respective requests. They all gathered in great anticipation, nudging each other in the space outside his small house.

Mr. X took out some lists and gave away some of the items requested for by the respective list-givers. That still left a large contingent of unsatisfied 'customers', if we may call them so. To the voiced as well as unexpressed queries, he put out his response as follows:

"Friends and town-men,

After I reached Bombay, I went around a few days looking at city lights. It is a big and fascinating city. The number of people there is beyond belief. The number and size of the shops and the goods they sell is unthinkable. The next couple of days I went around various shopping centres in order to get an idea about availability of various products and their comparative prices. The day previous to my departure, I went to the famous seaside resort called Chowpati. There, on the parapet, I took out and kept all the lists given by you, one after the other in a line. I then took out the money (in coins) given by some of you and kept it on top of the respective lists. It was early morning and a nice sea breeze was blowing. After I had arranged all the lists along with the money provided for them, a particularly strong whiff of fresh air came and blew away all the lists for which no money had been provided. The coins provided by others acted as a paper weight and kept the lists from flying away. I have, therefore, been able to bring things only for those of you who had given money for the purchase of the items requested for. For others, I have to say sorry, I couldn't do much in the absence of the lists that were blown away."

There was a murmur of approval, particularly from those who had given the money and had, therefore, got the things they had asked for. Gradually, the assembled crowd melted away.

Part IV

Tributes

44 Intelligence Test

In recent times, the newspapers, off and on, have carried reports regarding young achievers attaining high score on Mensa IQ test. On 11 January, 2016, there was a news item that Ms. Kashmea Wahi, an 11 year old girl of Indian origin in the UK, had achieved the highest possible score of 162, leaving behind the likes of Albert Einstein and Stephen Hawking, as both are thought to have an IQ of 160. A prominent Hindi newspaper has instituted an Indian Intelligence Test (IIT), which assesses a student on several parameters, such as kinesthetic, linguistic, mathematical (logical), naturalistic, interpersonal, intrapersonal, visual and musical.

I have no claim to be in the league of Mensa geniuses; but the context of my IQ test speaks a lot about the sagacity of my father. When I was in school (1953-60) in the BNSD College, Kanpur, a choice between science and arts streams had to be made after passing the 8th class/standard examination. After passing the examination, when the new academic session began after the summer vacation, all those who had passed the 8th class were asked to assemble in the common/prayer hall. The hall was segmented into two parts. Those opting for the science stream were required to remain on the floor, the regrettable ones were asked to go to the dais (as if to showcase there assumed incompetence). As directed by my father, I went and joined the unchosen ones on the dais. My mathematics teacher from 8th standard came up and asked me whether I had heard the instructions correctly. (He was a mathematical genius and liked my performance in the previous class. His categorisation of human intelligence I still remember: blanket, leather and bamboo types. (See box.) I said 'yes', and stood my ground. I told him about my father's orders. He was disappointed, but couldn't do much about it.

My father's direction to me was based on the result of an intelligence test, which I had been put through during the summer vacation. What shocked my teacher was actually the dilemma that my father was grappling with. I was doing equally well in all the subjects, so there was no obvious indication about the subject stream I should join. The year was 1956, the place was Kanpur and it is not that the problem was identified during the preceding summer vacation. Imagine the sagacity of my father to have found an institute in Kanpur in 1956 to put me through a test to identify my proclivities! I wonder how many parents do it today. My father too did it only for me, because about my older siblings there was no confusion in respect of their academic propensities.

I vaguely remember the test procedures. It was spread over a few days. I was put through several sessions which *inter alia* not only tested my mental abilities and acumen but also my imagination and mechanical agility. I distinctly remember two tests. One was an Inkblot Test in the course of which I was shown several sheets.

I was then asked the question: "What do you see?" I remember liking the question and also recollect telling the faculty all kind of things; such as 'I see a dog',/'I see a monster on four legs'/'I spy a lion', and so on. I continue to make similar visualizations in cloud formations today. I recently clicked on my mobile camera a configuration that distinctly looked like the map of Jammu and Kashmir. Even in the tiles of my bathroom I see figures which amuse me no end.

The other test required me to insert a small iron rod into an object which had holes of several sizes. The test started with making me put the rod into the biggest hole and then gradually progressed to smaller and smaller ones. The catch was that if the iron rod touched any part of the rim of the hole, a bell would ring. I failed the test and was perhaps, therefore, found unsuitable for the engineering discipline. My father was an engineer and my elder brother was well on the way to becoming one.

I do not remember my father showing any disappointment with my performance; but that was the reason for his direction to me to stand with the art-wallas at the time of deciding the stream for which I should opt. But the good news was that I had an above average IQ. It was somewhere between 120 and 130, perhaps 127. I carried that test results with me till about 1970, after which, in the course my usual postings and transfers as an IAS officer, I lost them.

What is more, the test not only recommended the stream but also suggested the subjects I should opt for in my High School. I suspect that one of my uncles, who had already joined the civil services after post graduating in economics and had studied Sanskrit as one of his subjects earlier, had a say in the final choice. So I was saddled with economics, Sanskrit and geography (in addition to Hindi, English and mathematics). So be it.

I did quite well in the final examination but economics turned out to be my *bête noire,* in spite of my father having bought several tomes or volumes on the subject, much above the High School standard, for me to read. I scored very poorly in the subject, but still managed to pass with 'distinction' (75% marks), as it was termed those days. Of course, by today's standards, I would not have got admission into any good school for pursuing my higher secondary education. But things were not that bad those days. I continued in the same school and topped in the Intermediate Arts stream of the UP Board two years later.

But Sanskrit was a different kettle of fish and I took to it like duck to water, and continued with it till my graduation. It was also a subject I offered for my civil services examination and, I think, I qualified for IAS because of getting a 'distinction' in that subject. It is a different matter that my heart was never in the job. And that is why, post retirement, I am devoting myself to writing articles like the present one.

Types of Intelligence

The Math teacher of the 8th Standard in the BNSD College, of which I was a student, was in his elements as usual. He chided some students for not doing their home work; and made fun of others who were taken aback by the surprise test and couldn't answer any question at all. He then proceeded to tell us about three types of intelligence.

"First one is the *wool intelligence*", he said. "You put a needle through a woollen sweater, it goes in and comes out smoothly; but look at the sweater after withdrawing the needle, there is no hole, not even an iota of trace to suggest that anything had been through it. Some students' intelligence is like that. When something is explained to them, they seem to understand it very quickly. But when the period is over, the understanding disappears without a trace. That is why some of you have not been able to answer any question of this surprise test, even though all the questions were from the syllabus covered by me so far in the class."

He continued, "Second is the *leather intelligence*. If you try to pierce a piece of leather with a needle, it doesn't go in easily. But once it is through, it leaves a permanent mark. These are the students who take time to understand, but once they have understood, it is permanent.

"And third is the *bamboo intelligence*. That is the best. You drive a nail into a piece of dry bamboo. The bamboo gets split: up and down. If you tell something to students with 'bamboo' intelligence, they understand not only what you have told them, but all related matters too."

He stopped, smiled and said: "Think over it".

45 A Fresher's Friend

July 1962: I distinctly remember that it was the first Sunday after I had joined the A.N. Jha hostel of Allahabad University. I had encountered a bit of ragging during the week-days and, hence, was dreading being subjected to it for a full day by the seniors, at their leisure. Even though I was only 17, I had joined Allahabad University as a post graduate student in the Department of English Studies. Being ragged largely by a pack of B.A. (Part II) students (the first-time seniors) was none too palatable an experience. On top of that, it was my very first time out-of-home stay. Therefore, to say that I was dreading it is perhaps a bit of an understatement.

But, in a way, I was prepared for it. During the week I had bought a pocket dictionary to go with my text books. That Sunday was cloudy and quite pleasant. So, armed with a book and my pocket dictionary, I left the hostel early in the morning, and parked myself on one of the benches under a shady tree in the main university campus. Thus, from about 08:30 a.m. and up to almost Sunset, I sat on the bench and studied the book I had taken with me, consulting the dictionary as and when necessary. I took a couple of rounds in the central park in between, but never left the university premises; not even to have a cup of tea. When it grew dark, such that one could not be recognised from a distance, I cautiously walked back to the hostel. I thought I had weathered the storm. Monday would be another day and, hopefully, by next weekend the ragging mania would have somewhat subsided. I really thought I had acted smart.

But how wrong I was! The moment I tried to sneak in through the wicket-gate, a pack of seniors, who were sitting on the bench on the gravel path, outside the entrance to the main hall, jumped up and rushed to meet me. I was surrounded and put through an excruciating interrogation for my absence from the hostel throughout the day. I had thought that my early disappearance would go unnoticed because, in deference to my academic seniority and other credentials, I had been allotted a single room (No. 52) in the corner of the first-floor fifth block, near the staircase and overlooking the Hostel Superintendent's residence. But apparently one among the pack, which accosted me on my return, had seen me leaving the hostel premises. He was a very senior 'senior', who had completed his post-graduation in Chemistry and was waiting to take up a job. He had a laugh, which combined mirth with snigger; so one was never sure whether he was enjoying himself or merely expressing the ingrained contempt of a senior for the fresher in question. Be that as it may, I went through hell for the next couple of hours, and it ended only after I had memorised the hostel anthem and done a dozen or more of *furshies* (a ritual which required bending down at the waist, slapping the backside with the left hand, and doing three *salaams* with the right hand). I was feeling very miserable and started crying. Thereupon I was allowed to leave and went straight to my room in a very despondent state of mind.

Fifteen minutes later, there was a knock on my door. I got up and opened it. There was this very senior 'senior' standing there. He had that smirk on his face; and this time, he really sniggered or at least that is what I thought he did. I thought that I would have to go through the nightmare all over again. He asked me to come out of the room, which I did with a great deal of trepidation. We walked down the stairs, through the corridors, onto the gravel path, and out of the hostel wicket-gate. Not a word was spoken, while he walked ahead and I followed him. My mind was in a turmoil. I did not know what was in store for me. Once outside the main gate, he crossed the road to the corner cigarette-shop and bought a packet of Charminars. He lit a cigarette and started walking towards the university, with me in tow. After a few yards, he turned into *Jagati*, a restaurant, the popularity of which I came to realise much later.

There he ordered a lavish dinner, which I really hogged, having not eaten anything since the morning. During that dinner, the taste of which still lingers in my memory after 50 years, I really grew up as a fresher. The senior told me about the hostel culture, the need to take things lightly and not to be perturbed by verbal abuse during ragging. We shared information about our families, hobbies and other interests. Thereafter, he literally took me under his wings. We actually had nothing in common; but under his tutelage, I picked up playing the game of Bridge, which later became a passion. It took me to great heights as well as great lows; but that is another story.

46 My Adorable Dictator

I first came to know him in mid-1969 when I received a hand written letter from him as the Collector and District Magistrate of Nizamabad district. I received the letter while I was about to complete my training at the National Academy of Administration, Mussoorie, and was expecting to be relieved soon to proceed to Nizamabad, a district in Andhra Pradesh assigned to me for my field training. When I met him in his office, on reaching Nizamabad, I did not at first realize that it was he who was sitting in his residential office. When I told him that I wanted to meet the collector, he said that he was the collector. May be the confusion arose on account of his most un-IAS like unassuming manners, coupled with his short stature.

District training of newly recruited IAS officers was a serious business in those days; and, of course, I can vouch only for Andhra Pradesh in this regard, though it may have been true for several states. The trainees were sent to districts whose collectors were senior officers and were expected to instill the right values and administrative acumen in the young officer. During my first meeting with the collector (let us call him DS), I was provided a broad outline of the training that I was required to go through over the next year and a half. He then told me that there was no dedicated government accommodation available for my stay in the district; but I did not have to look for private accommodation since he had got an old and unutilized camp office, inside the compound of Collector's bungalow, all done up for my stay. It was a functional one-room apartment with an attached bathroom of modest means. It was perhaps used as a proper camp office during the Nizam's rule when a residential office could not have been located within the *sanctum sanatorium* of the living quarters, which had the restrictions attached to the harem (ladies quarters). In several other districts of Andhra Pradesh, the camp office is part and parcel of the collector's bungalow. It was so in Visakhapatnam where, much later, I served as the Collector and District Magistrate.

The two opening gambits, put me in the right frame of mind: training had to be taken seriously and I would be taken care of. Soon after joining the district, the fireworks began. I was sent for my village training to a place called Mortad, which was quite some distance away from the district headquarters. It was a biggish village, and for my month-long training, I was provided a room with electricity, water and only a modicum of toilet facilities. The village had been chosen because the village Patwari was an experienced person, who had trained officers before me too. The collector had arranged for a jeep to drop me at the village; but thereafter I was left to fend for myself.

Later when I got to exchange notes with my cohorts, I found that some of them were assigned villages close to the district headquarters so that they could comfortable stay at home and visit the village once in a while. My collector was a hard task master and had other ideas. After about 28 days (technically 2 days short of a month), a junior officer came to the village and told me that the collector wanted to see me. I left immediately for the headquarters in the jeep sent to pick me up. Upon meeting the collector, I came to know that he had decided that I had had enough of village training and wanted me to return to Nizamabad to start the next assignment. Since I was not informed about this by the person who came to pick me up, I had left my baggage in the village and somebody had to be sent to go and pick it up. Over a period of time, I started playing badminton and billiards with the collector in the town club, which was conveniently located within the collector's compound.

After about ten month of stay in the district, I took a month's leave to go home to get married. The marriage was fixed on the basis of a long distance trunk-call from my father (during which the female telephone operators giggled all the time), for which I had to make a couple of visits to the collector's bungalow, since I had no telephone of my own. When the news of my imminent marriage spread in the district, as everything does in a small town, one of the persons who came to call on me was the District Manager of the Indian Oil Corporation. He was quick to spot an opportunity to market an LPG connection in view of my impending marriage. He succeeded.

When I came back with my wife I found that an additional room had been added to my camp office accommodation during my absence in order to make my married life more comfortable. But, on account of my absence on leave, my training period had been extended by one month.

Often during my bachelor days in the district, the collector's wife used to send me savoury snacks to eat and I used to be invited for lunch and dinner from time to time. Once my wife joined me, our links with the collector's family became stronger. The collector's wife used to treat my wife as a daughter-in-law for all practical purposes. Their two children used to visit us often and treat us as a part of their family. When, towards the end of our stay in the district, my wife started expecting our first child, the concern of the putative mother-in-law increased many fold.

The life in the district was sedate and routine; but it was not devoid of small excitements. The collector's wife was hawk-eyed. She used to keep a distant watch over our routine. Having observed our out-house at night for some time, she told my wife that we should go to bed early. But we had other ideas. Both of us being movie buffs, we used to switch off the lights of our tenement early in order to pretend that we had gone to sleep. A little later, we used to sneak away by jumping over the wall of a school adjoining our abode to go and watch late shows. On one such occasion during the rainy season, when we returned from the movie, it was raining heavily and we were drenched. Our spectacles (we both wear a pair) were clouded with water vapours. As we approached the small verandah in front of our house, we saw two big figures standing there; but before we could react, we heard a mooing sound and realized that two cows had taken shelter in our verandah. On another occasion, we were woken up at night by a persistent knock on the window of our newly built bedroom. We were a bit scared and tried to peep through the glass; but could not see any one. Then suddenly, we heard something hit the window and found that it was the tail of a cow, which was the culprit.

Apart from the LPG connection which I had fortuitously acquired to help my wife with her cooking duties, I had also bought my first white good in the shape of a biggish transistor radio in order to provide some entertainment at the end of the daily routine. It cost me my one month's salary. It used to be kept on the sill of the bedroom window. One day, when it was on and one of the latest film songs, with a happy lilt, was playing on it, we saw a garden lizard swaying in front of it from side to side. My wife is terribly scared of the lizard and its ilk; they petrify her no end. The toilet attached to the tenement was an apology of a bathroom. One day, when my wife entered the toilet, she found a snake leader peeping out of the Indian style commode. I shall leave the rest to the reader's imagination.

There were many more such incidents and episodes, which, in retrospect, provide us entertaining reminiscences. But the elder brotherly care and concern that I received from the collector and the daughter-in-law treatment of my wife by the collector's wife, linger in our memory more than anything else. We were in touch off and on, particularly during his annual visits to Delhi to meet his elder brother. I had a long chat with the couple, a few days before he passed away in October, 2016. His son, when I met him a couple of days later, told me that DS treated me as his elder son.

DS's wife told me that he was planning to visit us and stay with us for a week before going to spend time with his son in Singapore. He had packed three suitcases for all the accompaniments and gifts for the Diwali festival in the offing.

I think my wife had a premonition about three weeks before his death, when she pushed me to call him up to check as to when he was planning to visit Delhi. He told me then that his brother had shifted to Lucknow.

47 A Personal Touch

It was around 8 am during an early winter morning when my landline telephone rang. The year was 1980 and location Hyderabad, much before the era of the mobiles. I had recently returned to Hyderabad after a stint in Delhi.

"Hello Agni", the caller said, when I picked up the phone, in his recognizably cheerful tone. The time of the call was not unusual, as having been my boss about a decade earlier, we were quite friendly. But the request was hugely unusual.

"What is it, I say?" he said somewhat sheepishly. "What is the second line of the lyric, *Aap jaisa koi meri jindigi may aye*?" The film Qurbani had recently been released and the song had gained considerable popularity. Even though he belonged to the south of the Vindhyas, he was very fond of Hindi movies and loved to listen to their songs on his small portable transistor. We used to watch Hindi movies together off and on, particularly during our earlier association.

"*Toa baat ban jaye*", I responded helpfully.

"Thank you", he said and promptly disconnected.

I first met UB in his office in Hyderabad Collectorate way back in 1971, when I had my first posting as Assistant-Collector (Hyderabad East) after the initial training. (The then Hyderabad District was subsequently divided into two districts and my jurisdiction then became part of Rangareddy District. In 2016 it was further sub-divided into a couple of districts.) He was wearing a bandgala made during his Mussoorie Academy days (about 6 years ago). It was early summer of Hyderabad and quite hot. Seeing his attire, I felt a little uncomfortable.

Looking under his table, I found him wearing sandals which bespoke his simplicity. My first impression was of a serious but somehow benign appearance.

He was my immediate boss and a hard task master at that. Even though I was on a regular posting, he decided that I was still under training, in a sense. The very first task assigned to me was distribution of taccavi (distress) relief to farmers, who had suffered crop loss due to a hail storm. (Earlier I had done pesticide spraying of field afflicted by pests, as in-charge BDO of Nizamabad block in Nizamabad District as Assistant Collector under Training.) I took it as a challenge and went personally from village to village for several days and distributed the taccavi relief in cash to famers in my presence.

Over a period of about two years of our working relationship together, we somehow developed a rapport and interacted with each other socially on a regular basis and watched movies together, particularly because our wives too developed a bond. He was a great movie buff; but interested in only commercial and light hearted movie. Sad and serious movies left him cold. His logic was that one went to movies to get relief from tension and not add to the headache. He suffered from migraine. We watched 'Anand' anyway.

We were out of touch thereafter because I moved to another district (Khammam) on promotion and then to Delhi (on somewhat of a demotion, as another episode has described in detail). We got back on the same wavelength when I returned in 1980 and the call came about the Qurbani song. When my father visited me in 1981 (first time after I had joined service in 1968) on the occasion of my house warming ceremony, I took him to UB's house. After interacting with him over a cup of tea (not coffee, which was UB's favourite), my father concluded that I was in good company.

When I was in Delhi (1975-80), UB came to Delhi and told me that he was going to the US for a conference for a period of five days. It was about cashew nut farming, an undoubted asset of the then Andhra Pradesh. It was his first and only trip abroad which he literally could not stomach. He returned to India prematurely because he did not like the food offered to him there.

It is not very often that two successive Chief Ministers belonging to very different political streams choose the same person as their principal advisor. Given his straightforward and reticent nature, UB becoming a part of a Chief Minister's team was actually a bit of a surp-ise. But he not only did that, but did it with élan. He was Principal Secretary to two very disparate political Chief Ministers, belonging to two political parties opposed to each other, namely T. Anjaiah (Congress Party) and then to N. T. Rama Rao (the founder of Telugu Desam Party). During that period we had a tacit understanding that we shall meet only on official business and have no social interaction. The greatest tribute, to his impartial and object performance during his tenure as the Principal Secretary to these Chief Ministers was the fact that on the occasion of the condolence meeting held in Andhra Pradesh Bhawan in Delhi after his untimely demise, all the MPs from Andhra Pradesh State belonging to various political parties assembled to pay their tributes to him.

As long as I can remember, come what may, UB always, almost religiously, used to go on about a month's leave in May-June every year, which coincided with his children's school holidays. The destination was always Vijayawada, which was his native place and home to a large number of his school and college friends. Going back to the roots and living a childlike existence, free of official care, was the objective. He wanted to unwind.

Again I moved to Delhi in 1984. In the era when mobile phones had not yet made their presence felt, going out of place was also going out of mind. Writing personal letters was falling into disuse and ringing up long distance on land line was costly and sometimes quite a hassle. We again lost touch, till an unexpected phone call came. It was a very unusual call given the fact that, in the context of the communication systems available then, we were hardly in touch whenever we were not together in Hyderabad. It was not a business call *per se*. We exchanged pleasantries and he told me that he was off with his family to Vijayawada on his annual leave to meet up with his school friends and relatives.

In retrospect I think that there was no need for him to ring me up just to apprise me of his holiday programme. But perhaps he was trying to say the last bye-bye. A few days later, I got the news that he had died in an accident, when a bus rammed into his friend's scooter on which he was doing pillion riding. He was Principal Secretary to N. T. Rama Rao then.

48 Fate Accomplished

I got to know him during the summer of 1976. We were almost next-door neighbours in a multi-storeyed sports complex, being used as transit accommodation for government servants posted to Delhi on transfer. There were 8 floors and each floor had 32 apartments. It is difficult to imagine how the architect managed to conceptualize it; but he did. Add to that the fact that most of the occupants were young couples with small children; so each floor had about 64 children @ two for each flat. There used to be quite a scene in the evenings, with the children chit-chatting, skating on the floor landing and doing all other kind of things that the children normally do. The kitchens of all the flats were facing the landing. Walking down the landing on a languid afternoon or late evening, you could get all kinds of aromas ranging from the north of India to the south and from the east to the west. Thus, families got to know each other through children bringing their friends to the flat or the wives exchanging cooking recipes.

Most of us did not have TVs. There was only one in the common room, which naturally turned into a 'commotion room' in the evenings, when the Doordarshan only programmes were aired for a few hours.

Mr. Prasada Rao (name changed) and I had had a nodding acquaintance for some time, before, on a particularly hot day of the ensuing summer, we simultaneously, and somewhat impulsively, decided to buy a room cooler. We went out to Daryaganj and bought a rather large-sized cooler each to match the degree of our discomfort. In due course, we discovered several common interests and passions, including a penchant for impulsive action.

Mr. Prasada Rao, a member of the Indian Forest Service and posted with the Government of India then, was an intelligent, witty and unassuming person. We mixed very well also because our spouses and children too liked each other. Both of us had two sons (his were a few years older), who provided plenty of opportunity to their mothers to compare notes. Moreover, the state (erstwhile Andhra Pradesh) to which I was allotted as an IAS officer was his native state too.

A couple of years later, my younger son, who was five years of age, decided to take a short cut to the ground floor from our second floor flat by sliding down the banister of the public staircase, as he had seen some older boys doing it. He could not quite manage it and fell headlong onto the hard ground below. Mr. Prasada Rao's elder son saw the boy lying on the tarmac, bleeding profusely due to a head injury. He carried him on his hands up to our flat, unmindful of the blood smearing his clothes all over. That brought us even closer and we went for several outings and spent many evenings together during our stay in the multi-storeyed haven for close to four years. At the end of it, Mr. Prasada Rao went on a secondment to the Food and Agriculture Organization (FAO) and, subsequently, got absorbed in it. I returned to my state government and got immersed in babudom. We met off and on, whenever our paths crossed, particularly when he visited his native state to meet his mother. In those early days of the computer age (1980s), he used to talk animatedly of the machine he had, which permitted touch-screen editing of text. I was fascinated.

Years later, in early 1990s, when I was doing a stint at the Lal Bahadur National Academy of Administration, Mussoorie, I received a surprise call one day from Mr. Prasada Rao from Dehradun inviting us to dinner. He had come to Forest Research Institute, Dehradun on a consultancy assignment on behalf of the FAO. I and my wife spent a nice evening together reminiscing the days gone by. At the end of it, we invited him to pay a return visit to our place in Mussoorie, which he did. In the course of the conversation, he mentioned to us that he was going to the USA to visit his son, who had been blessed with a son. In parting, we hoped to meet again during his next trip to Dehradun.

Ten days later, he was dead; although we came to know about it only about a month later through a chance meeting with a common friend. As it transpired, Mr. Prasada Rao went to Hyderabad to look up his mother before proceeding to the USA. On the spur of the moment, he decided to request his mother to accompany him. That would have, in his opinion, provided an opportunity for four generations of the family to be together under one roof at the same time. But this required a change in his itinerary. He had booked himself to fly out of Mumbai on a particular day. But in order to take with him his mother, an aged lady unused to long air travels, he needed a brief halt in Mumbai to give her some time to recuperate before she undertook the long journey to the USA. He, therefore, postponed his departure by a day. The airlines he was travelling by gave him a stopover in Mumbai in the Centaur hotel. On reaching Mumbai, he sought a change in the room allotted to him in the hotel to suit the convenience of his mother. His sister and brother-in-law came to Mumbai to see them off. As there were several hours available before the departure of the flight, his sister suggested that Mr. Prasada Rao and her husband might like to go into town. Mr. Prasada Rao differed. He said that he wanted to be with his mother to prepare her for the long journey ahead and, therefore, persuaded his sister and the brother-in-law to go to the city to make some purchases for him.

A little later the infamous bomb blasts of 1993 in Mumbai took place. One of the bombs went off in the Centaur Hotel, right next to the room where Mr. Prasada Rao and his mother had checked in. They died instantaneously.

We are still in touch with his two sons, who are in the USA and his unassuming and a very homely wife, who is periodically in Hyderabad and serves lovely *dosas* to us whenever we happen to be there. But we miss the cheer and the camaraderie that we enjoyed in the early days of our friendship.

49 The Halcyon Handloom Days

It was a visit that gave a new turn to my career and put me on way to an assignment, which I consider as perhaps the best period of my working life. I had just been transferred from the post of Collector & District Magistrate, Visakhapatnam, as a consequence of a collateral damage caused by a rivalry between two politicians, none of whom was either for or against me *per se*. I was posted as Director of Handloom and Textiles in Hyderabad.

Mr. S.K. Misra (SKM) was then the Development Commissioner for Handlooms, Government of India. He made a programme to visit Hyderabad to generate a consensus for setting up of the Association of Corporations and Apex Societies of Handlooms (ACASH) to provide a common platform for the diverse organizations created by various state governments to promote and support the handloom weavers, in order to take up joint ventures and consider issues of mutual interest. ACASH was a body set up in 1984 to make available a united front and give bargaining power to these handloom organization. Some of its other objectives were to disseminate information for marketing of handloom products, to undertake activities such as market surveys, research, exhibitions, publicity and publications in order to promote the handloom sector in India and abroad, and to work for legislative and other safeguards for protection of the handloom industry. In due course it led to ACASH being designated as the nodal agency to arrange supply of handloom products to Ministries/ Departments and other government agencies under a Single

Tender System (STS) through its members. But that was only one of the several new and unique initiatives to which I was a witness during the next few years.

But, first things first. At the end of that visit of Andhra Pradesh in 1983, Mr. Misra made an offer to me to join the office of the Development Commissioner for Handlooms as an Additional Development Commissioner (ADC). It was a great honour, but it being mid-session for my school going children I politely refused. I also sought his indulgence to give me some more time to gather field experience. (I had been on my post as Director of Handloom Textiles only for a few months then). Several months later, when the next school session was drawing to a close, Mr. Misra repeated his offer and said that he would not take 'no' for an answer. By that time, I was much better informed about the SKM or 'Chappy' way of administration. I knew that it was an offer I could not refuse; it was ADC (Handloom) or nothing. I made a deal. I requested him to help me getting my children admitted in a good school in Delhi. He agreed.

I landed up in Delhi in April, 1984. Mr. Misra kept his word and my children were admitted to a very prestigious school. A few weeks later, he called me and told me that a letter had come from the Government of Andhra Pradesh making an offer to me to return to Andhra Pradesh, if I wanted the next promotion equivalent of Joint Secretary to Government of India (the post Mr. Misra was occupying, but had been upgraded personal to him). I said that I had made the decision to come to Delhi, with full knowledge of the fact that if I had continued in Andhra Pradesh I would have got that promotion, which would hopefully come my way in Delhi only after about two years. But it did not matter. He then gave me the letter of the Government of Andhra Pradesh. From the date of the letter, I could make out that Mr. Misra had kept it with him for quite a few days before broaching the subject to me. I did not respond to the letter.

During my stay in the office of the Development Commissioner (Handlooms) for the next five years, two years were spent under the strict but benign leadership of Mr. Misra.

He was then promoted and posted as Secretary to Government of India in the Ministry of Tourism. I too got my promotion and moved into the position vacated by him, but continued to be under his tutelage, as we continued to work together on a project which put handlooms & handicrafts of India firmly on an international map, till then unchartered.

In the course of two years I spent working directly under Mr. Misra, I was always in awe of his vision and network. I found him to be a great institution builder. During those years (1984-86), not only did ACASH come into its own, but two more institutions were established. One had already been formally set up in 1983 under section 25 (now Section 8) of the Companies Act, namely, the National Handloom Development Corporation (NHDC), in pursuance of the perceived need for speedy development of the handloom sector through procurement and supply of inputs at reasonable prices, augmenting marketing efforts of the State, and upgrading technology to improve quality and productivity. I was made the in-charge Managing Director and had the responsibility of formulating the company's byelaws and undertake recruitment of requisite personnel. Mr. Misra was, of course, the Chairman. In due course, NHDC established several regional offices and raw material depots. It organized National Handloom Expositions on a regular basis, in collaboration with ACASH. Later, it set up marketing complexes for the members of ACASH, which came to be known by the generic name of 'Handloom Haveli' (since the first one was set up in Jaipur under that monicker).

The other institution, which was in the conceptualization stage when I joined, was the National Institute of Fashion Technology (NIFT) to provide skilled manpower to the garment industry, particularly the garment export industry, in India. I was assigned the task of giving shape to the idea. A collaborative arrangement with the Fashion Institute of Technology (FIT), New York was entered into for the purpose. NIFT came into being in 1986, with a vision to fulfil a growing need for professionals specialised in the field of fashion. Since its inception under the Ministry of Textiles, it has emerged as a prominent leader in the field of professional education, deftly combining design with management and technology.

The NIFT Act, 2006 has now accorded statutory status to the Institute for the promotion and development of education & research in Fashion Technology with President of India as the Visitor. The Act signifies public confidence in NIFT as a thought leader, with 'fashion' as a business strategy for value addition. The Act also empowers NIFT to confer undergraduate and postgraduate degrees. The Institute is a pioneer in envisioning and evolving fashion business education in the country through a network of fifteen professionally managed centres located at Bengaluru, Bhopal, Bhubaneswar, Chennai, Gandhinagar, Hyderabad, Jodhpur, Kangra, Kannur, Kolkata, Mumbai, New Delhi, Patna, Raebareli and Shillong. *What an idea sirji*!

It is not now in common knowledge that the initial programmes of NIFT were held in the shopping Plaza of Samrat Hotel, Chanakyapuri. The short courses initially organized by the faculty of FIT, New York, related to garment design, manufacturing and marketing. The consultant (Mr. Richard Streiter) and the faculty from FIT, New York were accommodated in that hotel. Another example of Mr. Misra's innovative and networking abilities. I also remember the phone calls of Prof. Arthur Price of FIT during early days, always made at an unearthly hour, which my wife was unable to cope with. And then later came an unearthly phone call from Mr. Streiter, when he was detained by the local authorities in Leh (Ladakh) for want of adequate papers.

By the time Mr. Misra left the office of Development Commissioner for Handlooms, he had already conceptualized an International event to showcase the exquisite handloom and handicraft products of India, namely, the Surajkund International Crafts Mela (Fair).

His elevation as Secretary to goverment of India in the Ministry of Tourism greatly facilitated speedy grounding of the event. Eversince 1987, this colorful craft festival of India is held in the backdrop of the Surajkund Lake in Faridabad, Haryana, during the spring season every year during February 1–15. Traditional craftsmen (artists, painters, weavers and sculptors) from all parts of the country as well as SAARC countries participate in this annual celebration. Designer items created by best designers and craftsmen in wood, metal, bamboo, iron, glass, textiles and stone can be seen here. This Fair is visited by lovers of arts and crafts from all over the world.

Every year has a theme, specific to a State of India, which is depicted at the entrance to the Mela grounds and provides an ambience of that particular state with characteristic colours, materials, architecture, furniture and decorations. The Mela also includes a food festival covering some of the popular cuisines from different parts of the country. Entertainment in the form of famous rhythms and dance of folk theatre are also held during the Fair.

The real icing on the cake, and another example of Mr. Misra's gargantuan network, was production of a film on the trials and tribulations of the handloom weavers, directed by Mr. Shyam Benegal. It was called *Susman* (The Essence) and was released in 1987. It had a star cast of about twenty well known cinema and theatre character actors, some of them up and coming at that time. Shabana Azmi and Om Puri played the lead roles; others included Neena Gupta, Anu Kapoor, Kulbhushan Kharbanda, Pankaj Kapoor, Mohan Agashe, Anita Kanwar, Jayant Kripalani, Satish Kaushik, Ila Arun, Harish Patel and K. K. Raina. It was, in a sense, a sequel to *Manthan*, the film on milk cooperatives of Gujarat (The Amul Story); and sought to showcase the plethora of problems that the weavers face in their lives. It is as realistic and relevant today as it was then. Only a few years ago (in 2014) I received a request from one of my friends, who works for an NGO, that she wanted a copy of the film to show it to the members of the Craft Council of India and a group of weavers in Tamil Nadu. Mr. Shyam Benegal promptly arranged a DVD copy for the purpose through his organization (Sahyadri Films).

The unique thing about all these innovations is that they have stood the test of time and have not at all faded away as many public institutions do, after having been set up with a lot of fanfare. I distinctly remember that when the NIFT was being set up, a meeting was organized with the leading garment exporters in the country to seek their cooperation. They came and listened to the project proposal with some reservations and did not at all look convinced, since they thought it was their territory. They, therefore, did not make any definite commitments to support the project. A few years later, however, they were recruiting the students passing out of NIFT with great alacrity, which continues unabated till date. They thus literally, came on board.

50 My Benefactors

In my reminiscences in this compendium, I have, most of the time, tried to avoid mentioning names of the characters. Occasionally, in respect of the articles already published, some readers could not suppress their curiosity and, even though perhaps they knew the person concerned, asked me to name him/her. However, I have been able to parry the queries. But in this fiftieth chapter, given its thanks-giving tenor, I think I can take the liberty of naming a few of them, except one Who-Must-Not-Be-Named (*à la* Voldemort, a Harry Potter character). So be it.

I would like to begin with paying obeisance to my parents (late Narayan Prasad and late Savitri), who brought me into being and contributed immensely to my becoming. They drilled into me, by example, the virtues of devotion to duty, integrity, meticulous attention to details, frugality and humility, which have been the guiding principles of my life.

Next, of course, comes my dear wife (Vijay) and our two children (Abhishek and Amitesh), who have borne the brunt of my idiosyncrasies, with exemplary fortitude, patience and decorum. The encouragement I received from my wife in putting together this book was indeed heartening.

Going back to my school days, I have to mention Gandhiji (the name by which the teacher was popularly known; and we did not dare ask for the real name), my Mathematics and English teacher in High School, who reinforced some of the virtues instilled in me by my parents. The love for mathematics that he created in me got me 98 out of 100 in the final examination (nothing great by today's standards, when students are scoring centum in English and Economics, the latter being my most hated subject).

Another mentor I would like to name is Prof. K. K. Mehrotra, Head of the Department of Allahabad University, who not only provided me access to his personal library when I joined the Department as a post graduate student, but also offered me the job of a lecturer, two years after I had left the Department.

I am also beholden to Col. S. G. Tiwari, my maternal grand uncle, who, as a member of the Allahabad University Senate, scuttled my confirmation in the job of the lecturer in the English Department and, thereby, left me no option but to focus on the IAS examination. There is no tongue in cheek here. I do not regret having not been confirmed, because the reason why I wanted to continue as a lecturer was, to some extent, an unvoiced peer pressure of two close friends (Alok and Harish), both of whom left the English Department after some time and took up jobs outside Allahabad. I might not have been able to follow suit, and would have been left high and dry. In any case, I do not think I would have made much of a mark as a teacher, least of all of the English language, given my initial handicap described elsewhere.

I got into the IAS, first shot, although my father was not very happy with my rank. He was of the opinion that had I worked really hard, I would have performed much better. Ironically, if I had got one rank above the one I got, I may have been allotted to West Bengal rather than Andhra Pradesh, given the roster system in place at that time. Getting a rank to get the home state (UP) was, of course, out of the question; and I thank God for that too. Be that as it may, I am grateful to T. N. Chaturvedi, my Joint Director in the LBSNAA, who perhaps saw some potential in me as a civil servant, a fact of which I got to see the proof of several years after my retirement. Generally speaking, the 'authorities' (be it parents, teachers, or superiors), in those days, were not very effusive or demonstrative in appreciating the good qualities or achievements of their wards. In between, of course, we occasionally met here and there, particularly in Galgotia book store in Connaught Place, New Delhi.

In service, late D. Shankaraguruswamy, my first collector, when I was under training, really trained me to perfection. There is a separate article on him in this section.

I think I need to get more personal now onwards. Mohan Kanda (an 'insider' cadre mate) was my friend, philosopher and guide from the beginning. I did not really know him, in the beginning, at the LBSNAA, till the cadre allotment order was posted on the Notice Board. He was the one who informed me that I had been allotted to Andhra Pradesh, along with him (of course). We came closer after that. The high point of our friendship, from my point of view, was when he rang me up from Hyderabad, while I was posted in Delhi (as an under secretary) during the later half of 1970s, to ask me whether I would like to join him in buying a plot in the Banjara Hills in Hyderabad to build a house. I said yes. He did everything thereafter to get the project going, without ever asking me to show up in Hyderabad. I am indeed grateful to him for his selfless munificence.

S. K. Misra (Chappy, as he is popularly known), picked me up in Hyderabad to join him in the office of the Development Commissioner (Handlooms) in the mid 1980s. There is a separate article on him in this section. I am particularly grateful to him for getting my children admitted in a prestigious school in Delhi, upon my arrival. Given the hopeless situation in finding a berth for children in Delhi schools at that time (and, from all accounts, it is no better now, even though the Sanskriti school has come up), I shudder to think what would have been my children's fate, had he not come to our rescue.

Around the same time (*circa* 1985 AD) I found a messiah in Dhananjay P. Singh, the Director of Estates, who provided me a decent government accommodation in Kaka Nagar colony (on Mathura Road). On the housing front, I once again found a deliverer in Ajay Mishra (*circa* 2000 AD), who facilitated my getting an 'appropriate' government accommodation in Tilak Lane (on Tilak Marg, near India Gate), after I had spent about nine months in the Andhra Pradesh government's guest house (AP Bhawan) in my next foray in Delhi.

Another benefactor was Prof. M. Gulrajani, who facilitated my admission in the Department of Textile Technology in IIT Delhi to do my Ph. D. Going back to school at the age of 40+ was a tough call; but with Prof. Gulrajani as my mentor, I managed it quite well. There is a separate article on my working for the Ph. D. degree.

While I was doing my Ph. D., my younger son was looking for admission in an engineering college. Dhirendra Singh, my colleague, facilitated his admission in MIT, Manipal. It was indeed hell of a good turn.

I would like to profusely thank Ms Sindhushree Khullar, who nominated me for the Queen Elizabeth (QEH) Fellowship in Oxford for one academic year, although all I had asked was a short three months exposure to a UK or US university so that I could access some good literature to embellish my thesis. It not only gave me a surrogate foreign posting along with my wife, but also helped add icing to my thesis, the final frontier, by way of an artificial intelligence based application called Handloom Technology Tutor. That put to rest all doubts, albeit retrospectively, about my eligibility to join an IIT, because I was not from the science stream. The fellowship was very comfortable and I could save enough money to fund my younger son's post graduate diploma in computer science, which led to his landing a job in the USA.

I owe a debt of gratitude to B. N. Yugandhar, the Director of LBSNAA, which I joined on return from Oxford, for 'facilitating' my posting in LBSNAA. It helped me immensely in completing the writing of my thesis, on account of its academic environs.

I am grateful to P. C. Hota for retrieving me from an indifferent Annual Confidential Report (ACR, now called Annual Performance Appraisal Report or APAR), which would have come in the way of my promotion as Additional Secretary to Government of India.

I am obliged to Prabhat Kumar, the then Cabinet Secretary, for giving me an opportunity to work with him as Additional Secretary, DARPG.

I would like to place on record, my heartfelt thanks to late Ashok Verma for pushing me to apply for the membership of

Delhi Gymkhana Club and Ms. Madhulika Shukul and Ganga Das for finally getting me there.

Probir Sen was instrumental to my getting the Membership of the India International Centre. Ravi Mathur allotted me the plot in Greater Noida in which, ultimately, I settled down after retirement. Suresh Pachouri, former Minister in the Government of India, facilitated my two post retirement assignments. I am extremely obliged to all of them.

There are many others who have helped me in various ways at different points of time in my life and career. I am beholden to all of them.

But there is one benefactor whom I shall not name. He is a colleague, who told my newly married wife at a party in Hyderabad that I was drunk and lying on the staircase of the venue of the function, when I had not had a drink at all. She was naturally very upset because we were just married and, since it was an arranged marriage, she had not known me much by then. As it was a well-known colleague who had broken the news to her, she really thought it was true and panicked. She came from a family which did not approve of drinking liquor. She was new to the State of Andhra Pradesh and did not know a soul in Hyderabad: no relatives or previous friends. In certain communities, there is a tradition of heavy drinking and some of them drink liquor like water and think nothing of it, but that is no reason to crack such a terribly sick joke. We have not forgiven that joker so far. Thanks to him, we have been made aware, from time to time, that we are not godly and that we have our weakness, such as not being able to forgive someone. Be that as it may, the discussion between me and my wife that followed this episode made me understand her concerns much better. It also, perhaps unbeknownst, helped set certain ground rules, for my future conduct, which, of course, have been broken off and on.

Why Didn't You tell me this Before?

There was a Brahmin, who used to be invited often for lunch during various ceremonies organised by people on auspicious and other occasions. He had a very young son. When the son grew up and his thread ceremony had been performed, the Brahmin decided to take him along for the lavish lunches, which earlier he used to enjoy all by himself.

On the first day, before starting for the lunch, the Brahmin briefed his son about the customs and rituals associated with such lunches. In particular, he told the son: "Stuff yourself with food, which you would not get often to eat. Don't unnecessarily fill up your stomach with water."

At the lunch, however, the Brahmin observed that his son was taking a sip of water off and on. When they returned home, the Brahmin gave his son a tight slap and asked him as to why he had not followed his instruction about not drinking water.

The son got a bucket and filled it with ash up to the brim. He then poured a little water in the bucket and the ash settled down. He then put some more ash in the bucket and poured some more water on it. After a few such operations, he told his father: "Look, now you can see why I was drinking water off and on. It was to make the food settle down a bit and create space for more food to go in."

The father slapped his son once again and said: "Why didn't you tell me this before?"

PART V

Musings

51 Senior Citizens in e-Land

Addressing the Governors and Lt. Governors of the States through video-conferencing on 5 January, 2017, President Pranab Mukherjee cautioned the Government: "Demonetisation, while immobilising black money and fighting corruption, may lead to temporary slow down of the economy. We all will have to be extra careful to alleviate the suffering of the poor...They need to get succour here and now so that they can also participate actively in the national march towards a future..."

Apart from the economically deprived, there is also a generation of digitally deprived persons who have been hard hit by the digital economy, which is being propagated as a necessary concomitant of demonetisation. My basic assumptions are that you are over sixty, literate, middle class, and not only not very comfortable with all the gadgets that your children and grand children play around with but perhaps even have come positively to hate them.

I do not wish to pontificate but would like to offer a few tips on how to manage the bogey of e-money, based on my personal experience, in order to provide you, in Pranab Mukherjee's words, "succour here and now so that (you) can also participate in the national march towards future."

Post-demonetisation, not only was I rendered cashless (except for my neat cache of hundred rupee notes, mentioned elsewhere), but my spouse too, much to her chagrin, lost her 'Swiss bank account', which she had accumulate over the years, with small secret contributions. We had money "to which I found no key", as Omar Khayyam would have said if he were in my predicament. I thought quickly and decided to start using my credit/debit cards, which were there but, in a sense, dormant. A couple of credit cards, I used to, no doubt, carry but I put them into use only when making large purchases, once in a blue moon. You see, I belong to the generation, which, initially, got salary in cash and cut the coat according to the cloth, as they used to say in those days. My father used to get his monthly salary in cash, which he used to distibute across a few cloth pouches labeled 'milk', 'groceries', 'school fees', 'servant', miscellaneous' and so on. When the Government shifted to depositing salary in employees' bank accounts, our generation switched to withdrawing cash once a month and made ends meet within the sum so acquired. Hence, use of credit card for all and sundry purposes was a big no, no.

I also decided to activate one of the debit cards, which banks routinely dish out these days when you open an account with them. Being a little more comfortable with the digital world than many of my ilk, I called a toll free number to set the PIN.

The euphoria surrounding the acquisition of crisp new ₹2,000 currency notes soon evaporate when the realization came home that they were of little practical use for daily needs. Apart from the trauma accompanying the long queues and the limited weekly disbursal of cash by the banks, the notes of smaller denominations, particularly the elusive ₹500 note, were not in sight. In order, therefore, to get more mileage out of my gradually diminishing stock of ₹100 notes, I ventured into a territory I had not explored before, namely an e-wallet. I downloaded the Paytm application myself and activated it with the assistance of a young neighbour. When I went to the Big Bazaar next day, with great trepidation, I told the assistant at the check out counter that I wanted to pay through Paytm. He asked me to tell him my mobile number and, after punching it into his machine, he asked me to tell him the OTP (One Time Password) that had been SMSed to my mobile. Voilà, it was so easy! In due course, I found that there were other methods of using Paytm too; such as punching in the mobile number of the person whom you want to pay or scanning the QR (Quick Response) code through my mobile.

My next foray into the digital world arose on account of a taxi ride. I had to pay ₹1,100 to the driver. I confidently fished out the newly acquired and largely unacceptable ₹2,000 note to defray the charges; but the driver had no change to return me the balance. I asked him whether he would accept a cheque, he declined and told me his predicament. It was his last duty before he proceeded to his village for his daughter's marriage. He had no time to stand in a queue to encash the cheque. Reluctantly, I parted with eleven ₹100 notes. I then decided to download another application (Ola), again on the advice of my neighbour, who said that Ola's service in our locality was pretty good; and I found it to be excellent. (There were only two options, you see, to rate the service, in a message I received after the ride: 'poor' or 'excellent' or something to that effect.)

In India, primarily three types of e-wallets are available: *closed* (which facilitate the purchase of goods and services from the entity issuing it, e.g. Ola); *semi-closed* (which, in addition to the purchase of goods and services from the entity issuing it, facilitate payment for select services, such as utility bills, e.g. Airtel Money); and *open* (which can be used for purchase of goods and services, including financial services like funds transfer at any card accepting merchant locations, e.g. Paytm).

The next stop was net banking. I received a notice through email from one of the clubs I am a member of that a certain amount was overdue. The club is located about 40 kms away from my home. I had no plans to visit it in the near future. The email offered a net banking payment option. Armed with the confidence acquired through the use of e-wallets, I took a leap into the dark and did it! The rest, as they say, is history.

Gradually, I have shifted from cash to less cash. I have made a subtle change in my manual accounting procedure. (I am aware that there are appilactions which enable you to keep your expenditure data; but I had not graduated to it till the finalization of the manuscript of this book.) I record my cash and e-payments separately by resorting to a simple device of putting 'e' or 'c', as the case may be, after the expenditure detail. At the end of each page, and, of course, at the end of the month, I have two totals (an overall total and a separate 'e' total), enabling me to calculate the %age of e-payments as compared to the total. My successive monthly accounts data have displayed a gradual shift towards more e-transactions, albeit with some fluctuations.

Based on these and other subsequent experiences, I would like to list some tips for the uninitiated, especially the senior citizens, for their forays into e-land, à la Alice's Adventures in Wonderland.

You may have several credit and/or debit cards; but carry only one or two with you. I carry one credit card of a bank in which I have no account, and a debit card of a bank in which I keep only a small amount. Carrying a debit card, which is linked to your main account, all the time, is daunting and gives me goose pimples. The smaller bank account may also be used for net banking.

In reputed establishments, which I often visit, I use the bank-linked debit card. In other well-known brand shops, I use my credit card, which is not linked to a bank. In other smaller establishment, I use my e-wallet, in which I put only a small amount, say about ₹2000, at a time. I, traditionally, issue cheques for paying electricity & water bills, advance income tax as well as investments, such as FDs, Mutual Funds etc. I am trying to move to non-cash modes of payment afap (as far as possible).

I have locked my e-wallets through the security system provided by my Android-based mobile; they can be opened only through an MPIN generated by me. For credit/debit cards, it is advised that one should change the PIN often, say on a half-yearly basis, which is easier said than done. Remembering a couple of PINs is difficult enough, let alone if they are often changing. I have tried two options, one is to have a single set of four numbers and use them in different combinations; the other is to have two PINs for two cards and keep them switching from one to the other. Write them down, if you have to, in some 'obscure' document, which you do not carry with you. For net banking, it is advisable to access only those URLs, which begin with https (i.e. a 'secure' http).

I now carry the old fashioned wallet with a few currency notes (of denominations of hundred and below) in the hip-pocket in which I used to carry it. My credit/debit cards and mobile are safely tucked away in other pockets. In case I am waylaid, I can always, as innocently as I can, hand over my wallet to the predator (s) and, hopefully, get away. In the digital world, I am only as safe as my mobile; because, I can block my credit/debit card, but not really my mobile, because the security features in it are easy to be hacked.

Accounting for daily expenditure with credit/debit cards and the e-wallets needs some organising. For accounting purposes, the money spent on each transaction using a credit or a debit card may be put down as expenditure straightaway. Similarly, any money transferred to an e-wallet too may be treated as expenditure on disbursal basis, for the sake of simplicity.

As regards accounting for any amount given to my spouse, I have a slightly complicated system, since a long time. The money given to her from time to time as allowance or advance for a likely expenditure is not treated as expenditure, since it does not really leave home. Only what she actually spends is treated as expenditure; the balance is kept in her Swiss ('safe') account. May her Swiss account increase till the next demonetisation, when it would once again be unearthed like the rest of them! Amen.

52 Humble Samosa on a High

That samosa is a quint-essential and iconic Indian snack 'is a truth universally acknowledged'; although it is claimed to have originated in the Middle East (where it is known as *sambosa*) prior to the 10th century. But what is happening to our dear samosa today is a matter of great concern to all samosa lovers, because it is a complete snack with all the ingredients of a popular Indian meal with basic ingredients of *poori* and *subji*. It is an anytime anywhere any which way (vegetable, paneer, mutton) snack; and all time is samosa time. And, as Sanjeev Kapoor, the famous super chef, has said: "We talk about health foods and salads but end up eating samosas."

The delicious samosa, had not in the past received adequate appreciation/recognition, except in the mid-nineties on account of the ditty: *Jab tak rahega samosay mein aloo, tab tak rahega Bihar main Laloo*: [Lalu (Yadav) shall rule in Bihar as long as there is potato in samosa] or the romantic version of the second line – *tera rahunga o meri Shaloo* (I shall remain yours, my dear Shaloo). You can, perhaps, ignore the fact that one of the crossroads in an obscure colony of Delhi is called 'Samosa Chowk'. In addition to these so-called aberrations, our dear samosa has been in the news, of late, also for a variety of, not so savoury, reasons.

From being a common man's snack, it has acquired the status of a luxury item. In order, perhaps, to grapple with the revenue loss caused by the introduction of prohibition, the Government of Bihar in early 2016 went on to slap a luxury tax on samosa, of all things. It has thus, acquired a status comparable to five star hotels, limousines, crystal bath tubs, among others. This 'samosa tax', if we may christen it so, found echoes in the far southern state of Kerala, where in mid-2016, the Government imposed a fat tax on junk food. However, according to some experts, imposing tax only on 'western foods', as Kerala did when it imposed the fat tax on burgers, pizzas, tacos, doughnuts and pastas sold by 'branded restaurants' such as McDonalds and KFC, could amount to discriminatory treatment inviting WTO action. Even though, as far as extra-terrestrials are concerned, we may be the loneliest lot, but when it comes to imposing such taxes, we Indians are definitely not alone. Taking a leaf out of tobacco's book to curb market activities that generate negative externalities, many countries all over the world (Denmark, France, Mexico, Japan, Norway, United Kingdom, and United States, to name a few) have introduced financial penalties known as 'fat tax', 'sugar tax', 'soda tax', 'sin tax' *et al*. Some of them, of course, had to withdraw such measures after popular protest.

Even in the normal taxation regime, a controversy was raked up regarding whether samosa or, more specifically, its step-brother 'aloo bonda' should be categorized as 'processed vegetable' (which attracts 4% VAT) or 'snack' (which attracts 13% VAT). The defendants unsuccessfully argued before the Supreme Court of India that since these readymade snacks had over 50% potato content, they should get the benefit of lower VAT as applicable to processed vegetable. The GST regime unleashed on 1 July 2017 has made the controversy irrelevant.

Then came the disturbing news that in Mumbai, the vendors of *vada pav*, *pan*, fruit juices and other assorted items have come under the radar of the income tax authorities because of their huge income from the sale of those items, for which they had evaded filing income tax returns so far. It is part of the campaign to crack down on black money in the informal sector. If *vada pav* is under the scanner, can samosa be far behind? The calorific value of both, according to one study, is just about the same (300). The counter argument of the vendors of these savouries, of course, is that they are willing to file tax returns provided they are not constantly required to bribe the officials for licensing and other permissions.

It is further to be noted that the controversy regarding the definition of 'public servant' under the Lokpal and Lokayuktas Act, 2013 notwithstanding, every public servant is required to file a declaration regarding his assets and liabilities as on the 31st day of March every year, under the Public Servants (Furnishing of Information and Annual Return of Assets and Liabilities and the Limits for Exemption of Assets in Filing Returns) Rules, 2014. The time for filing of first returns under the rules has been extended from time to time and the last time it was 31st December, 2016. Form II prescribed for the purpose *inter alia* requires a declaration relating to movable property including 'valuable things'. Going by the tenor of developments aforementioned, I am quite sure that possession of samosas would come within the ambit of this law. Moreover, in case you do not possess a legal receipt for the purchase of your beloved samosa, you would have done well to file a declaration under the Income Declaration Scheme by 30 September, 2016.

The typical Indian ambivalence has also recently come to the fore and a purveyor of the item in question has been downgraded from the status of a vendor of a luxury item to a 'peddler' of samosas within the portals of a very high class educational institution. The occasion was a memorial service organised on the passing away of Rohtas, who, as the owner of a popular dhaba, used to sell samosas and *nimbu pani* to the students and other stakeholders of the St. Stephen's College, Delhi. A number of alumni gathered to mark the event. The guards stopped some of the former eminent ones, including Ramachandra Guha (the famous historian) and Arvind Subramaniam (Chief Economic Adviser to Narendra Modi) from entering the college. Valson Thampu, the Principal of the college raked up a controversy by posting a vitriolic on his Facebook entitled 'Alumni and Samosa Worship'. *Inter alia* it stated, "I can't understand how a peddler of samosa is more important than the bursar or college on which he thrived: so much so that politics can be unleashed around his death to the embarrassment of the college."

No wonder there was a huge uproar from all conceivable quarters. It was observed: "Why did the taunt by St. Stephen's College principal anger us all? Because there are few who haven't spent their college years at those warn snack shacks, discussing projects, love and politics over tea and samosas." Even within the sacred portals of the JNU, there was vociferous protest when the authorities attempted to shut down the iconic Ganga Dhaba.

It cannot be gainsaid that samosa does stimulate intellectual activity. The high point of the weekly meetings of a very staid NGO (the senior citizen members of which get a huge amount of joy in doing something useful and worthwhile instead of just playing golf and watching TV) is the serving of samosas at about 12 noon, when all discussion comes to an embarrassingly salivary halt while the participants crunch away at their much awaited snack. When asked as to 'what do you get in return for all your labour', one of them is actually said to have observed: "We work for a samosa that is served in the Thursday meetings."

In Greater Noida, where I live, the joints peddling (sorry selling) samosas are next only to outlets for sale and/or repair of mobiles. But one of the popular ones has chosen to call itself '*Badnam Samosa Wale*' (infamous samosa peddler (sorry).

During my stay in Oxford, *inter alia* I and my wife went looking for the homely samosa. We found a road-side stall selling it. We tasted and found it quite bland. If the British Prime Minister went gaga over *chicken tikka masala*, surely the common man there deserved better samosas. My wife offered to prepare a sample of authentic samosas for the stall to sell. The price and other arrangements were agreed upon. My wife prepared a rather large sample of a dozen samosas and gave it to the stall-owner for test-marketing. He said he would get back. We went back to him after a week. The samosas were not on display but he said that there was no demand so the contract was off. What happened to the bloody samosas? Did he sell them or ate them all, along with his family members, and had a good laughing belch. No wonder the English are called a nation of shopkeepers.

If samosa comes can dosa be far behind? Like not-so-humble samosa now, dosa too has seen its ups and downs. It wouldn't come as a surprise if it too comes under the scanner, for taxable income or for the fat tax. As a matter of fa(c)t, a student is reported to have asked Raghuram Rajan, the erstwhile Governor of the Reserve Bank: "If inflation is down, why dosas cost more?" The reply of the Governor was crisp: "You pay for the pan and the dosa maker's wages." Across boardrooms and banquet halls, there is this hiss and sizzle of dosa dialogue.

However, samosa alone is the ultimate benchmark of purchasing power or inflation index. During my school days it used to cost an anna, i.e. 6 paise. Today it costs ten rupees, on an average. This means that since the late fifties, the price of a samosa today has gone up by about 166.66 (recurring) times. Take petrol for triangulation. It used to cost 13 and a half anna for a gallon. In modern times, its price is 65 rupees or thereabouts, per litre. This means an increase of 361.11 (recurring) times. That gives one the satisfaction that the samosa is not as costly as it could have been.

But all this has not dampened the spirits of the samosa makers of India. There was news from Maharajganj in Uttar Pradesh that they made the world's largest samosa, which beat the record of the students of Bradford College of United Kingdom. The Maharajganj samosa weighed 387.750 kilograms. How the hell does one eat a samosa of such a gargantuan proportion? No wonder the news came a few days later that after being on display for three days it got spoilt and was disposed of in a nearby canal like the statues of Ganesh and Durga. What a waste!

And as I write this piece, I am reminded of an article written by Usha Raman for the Education Supplement of *The Hindu* dated 29 February, 2016 ('Bringing your thoughts together'), wherein she propounds that we 'unpack' a dense idea by exploring it through the works of many writers. As we try to 'dissect' an idea, we explore its different aspects from a variety of angles. The article's opening sentence reads as follows:

"Last year, I learnt a simple and efficient way of folding plastic bags from a young woman who had learnt it from her grandmother. We now call it the 'samosa' fold, as it makes a small triangle that can then be neatly stacked away – a handy space-saving approach."

As a child, I was vaguely interested in the goings on in our family kitchen. Encouraged by my mother, I picked up a few recipes by just observing her. One such recipe, which I successfully replicated later in life, to the surprise of my young friends, was about making samosas. The secret of its unique flavour was using the powder of dried seeds of raw pomegranate as a souring agent.

Pathan paise khata hai (Pathan is eating money)

A Pathan from Afghanistan had come to India first time, a little after India got independence. He was walking down a street full of shops and looking with keen interest at goods on display. In a general merchant's shop, one particular item caught his fancy. He asked for its price, which appeared to be within his reach. He took the product and smelled it; the smell was very appealing. He bought the product and, while walking down the street, started to eat it. Within seconds, he was coughing uncontrollably and spitting out the piece he had bitten. Very agitated, he returned to the shop and asked the merchant, what kind of cookie he had sold to him. The merchant laughed and told the Pathan that the product was not a cookie but a cake of soap, meant for bathing. The Khan understood that he had made a mistake; but nothing could be done about it. He stood there thinking for some time, and then started to eat the rest of the soap, bit by bit. The merchant was amused and asked the Pathan: "Why are you eating soap?"

The Pathan smiled and said: "Pathan paise khata hai", meaning thereby that since he had spent money to buy the product thinking it was sweetmeat, he had to eat it anyhow.

53 How to be an Intellectual

The Secretary, Ministry of Textiles convened a meeting to discuss some ticklish issues, particularly the eternal rivalry between and related conflicting demands of the mill, powerloom and handloom sectors. As the then Development Commissioner for Handlooms, I was one of the invitees to this high profile meeting. Each of the participants was asked to present his or her point of view. After the officers had had their say, the Secretary called upon the Ministry's Economic Adviser to sum up and give his advice. While the officers had spoken in everyday language, the Economic Adviser proceeded to pontificate in an esoteric language, which we vaguely understood. He had a field day. The Secretary, one of our ilk, nodded gravely at the end and agreed with the Economic Adviser. We were aghast, not so much because our points of view had been ignored, but because we failed to understand what had been agreed to. The minutes of the meeting were drawn up by one of the officers, who perhaps had a degree in economics, and made some sense.

This was perhaps one of the episodes, among several others, which made me take a plunge and register for a Ph. D. degree, to get even with the intellectuals as well as pseudo-experts of this world. The title of my Ph. D. thesis said it all. Instead of simply calling it: 'An Analysis of Textile Policy of Government of India', it is titled 'Systems Engineering Approach to Public Policy Analysis and Design'.

Some of the highfalutin words and phrases learnt as well as coined by me during my Ph. D. work were: Analytical

Hierarchy Process; Integrated/Unified Programme Planning; Interpretive Structural Modeling; Logical Processual Framework; Nominal Group Technique; Policy (deficit, arena, entrepreneurs, window, paralysis); Options Field and Options Profile Methodologies; Protocol and Algorithm (for procedure/process); System Dynamics Modeling (e.g. 'urban dynamics' instead of urban issues); Trigger Question and so on.

In order to toughen oneself for the rough and tumble of the world of experts and an assortment of advisers, one must acquaint oneself with a modicum of economics to begin with. Without that you are somewhat of a non-starter, as I continue to be. I have, however, acquired a rudimentary knowledge of and a nodding acquaintance with economic terminology by reading a few economic newspapers and magazines. The words that readily come to my mind are: actuarial calculations; amortization; annuity; balance of trade; bullish & bearish market; capex & forex; CRR & SLR; cost-benefit analysis; debt & equity; derivatives; dear and cheap money; debentures; demographic dividend; discounted cash flow; ecosystem; escrow account; externalities; framework; general equilibrium and disequilibrium; economies of scale; elasticity of demand; factors of production; fiduciary relationship; fiscal and revenue deficit; laissez faire; law of diminishing returns; laws of demand and supply; liberalisation, privatisation and globalisation (LPG); linear programming; marginal cost/utility; 'masala' bonds; mergers and acquisitions; micro- and macro-economics, perfect and imperfect market/competition; NPA; NPV; public goods; pump-priming; ratios and curves; rent seeking; securities; shares (ordinary, deferred and preference); social accounting and audit; subsidiarity principle; supply chain management; stressed assets; theory of constraint; value addition; verticals; X-Y axes, among others.

The terminology of social research methods is also useful in flummoxing others with your expert demeanour. Some useful terms and expressions are: cohort; conceptual framework; conditioning; correlation co-efficient; construct; definition (working and operational); error (Type I and Type

II); frequency distribution; group (control and experiment); halo effect; Hawthorne effect; hypothesis (alternate and null); longitudinal study; participant observer; placebo effect; predictive validity; questions (closed, double-barrelled, leading, and open-ended); research (action and applied); regression analysis; sampling (design, error and population); sampling methods (accidental, cluster, expert, judgmental, probability, proportionate stratified, quota, random, snowball, stratified random, and systematic); scales (interval, Likert, nominal, ordinal, ratio, and Thurstone); Stockholm syndrome; theoretical framework; variables (attribute, chance, continuous, dependent, dichotomous, extraneous, intervening, independent and random); time series data; and variance analysis among others.

Some management and business jargon could also come in handy. Words and expressions such as ambush marketing; bandwidth; break-even analysis; business cycle; corporate culture; capacity building; confidence building measures (CBM); demand-side & supply-side; design & execution; disruptive (innovation/strategy/technology/thinking); downsizing; Enterprise Resource Planning (ERP); holistic approach; human capital; ideator; learning organization; opportunity cost; organizational behaviour; paradigm shift; ping; positioning a product; re-engineering; rightsizing; role play; SAP (Systems, Applications and Products); situational leadership; strategic planning; synergy; value addition; value chain etc. could be used to create an impression.

Quality terminology is equally effective. Some of the basic terms and phrases are: bar charts; benchmarking; brain writing; cause and effect analysis (fishbone diagram); check sheets; conformity and non-conforming outputs; continuous/continual improvement; control chart; corrective action; cost of quality; customer focus/satisfaction; DMAIC (Define, Measure, Analyze, Improve and Control); engagement of people; evidence-based decision-making; external providers; force field analysis; Failure Mode and Effect Analysis (FEMA); flow chart; histogram; *hoshin kanri* (quality policy deployment); *kaizen* (change for the better); leadership commitment; lean;

measurement traceability; Pareto analysis; PDCA (Plan, Do Check and Act) cycle (Deming Wheel); PERT & CPM; pie chart; process approach; Quality Function Deployment (QFD); relationship management; risk based thinking; six sigma; Statistical Process Control (SPC); Total Productive Maintenance (TPM); Total Quality Management (TQM) *et al.*

If you are unfamiliar with some of the words and expressions used above, a little bit of 'googling' may help.

A Smattering of thinkers and well known authors is also of great help in making your conversation sound intellectual. A few books you can use for this purpose are mentioned in the references appended at the end.

Please also familiarise yourself with the pet words and expressions of the current establishment, such as start up India; skill India; make in India; digital India; stand up India; zero defect & zero effect; reform, perform, transform; Ek Bharat, Sreshtha Bharat and so on.

A mention of leading and lagging indicators will give you the final imprimatur to call yourself an intellectual who has arrived. 'Leading Indicators' are predictors of future outcomes. First, leading indicators are antecedents (a thing/event that logically precedes another) to important events that predict or foreshadow those events. Second, leading indicators are not fixed characteristics of individuals or systems; rather, they are conditions or activities that can be changed by action. Third, the search for leading indicators catalyzes a productive inquiry that results in the rethinking of organizational resources or supports. Fourth, the search for leading indicators may help identify or develop more relevant and precise indicators. Think of how the amber traffic light indicates the coming of the red light. A 'lagging indicator' is one that captures the past outcomes. Unemployment is one of the most popular lagging indicators. If the unemployment rate is rising, it indicates that the economy was not managed properly in the past. Similarly, air quality index is also a lagging indicator, it tells us about the problem *post facto*.

Then there are a few expressions that you must use often in preference to their 'common parlance' equivalents in order to give your interventions an intellectual ring. Thus, instead of saying that "something has been taken into account", say "it has been factored in". Similarly, learn to use the expression "is a function of (*f*)". For example, instead of saying "the success of Panchayati Raj depends on allocation of finances, functions and functionaries to it", say "success of Panchayati Raj is a function of finances, functions and functionaries". You may even write it as "Panchayati Raj (*f*) finances, functions and functionary".

Whenever you find yourself in a situation when you are unable to defend your point of view, you can easily wriggle out of it by using the expression: "ultimately, it is a state of mind".

If nothing else works, then there is the following Buzz Phrase Generator to give a studious flavour to your expressions. Pick one word at random from each of the three columns, and you are armed with a unique phrase, which could confound the best of so-called experts. It is literally, an armoury of intellectualisms!

Buzz Phrase Generator: The Complete Plain Words (1978: 308)

Column 1	Column 2	Column 3
0. Integrated	0. Management	0. Options
1. Overall	1. Organizational	2. Flexibility
2. Systematized	2. Monitored	2. Capability
3. Parallel	3. Reciprocal	3. Mobility
4. Functional	4. Digital	4. Programming
5. Responsive	5. Logistical	5. Concept
6. Optimal	6. Transitional	6. Time-phase
7. Synchronized	7. Incremental	7. Projection
8. Compatible	8. Third-generation	8. Hardware
9. Balanced	9. Policy	9. Contingency

Courtesy: Canadian Defence Department

References

Adams, Ian and R. W. Dyson (2007) *Fifty Great Political Thinkers.* London: Routledge.

Gleeson-White, Jane (2005) 51 *Great Masterpieces you should have read (and probably you didn't).* Delhi: Orient Publishing.

Gowers, Sir Ernest (1978) *The Complete Plain Words.* London: ELBS & Penguin Books.

Kanji, Gopal K. and Mike Asher (1996) *100 Methods for Total Quality Management.* New Delhi: Response Books (A Division of Sage Publications).

Kumar, Ranjit (2011) *Research Methodology.* New Delhi: Sage Publications.

Walsh, George (2009) *51 Great Books You Should have Read (and probably you didn't).* Delhi: Orient Paperbacks.

54 An Ode to South Indian Savouries

The culinary delicacies of south India are indeed *nonpareil.* Nothing can beat the wholesome first-thing-in-the-morning taste of *idlies, dosas* (of infinite variety), and/or *vadas* with *sambhar* and the coconut/ginger chutney. 'Oh to eat a dosa' is, in some ways (pardon the blasphemy, if any), comparable to 'Oh to be in England'. If you are a south-Indian-foodophile/foodie, the list of mouth-watering dishes, dished out at the speed of light (an exaggeration, of course, in terms their preparation, but OK as far expectations of the person waiting to be served) will be nearly interminable. Just imagine, after a mouthful of *payasam* having been served on your plate, followed, in quick succession, by lime rice, curd (yoghurt) rice and tamarind rice, in one fell sweep, not forgetting the omni-present *dahi vada* (even small ones at that). Pre- or suf-fix it with *rasam* and add to it *sambhar* with plain rice. Top it with curd and plain rice combination, supported by lime pickle or *gongura pachari* or even the simple table salt; and you literally have heaven in the scoop of your hand, especially if all this is cooked by your loving spouse. (In order to maintain a certain salivary focus, I have avoided discussing some of the other savoury south Indian dishes like *pongal, uttapam, avial, puttu et al*). If my southern gastronomical diatribe has not made sense to you so far then you may perhaps like to move on.

This is not to say that other parts of our great country are not blessed with delightful cuisine. At the top of the list is, of course, the near universal *samosa,* which comes with various fillings and in a variety of sizes as well as with variable shelf life. The great thing about it is that no authority has so far attempted to standardise and/or prescribe its contours and weight, as was done by the government in the 1980s in Andhra Pradesh for *idlies, vadas et al.* And how can I afford not to mention the luscious *jalebee*?

There are many other mouth-watering delicacies, which are temptingly advertised in the media in the context of food festivals springing up everywhere all the time. Thus, there is the famous Indo-UK dish called *chicken tikka masala;* not far behind are *tandoori* chicken, butter chicken and Hyderabadi *biryani*. I would like to name a few inseparable pairs, such as *litti-chokha, dal-bati & churma*, and *jhunka-bhakar* among others. If we take a cursory look at some of the States of India, *sattu* from Bihar, *machher jhol* of Bengal, *singju* salad of Manipur, steamed fish of Assam, among many others (which I am not listing for constraint of space) need an honourable mention. But Jammu and Kashmir stands apart with its yummy dishes comprising *yakhni, rista* and *gostaba*, washed down with a cupful of *kahwah* poured from the *samowar*. I may be pardoued for other unintended exclusions.

Be that as it may, the extraordinary thing about the southern eminently edible delights is that they are easy to cook, easy to serve and, wonder of wonders, conducive to your good health (provided, always, that you are a connoisseur and not a glutton). Forget the royal/feudal menu of 56 or more courses (*chhapan bhojan*, and not 'ab tak chhappan'). Keep off the non-

North Oxford Oversees Centre, 107 Banbury Road, Oxford (UK)

vegetarian as well as so-called vegetarian specialities, even if they are kept on the table temptingly close to the wholesome ones and smell even better. A recent study states that if the whole world turned vegan or, at least, vegetarain, the global warming disaster could be averted for some time. Not only is the way to hell paved by good intention; geographically too, heaven is quite close to hell for comfort.

My wife and I spent a year in Oxford some time ago. I was deputed by the Government of India as a Visiting Fellow to the Queen Elizabeth House, Oxford for one academic year (read nine months). We were accommodated in a suite in North Oxford Overseas Centre (lovingly called the 'NOOK', following the abbreviation NOOC). We found that Indian food was quite a rage in Oxford. We met a professor, who actually professed that he held his tutorials in Indian restaurants; he and his students picking up the tab alternately. During the long winter evenings, we took to entertaining our local friends at our modest accommodation with a variety of Indian dishes. We became quite friendly with an English couple who ate only vegetarian Indian food. The husband told us that he could win the affection of his would-be wife only by demonstrating his unfailing ability to cook quality Indian vegetarian meals.

Every community not only has its peculiar culinary skills but also a certain culinary etiquette, which *inter alia* prescribes the permissible combination of constituents. This type of etiquette is largely inherited and cannot be easily acquired. It is one thing to enjoy the taste of *bhindis* (ladies fingers) and *baigan* (brinjal/egg plant) in *sambhar*, but cooking these two vegetables together with *garam masala* and a host of unrelated assortment of condiments is something quite different. Till the time we met this English Indian-vegetarian-food-besotted couple, we could never have imagined that it was possible to make an Indian dishes taste exotic to the Indians.

But the lonely winter brought much greater trial. There was a particular priest whose late lamented father, an army officer, had served in Pondicherry before India got independence. The priest, as we found out during the long and languid winter evenings, was addicted to south Indian food. The first time we met at a common friend's house, after realising that we were from India, he soon started dropping broad hints to be invited to our apartment for a meal. At another external encounter, he confessed that *dosa* was the 'food of the gods' (*a la Chariots of the Gods?*: Erich von Daniken). Having taken our indifference to invite him for a meal as a good breeding ground for consent, one day, he came around to NOOC. For security reasons no one, other than the residents who had a key to the main door, could enter the building. Since our apartment was on the first floor, he went round the building and knocked at the bay windows of ground floor rooms/apartments, the occupants of which happened to be awake/available at that time. After considerable effort he found a willing accomplice in a particularly nosey neighbour, the spouse of a fellow scholar, who let him in. We soon heard our doorbell. We were quite surprised to see the priest at that dark winter hour (though not late in real time) when we opened the door. After having been admitted, he jocularly described his trials and tribulations in reaching us. He was indeed full of praise for our neighbour(?) for her willing co-operation. The evening was full of amorous references to the variegated/virtual *dosa*, the 'food of the gods'. The end of the evening, saw us deciding to invite the priest, along with some other waiting-in-the-wings friends for a meal comprising *dosa, idli, poori*, chicken curry and what have you.

In the end, I would like to redraw the attention of the reader to the 'samosa episode' in Oxford, described in detail earlier.

55 Distinguishing Marks

India, they say, is a country of unity in diversity. Which is, no doubt, true. *Holi, Diwali, Eid(s), Guru Parb, Buddha Purnima, Mahavir Jayanti,* and a host of other festivals are celebrated across the length and breadth of this country. Quite some time ago in the mid 1990s, when I was in Bihar as an election observer, driving down from Patna to the constituency allotted to me I found several cars, buses and tractors with trailers bedecked with flowers and paper stickers announcing the marriage of Indu with Deepak and of Shekhar with Madhuri, while all the auto-repair shops on the route were closed on account of *id-ul-zuha*. I found persons of different communities crowding together on two or three wheelers, trying to reach their diverse destinations in considerable haste. Some of them were bound for the marriages and others for the festival. The Hindu auspicious days coincide with the Muslim festivals with considerable regularity.

Election time, in those days, was all about ballot papers, which were inseparable from the distinguishing marks affixed on them, including their counterfoils. As the passions mounted with the approach of the polling day, things were a bit different. Similarly, as one came closer to the ground, there was more, and perhaps richer, diversity, which makes India such an exciting destination. In order, however, to adequately appreciate the nuances of this distinguishing diversity amidst overall unity, one has to be, perhaps, necessarily an outsider. Otherwise how could one's gaze stumble upon and get transfixed on things which are sub-consciously known but are still not distinguishable from other humdrum sights, in a manner of speaking?

During my election tour of Bihar, I not only got to understand the meaning of *tola* (a locality) and *litti* (a preparation made with a mix of wheat and Bengal gram flours and a host of other ingredients) and its inseparable companion *chokha* (a vegetable preparation with brinjal and tomato), which I had tasted before; but also several other distinguishing marks of northern Bihar, some of them reminiscent of Indus Valley Civilisation. But, in India, there is not only diversity within the country, but also about how things are done differently from region to region, depending upon how you define the region, which could even be a village.

To start with the Indus Valley Civilisation, I saw *bakhar*, the grain storage bin, a cylindrical granary (about 4 to 6 feets in height; and about 4 feet in diameter, on an average), slightly tapering at the bottom or, in some cases, at the top, and mounted on a brick platform, most of the time. *Bakhar* is made of bamboo strips or a local wild weed (of which the hut and thatched roofs are made), and woven, as in the case of a basket. It is covered with a thick coat of paste made of mud and straw. Its size depends of how much grain the household wants to or is capable of storing. And that is where lies the rub (rich variety) of *bakhars*, which I found strewn around, in large numbers, in all villages. Again, depending on the resources of the household, it is white-washed and its base is made with brick and mortar. Sometimes, a separate *bakhar* is made for storage of fodder, which is, generally, of a frugal quality. At all times, of course, it was reminiscent of the grain storage devices I had read about in the history of Harappan civilisation.

Next object of my curiosity was *sisopata*, a monument (though, at most places, a modest one of about 2′×2′×2′ feet) built to honour *chhat ma*, i.e. the goddess representing the sixth day of the bright fortnight of the Indian lunar *kartik* month (October-November). A promise to build it is made upon fulfilment of a wish. Generally again, it is a square-shaped structure, with five steps tapering towards the top and finished with a small dome. The resources of the person/family concerned, decide the shape, size, the number of steps (in some cases), and other features of this monument dedicated to *om chhat ma*. Made of brick and mortar, it is built by the villagers at a single site (preferably, the village commons), usually the land adjoining or on a road or a culvert. The numbers at a given site, the size and shape of the monument and the colours covering them, are a sight to behold. But, one finds all these rich as well as poor monuments ranged along the same site. Most of them do not bear any inscriptions; but some of them proclaim their dedication to *om chhat ma*, and bear the name(s) of the dedicater(s).

Some of them are very colourful, others are just plain white-washed. At one place near the canal I saw a large set of very high (almost 7 feet) *sisopatas*, some with even seven steps, very imaginatively painted in various colours. It was indeed a site to behold and, naturally, spoke of the intensity of devotion and well-to-do status of their providers.

And, finally, it was *koetha* which took the (dung) cake. Prepared with rolls of dung cake and straw, stacked in cross-stitch fashion, it is a fuel item used for preparing special meals, particularly on festive occasions. *Litti* is one of the items cooked on a *koetha*, which burns slowly to roast it properly. Brinjal, which is the main vegetable used to make *litti*'s companion *chokha*, is also roasted on a *koetha* before mashing it. The rolls are arranged in sets of five and heaped, one on top of another, up to ten levels, with their ends alternately projecting on opposite sides. Slightly tapering towards the top, the base of the *koetha* (also called simply *upla* or cow-dung cake) is prepared with the same material to provide a platform. The normal size is 2′x2′x4′, but could be larger, depending on how much cattle the household has, a factor which also obviously determines how many *koethas* a family would prepare and store. At one place, while inspecting a school building selected for setting up of a Polling Station, I found that a few sadhus were comfortable parked at the proposed site of the Polling Station and were busy cooking their food on a *koetha*, provided by one of their genuine or willy nilly devotees in the village.

56 Skill Development: A Parable

Note from the Author

This is a parable on Skill Development of yore (may be a 100 years ago, give or take a year or two here and there, from nowhere). I am sorry and apologise in advance for its sexist approach or gender insensitivity. But, at the same time, one must appreciate the acceptance on part of the mother-in-law of the lack of skill in a newly married and naive daughter-in-law. Should I begin now?

False Start

OK. Here I go. Oh, I forgot. I must first explain a few local words, phrases and idioms which will recur in this parable:

- *lok mehar kee kukur?:* (spoken by the daughter-in-law): Am I a cultured/skilled housewife or a dog (sorry, can't use the appropriate word)?
- *banaa pahiyo/kar pahiyo/phenk pahiyo?* (spoken by the mother-in-law): Will you be able to make it/do it/throw it (respectively)?
- *naa bano:* (spoken by the daughter-in-law) could not make it.
- *pua/puo:* fried sweetened (with sugar or molasses) *poori*.
- *gulagula/gulagulo:* dumpling made with a lighter flour batter than pua.
- *cheelara/cheelaro:* pancake made with a lighter batter than gulagula.

The Parable

And here goes the parable. Since all stories as well parables begin from the beginning of time, this too would.

Once upon a time [about a hundred (or is it a thousand?) years ago] there was this family of four persons (unusual in those days, at least in India) comprising father, mother, son and daughter-in-law. The son had got married recently and the daughter-in-law was trying her best to ingratiate herself with her mother-in-law. One day, the daughter-in-law, even though 'unskilled', thought of cooking something special to please the mother-in-law. She went up to the mother-in-law and said: "*Puo banaa loon*?" (Should I make some pua?)

- Mother-in-law: *"banaa pahiyo?"*
- Daughter-in-law: *"lok mehar kee kukur."*

The daughter-in-law went into the kitchen and, eager to impress the mother-in-law, started preparing the dough in a great hurry. After it was ready, she found that she had put a little more water than was necessary. She realized that it was not possible to make the *pua* with that dough, but she could make *gulagula* with it after adding a little more water. She went back to the mother-in-law and, having explained the predicament to her, said: "*Puo to naa bano, gulagulo banaa loon*?" (It is not possible to make the *pua*, should I make *gulagula*?)

- Mother-in-law: *"banaa pahiyo?"*
- Daughter-in-law: *"lok mehar kee kukur."*

The daughter-in-law promptly returned to the kitchen and added some more water to the dough. Upon closer inspection, she found that she had added a little more water than was necessary. *Gulagula* was now out of the question, but luckily by adding a little more water, the dough could be used to make *cheelara*. She again went up to the mother-in-law and having explained the problem, said: "*Gulagulo to naa bano, cheelaro banaa loon*?" (It is not possible to make the *gulagula*, should I make *cheelara*?)

- Mother-in-law: *"banaa pahiyo?"*

- Daughter-in-law: "*lok mehar kee kukur.*"

Post haste, keen to prove her cooking abilities, the daughter-in-law went into the kitchen once again and attempted to add a little water to the dough in order to make it suitable for *cheelara*. But as luck would have it this time too she poured a little more water than required. The watery concoction stared back at her. The situation now was irretrievable. She went back to the mother-in-law and honestly told her what had happened. In the end she said: "*Cheelaro to naa bano, phenk doon*?" (It is not possible to make *cheelara* now, shall I throw away the batter?)

- Mother-in-law: "*phenk pahiyo?*"
- Daughter-in-law: "*lok mehar kee kukur.*"

As the family was living on a first floor apartment, the daughter-in-law went into the balcony and threw the dough on to the street. Unfortunately, it fell on the head of a passerby.

The parable, by implication, tells the reader about the fundamentals of making three different dishes with the same ingredients, but with a little more water added, of course, judiciously.

Talking about the consistency of dough for various purposes, the same is true of the batter for *idli, dosa* and *uttapam*. There may be a parable in the south based on that or could now be made.

It I would like to conclude with a supportive proverb: *gareebi main atta geela* (as it is I'm poor; now my dough has too much water).

Bahu, na hoi toa, tanik gudari kari deo (Daughter-in-law, if you don't mind, please make them a little thicker)

An elderly uncle of my father from our ancestral village used to visit us once in a while, when we were located in Kanpur. My mother, being a dutiful daughter-in-law, used to serve him lunch and dinner before any of us could have a go at it. Those were the days when food used to be cooked in *chulhas* (firewood-based cooking appliance) and *angithis* (coal-based cooking appliance). There were no LPG cylinders or piped gas then. She used to cover her face with the *pallu* (about which the Chief Minister of Haryana has raked up a controversy recently) of her sari while blowing air into the two cooking appliances to keep them going simulataneously. In order to what she thought would please the old man, she prepared thin and puffed *chapattis*, when he visited us the first time. The *chapattis* were being passed on to him one at a time; a slow process indeed. He was able to consume one, much before the next one arrived. He observed the operations with some indulgence for some time. After he had been through with about half a dozen of such delicate delicacies, he told my mother: "*Bahu* (daughter-in-law), *na hoi toa* (if you don't mind), *tanik gudari kari deo* (please make them a little thicker)". It was his solution to the process which was laborious to my mother and somewhat unsatisfactory to him. If the *chapatti* was made a little thicker, he would take a little more time to eat it and my mother would, in turn, have to prepare a lot fewer of them to satisfy his appetite. It was a win-win situation for both of them.

57 Ten Commandments of Weight Management for Dummies

1. Take a Measure of Yourself

Keep a record/log of all inputs and activities during your waking hours for one week. Consult an expert/nutritionist to assign a calorific value on all your inputs and activities. Find out the optimal number of calories you need to consume per day, given your sex, age, body structure, height, weight, physical activity level etc.

There is a 'Twenty-minute Rule', i.e. it takes your brain 20 minutes to register the adequacy or otherwise of a meal consumed, particularly the traditional 'three main meals of the day'. So, initially, remember to check the feeling you get after 20 minutes of having a meal and decide whether you are feeling 'still hungry'/'nearly full' or 'full' or 'over full'. Alternatively, eat/chew slo-o-wly. Experiment with yourself to identify the 'still hungry' or 'nearly full' state of feeling within your stomach, particularly during the three main meals.

2. Make a Plan: Activity is of the Essence

In consultation with an expert, prepare a plan for weight reduction (with milestones to be achieved) by reducing inputs and/or increasing physical activities (including aerobic exercises, yoga, Pilates etc.). But do not plan a rapid weight loss; aim to lose about 2 kgs. per month, till the ideal/desired weight/BMI (Body Mass Index) is achieved. It is all about input-output ratio. Ideally it should be 1 on a daily basis; if trying to lose weight, you may go down up to 0.7.

Please remember to limit your intake to stop at 'still hungry'/'nearly full' level.

3. Small and Frequent Meals do the Trick: Keep the Metabolism Revved Up

Take six small meals during the day, rather than 3 heavy (proper/regular) meals, in order to keep the metabolism active and match the inputs with energy consumption on a continuous basis. The 'fat' (calories) savings bank account should always be managed in the overdraft mode. The size of the meals taken during the day should follow the normal distribution curve, starting and ending with small inputs. A sample of Six Meals is as follows:

TIME (Hours)	NATURE OF DIET
0630	Tea with Nuts and/or Digestive/light biscuits
0830-1000	Breakfast
1300-1400	Lunch
1600-1630	Fruits
1730-1830	Tea with very light snacks
1930-2000	Supper/Dinner

Generally speaking, there should be a gap of about two hours between meals. Do not take fruits at the end of lunch or dinner (as an alternative to *gulab janum* or ice-cream, for instance). It does not do you any good; by the time the main meal gets digested, the fruits would have got rotten.

Please do remind yourself of the 'Twenty-minute Rule'.

4. Balance Your Plate: One-by-Four Rule

Your lunch/dinner plate should have four components in equal proportion (in volume if not in weight) comprising: (i) carbohydrates; (ii) proteins; (iii) vegetables; and (iv) salads/greens.

Chew every morsel 32 times, more or less, to match the number of teeth you supposedly have.

5. Give Yourself a Rough Edge: Be a Roughage Lover

Eat a lot of roughage (salads/greens); may be even more than the quarter of your plate.

6. Keep the Water Cycle Going

Drink a lot of water, several times during the day: up to at least 4 litres. take about half a litre of water, first thing in the morning and one hour before going to sleep. Drink at regular intervals. Drink water one hour before and after each meal; but do not take water during or immediately after a meal.

7. Meal and Sleep do not go Together

Have your last meal (preferably by 7 pm) at least two hours before going to bed. Afternoon *siesta* too should be taken at least one hour after lunch.

8. Beware of the Dark Powers

Beware of carbs and food with preservatives. Do not underestimate the dark powers of sugar, salt, liquor and tobacco.

9. Observe Yourself Relentlessly

Keep a constant eye on what you are doing with regard to inputs and activities; if possible, keep notes. Weigh yourself every day in the morning to find the connection between the inputs and activities of the previous day, and the consequent weight gain/loss. Derive your own lessons for future inputs/activities. Monitoring inputs is 90% of the battle against the bulge; exercise is the other 10%.

Weigh yourself every day approximately at the same time in the morning, preferably before breakfast, on the same weighing machine and wearing the same set of clothes.

10. Be at Peace with Yourself

Do not despair if things do not go as per your plan on a particular day or for a few days (*diwali, sangeet*, and office parties). You can always bounce back. Every day is a new day; you can always start afresh.

Do not starve yourself after a day of indulgence; it does not work. Do not also over-strain by way of activities; it too does not work and could even be counter-productive.

Be happy and calm and enjoy your food.

58 My Name is Vijay and I am a Woman: As Told by my Wife

At birth I was named Vijay Lakshmi (because I was born on Vijay Dashami day) by my grandfather. However, my High School certificate bears the name Vijay Misra. My father used to spell my name with an 'i' (i.e. Vijai). After marriage my name was changed to Vijay Agnihotri. My graduation certificate is in that name.

Normally, the female version of Vijay is Vijaya and is spelled as such. As a matter of fact, several of my friends and colleagues, particularly those from South India, invariable call me Vijaya (with a long 'a' as the end); and I don't bother to correct them. A woman having a male sounding name is, however, not a singularity. For example, in the Punjab, men and women routinely bear the same (gender-neutral or an androgynous) name, which is differentiated by the suffix "Singh' and 'Kaur' respectively. Even outside the Panjab in North India some names are quite common among men and women, e.g. Kamlesh, Vinod *et al*. Celebrity men sporting largely feminine names in India are not a common occurrence, but are present, e.g. Kanti Desai.

Looking at the bigger picture, according to Wikipedia, unisex names have been enjoying a decent amount of popularity in English speaking countries as well in the past several decades. Masculine names have become increasingly popular among females in the past century but feminine names remain extremely rare among males. Examples of masculine names, which have been widely given to females and thus have become unisex, include Ashley, Beverly, Evelyn,

Hilary, Jocelyn, Joyce, Kelly, Lynn, Meredith, Shannon, Shirley, Sidney, Vivian, and Whitney. Modern unisex names may derive from nature (Lake, Rain, Willow), colors (Blue, Grey, Indigo), countries or states (Dakota, India, Montana), surnames (Jackson, Mackenzie, Madison, Murphy), and politicians (Kennedy, Reagan). Examples of unisex names among celebrities include Jamie (Jamie Bell and Jamie Lee Curtis), Morgan (Morgan Freeman and Morgan Fairchild), Shannon (Shannon Leto and Shannon Elizabeth), Taylor (Taylor Lautner and Taylor Swift), Tracy (Tracy Morgan and Tracy Chapman), Jordan (Jordan Knight and Jordan Pruitt), and Hayden (Hayden Christensen and Hayden Panettiere). According to the Social Security Administration, Jayden has been the most popular unisex name for boys since 2008 and Madison has been the most popular unisex name for girls since 2000 in the United States. Prior to Jayden, Logan was the most popular unisex name for boys and prior to Madison, Alexis was the most popular unisex name for girls.

Many Indian names become unisex when written with Latin characters because of the limitations of transliteration. The spellings *Chandra* and *Krishna*, for example, are transliterations of both the masculine and feminine versions of those names. In Indian languages, the final '*a*' of these names is a different letter with a different pronunciation, such that is no ambiguity. However, when they are seen (and usually, spoken) by someone unfamiliar with Indian languages, they become sexually ambiguous. Other Indian names, such as Ananda, are exclusively or nearly exclusively masculine in India, but because of their '*a*' ending, are assumed to be feminine in Anglophone societies. Many unisex names in India are obvious and are never ridiculed. For instance Nehal, Sonal, Snehal, Niral, Pranjal and Anmol are used commonly to name baby boys or girls in western states of India, such as Gujarat. Similarly, names like Kajal, Sujal, Viral, Harshal, Deepal, Bobby, Mrinal, Jyoti, Shakti, Kiran, Lucky, Ashwini, Shashi, Malhar, Umang, Shubham and Anupam are also very common sex-neutral names or unisex names in India. Most Punjabi Sikh first names such as Sandeep, Gurdeep, Kuldeep,

Mandeep Surjeet, Gurjeet, Kuljeet, Harjeet, Manjeet, Harpreet, Gurpreet, Jaspreet, Kulpreet, Manpreet, Prabhjot, Harjot, Gurjot, Jasjot, Sukhjinder, Bhupinder, Jasbinder, Parminder, Kulvinder, Harjinder, Ranjodh, Sheeraz, Hardeep, Kirendeep, Sukhdeep, Govindpal, and Rajan are unisex names and equally commonly given to either sex. In addition, names derived from Persian and Arabic, but not used among native speakers of those languages, are common among South Asian Muslims. Since Persian does not assign genders to inanimate nouns, some of these names are gender-neutral, for example: Roshan, Parveen, and Insaaf.

But having a unisex name is not the issue; it is the problem it creates in day to day life. Once I had asked someone to reserve a railway berth for me in an overnight train from Allahabad to New Delhi. I got a seat in the train starting at 9:30 pm. I sat down and was preparing myself to go to sleep, when the ticket examiner arrived. He looked at his chart and my ticket and said: "Madam, but you are not a man." I could not understand what he was trying to convey, till he pointed out that in my ticket, against my name the abbreviation "*pu*" (meaning *purush*: male) was written. For obvious reasons, the ticket examiner was hell bent on deboarding me late in the night for travelling on a fake ticket, till I produced my voter ID card, which, fortunately, I was carrying because I had a senior citizen concession.

My problem has been compounded because my husband is called Vivek. When we are both before an authority, say the registrar of marriages, we make sure to identify who is who. But recently we slipped. Both of us had gone to an ophthalmologist for an eye problem, which we shared in common. My husband presented our test reports to the doctor. He picked up one of them and called me to occupy the stool near him. He checked my eyes and diagnosed that the problem mentioned in the report had ceased to exit. He then called my husband and checked him for a long time and asked for his name. It is only then he realized that the diagnosis he had made in my case was with reference to the test report of my husband.

Actually coming to think of it, if I had spelt my name 'femininely' by adding an 'a' at the end, my email ID (vijayaagnihotri) would have looked a bit odd and prone to incorrect usage.

As one subscriber to Quora has pointed out, it is truly confusing for non-Indians to tell the gender of Indians by their first names until they have seen the photo. I never even thought about it till now, as it is quite natural for me. However, by Indian first names you are actually referring to Hindu (and sometimes Sikh, Buddhist, and Jain Indian) first names. Because I do not think there should be much confusion in Indian Muslim and Indian Christian first names.

The problem arises from the way we (and the British) started spelling our names during the British era - completely *ad hoc*. Therefore, the same spelling can be applied to the name of both genders. For example 'Sudipta' - is it the first name of a male or a female? It can be both. When it is male, the last 'a' is pronounced like 'oe' of 'toe'; when it is female the last 'a' is pronounced like 'a' of 'bra' (no offence meant). Therefore, looking at the spelling of the name (without any other guidance) it is very difficult to figure out the gender. Some people are using spelling to distinguish between genders but there is a long way to go. For example, I know someone who uses the spelling 'Sudipto' (male) instead of the confusing 'Sudipta'.

The first sure shot way is to listen to the pronunciation of the name - male names end with "without any vowel", "with the short 'a' (like say in ball or tall, and are spelt with one 'a')", and "with short 'o' (like toll)". Female names end with two 'aa' (like the 'u' in hull or husk, but still spelt with one a) or with long 'i' but spelt with one 'i' (pronounced like 'eel' of greet)". Unfortunately there are many exceptions to this general *ex post* rule. For example, Nupur - it ends with a consonant but still is a female name.

But, these rules should help you to some extent. However, remember that I am only talking about mainly Northern, Western and Mid-Eastern Indian Hindu Names. The far eastern and Southern names probably follows different rules.

The other sure way to know the gender of the person is to have some idea about the 'meaning' of the name, as all Indian Hindu names means something - either an object or animal, or an emotion, or some action, or a name of some God. But that I do not think is going to solve your problem.

So, for the time being, follow this rule - names ending with 'a' or 'i' are female, everything else is male. You are going to make some mistakes with this rule as well but at least you have some guidelines.

59 From a House to the Home: The Final Resting Place

My father could never build a house of his own. The reading of his own horoscope (he was an amateur astrologer) showed that it was affected by *grih-dosh* (house deficit) and, therefore, he was not destined to own a house. He tried to defy providence and went ahead and invested Rs. 5,000/- (approximately rupees ten lakh, in today's context) in a housing society. He promptly lost the money and never thought of building a house of his own ever again. He found solace in the proverb: *Fools build houses and wise men live in them.* In those circumstances, I consider myself a lucky fool. But the journey to the destination was not smooth.

It all began very early; actually immediately after I got into service. It began with a text book on English language for the intermediate classes (11th and 12th), co-authored by me before joining the service, getting the nod from the Uttar Pradesh High School and Intermediate Board. Around the time I got my first royalty in 1971, a princely sum of about Rs 2000/- (which was, at that time, about four times my monthly salary), I received an offer from my elder brother to join him in applying for a plot in the up and coming Indira Nagar residential colony in Lucknow. Armed with my royalty income and some encouraging assistance from my father, I went ahead. In a few years I was owner of a plot.

A few years later, towards the end of the 1970s, I got another offer from a dear colleague to join him in the acquisition of a plot in Banjara Hills in Hyderabad, this time with a loan sanctioned by the Government of Andhra Pradesh. Since I was posted in Delhi at that time, he even offered to build the house on my portion of the plot. He lived up to his promise, and by the time I reverted back to Hyderabad, the roof of the house was ready to be laid. In due course I completed the house. My father complimented me on my achievement because I was the first in our nuclear family to do it. He came all the way from Allahabad to attend the house warming ceremony. Alas it was not meant for us to stay; first because it had to be rented out to repay the loans, and then the circumstances conspired. For the sake of house warming, we spent a night there and that was all.

In the late 80s, my brother decided to sell his plot in Indira Nagar, Lucknow. I was back in Delhi on a posting. Having already built a house in Hyderabad and with no prospects of working in Uttar Pradesh, I too decided to sell my property in Lucknow and invest the money received in a flat on offer in a cooperative group housing society in Patparganj, New Delhi. The deal, however, fell through, after I had paid the membership fee and waited for a few months. I needed to invest the money in some other property in order to avoid the capital gains tax. I received another offer through a relative to buy a plot in a cooperative group housing society in Dwarka, in Delhi. I paid a few installments too, but the proposal failed to materialize because the society was unable to collect adequate money from the members to pay the price of the plot to the Delhi Development Authority. Getting back the money that I had already invested, was a long drawn out battle.

By this time I had shifted to Mussoorie as Joint Director, Lal Bahadur Shastri National Academy of Administration (LBSNAA), and was quite desperate to invest the sale proceeds of the Lucknow plot in some property somehow. One officer from the Uttar Pradesh Cadre, who was holding charge of the Greater Noida Authority, on a visit to the Academy as a guest faculty, came to my rescue. I applied for a plot and heaved a sigh of relief when the allotment letter came. I paid the installments from time to time and left it at that, because I already had a house in Hyderabad.

But the destiny willed otherwise. Towards late 1990s, having got a posting as Additional Secretary to Government of India in Delhi, I realized that I did not have to return to Hyderabad before retirement. I had been away from Andhra Pradesh for almost 15 years and had no strong roots or contacts there. Had I retired during a posting in Hyderabad, I would have perhaps settled down there. Moreover, my friend who had persuaded me to build the house in Hyderabad had sold his own house and moved on. In the meanwhile, I had also started receiving letters from the Greater Noida Authority to construct a house on the plot allotted to me, or else it would be resumed by them. Initially, I paid the relatively small penal charges for non-construction. Then came an order that took my breath away. It required me to pay a penal charge of Rs 80,000/- if I failed to construct the house. Building a house appeared to be a better option than paying that kind of penalty. But I had no money and I was in a quandary. My son, who had started working in the USA, came to my rescue this time. I could have got away with a smallish constructed area to satisfy the requirements of the Authority, but having been in and out of Delhi, staying in National Capital Region (NCR) after retirement did not appear to be a bad idea. So I decided to go the whole hog. I also decided to sell the house in Hyderabad. The House was built with the loan taken by my son. The sale proceeds of the Hyderabad house came in much later and helped prepay the loan and buy a flat for older age living.

The house was ready before the original date of my retirement; but in the meanwhile the age of retirement itself was increased from 58 to 60. The destiny once again conspired to prevent us from moving into the house to live in it, not only on account of increase in the age of retirement but also because I got a couple of post retirement assignments, which kept us away for another seven years before we actually moved into our home in 2012. It appears that I suffered from another variety of *grih-dosh*, which ordained that I shall build a house but would not be able to call it my home, at least for quite some time.

My saga of house acquisition is strewn with sundry other episodes. Like my father, I too lost some money (though not very much) in trying to buy a plot and join various housing societies. Much before the Hyderabad house venture, I tried to get a plot on the famous Road No. 12 of Banjara Hills with a loan for a plot taken from the Government. But I got a posting to Delhi before the proposal could materialize. At that early stage in my career, I could not have managed the transaction from long distance. I surrendered the loan amount I had received. This made me ineligible to get another loan for a few years. Thus when, on reaching Delhi, I got an offer to buy a plot in NOIDA from a friend in the authority, I could not accept it. I have invested money in a housing society proposed by the officials of a Ministry I happened to be working in and another floated by the alumni of Allahabad University as well as residents of the hostel I was staying in there. There was another society organised by the faculty and staff of the LBSNAA, to which I made a sizable contribution. Nothing came out of these forays.

After completing the house in Greater Noida (which had since evolved into a conglomerate of erstwhile villages aspiring to semi-sophistication of a township), but before actually moving into it, we contemplated selling it and buying a flat, because friends advised that for senior citizens flat living is safer and more comfortable. But for various reasons it did not happen and we are now not unhappy about it.

On my last assignment as Secretary General, Rajya Sabha, I was accommodated in a duplex house with five bedrooms and three bathrooms, which would reasonably qualify not only as an 'independent villa', but also as a 'detached' house in UK housing terminology. After my retirement from that assignment, I was given a pension, which was half of the salary I had drawn on one of my previous assignments as Secretary to the Government of India. But luckily, due to fortuitous circumstances, I moved into an independent home of my own which had accommodation more or less equal to what I had been used to in my last assignment. However, for the current abode to become our real home, we needed time to get our coordinates right in terms of being able to avail the services of reliable maid servant, washer man, tailor, *kirana* merchant, a shop which repairs electrical goods etc.

But have we really arrived at our final resting place? I cannot stay. It being an independent bungalow, it may be difficult to manage as we grow older. Hence came the move to sell off one property and invest the sale proceeds in a low-rise multi-storeyed flat, situated nearby (so that we do not have to start finding our coordinates all over again) being built by cohorts. The DDA offer of studio apartments for retired civil servants in Dwarka and 'Antara' senior citizen homes in Dehradun also look tempting. Who knows!

60 Which God Should I Pray Today?

As a former Director of Lal Bahadur Shastri National Academy of Administration (LBSNAA), who had settled down in Dehradun, RP used to be often invited to the Academy to talk to trainees on good governance issues. His talks were found to be very motivational by the young recruits. Some of his experiences narrated in his usual dead pan manner, used to have the listeners in splits.

One particular incident, during the time he spent as Secretary to Lal Bahadur Shastri (after whom the Academy has been named), when he was Prime Minister of India, is worth recounting. Mr. Shastri was going to Moscow and he wanted RP to accompany him. He, however, was not feeling well and was running high temperature. He went to the PM and said: "Sir! I would like to be excused." Naturally the PM asked as to what was the matter. RP told him that he was running high fever and Moscow was going to be very cold in winter. Mr Shastri heard him out and said: "It doesn't matter; please bring an extra blanket and you will be OK".

RP's one particular talk, which included this Shastri episode, was delivered often to new recruits. It panned 4 sessions of about one hour each. For the faculty of LBSNAA, who had to sit through, it was amusing to find that the text of the talk and the manner of its delivery were exactly the same, talk after talk and year after year. The joke was that even the timing of his taking a sip from the glass of water kept on the podium was also always the same. He had taken it to heart.

One of his favourite jokes pertained to his days in the LBSNAA as the Director. The trainees (probationers then) often complained to him about not having enough time to think on account of the heavy daily routine from early morning to late in the evening.

"The problem was not about their not getting time to *think*; it was more about not getting time to *drink*", he used to quip with only a hint of a smile. Another experience, which he used to recount, related to his life after retirement. While in service, he was quite busy, but used to find time to pray to a range of gods and goddesses of the Indian pantheon, at home or in various shrines in different parts of the country. However, after retirement, he had little time for them. Every day in the morning he had to choose his special god to offer his prayers to: it could be a plumber, an electrician, a carpenter or any one from the assortment of functionaries without whose services your life could be really miserable.

I thought it was a nice joke, because at that point of time I was in service and had a retinue of officials, who took care of such and other sundry matters. But the truth of RP's quandary dawned on me when some 20 years later I settled down in a house of my own, for the first time in my life, after retirement. When I look at my predicament these days, I think RP used to make a gross understatement. The day begins with a prayer to our daily maid (Oh Lord, give us this day our daily maid!). If she comes, we are eternally grateful to her. If she doesn't, there is hang all we can do about it. We do not expect her to tell us in advance about her inability to come, nor does she ever bother to inform. In the meanwhile, as the usual time of her daily arrival goes by, our tension increases by leaps and bounds because the dilemma is huge: whether to wait for her any longer or to start doing the work ourselves, particularly if we have an engagement elsewhere, including an appointment with a doctor?

That brings me to the second set of gods and goddesses in our pantheon, namely, the doctors. The procedure to get 'medical attendance' as it is called, being an ex-civil servant, is somewhat complicated if you want to avail of free medical facilities. First comes the 'referral' to meet the doctor. The doctor then usually prescribes a set of diagnostic tests to be carried out. Armed with that 'prescription' you return to the CGHS Dispensary and request for 'permission' to carry out those tests, which takes a day or more, depending on the day of the week. Next comes the requirement to fix an 'appointment' with the authorised diagnostic centre for the purpose. That too takes a couple of days; by which time your problem has subsided or vanished altogether. I am not a hypochondriac and, therefore, I wouldn't like to go into the gory details of trials and tribulations of an aged civil servant on this score.

Let us change track. Getting the electrician, plumber and carpenter is next only to getting a maid to work, in terms of the degree of its impossibility. First, any good workman worth his salt, is generally too busy with large projects and has little time for small householders (you can call them investors, to get the perspective right). If he agrees to come, you have to be hugely lucky if he comes at the time he has promised to come. For example, if your plumber says that he would be there in half an hour, you can rest assured that it will stretch to nearly two hours, that is if it does not spill over to the next day or the next week. In the meanwhile you have no option but to wait and pray. Your appointments get postponed or cancelled; but you can do nothing but pray. Thus we pray by rotation and by rote to about half a dozen gods and goddesses of our household pantheon. And the list of gods in the pantheon has kept on increasing with growth in technology. So we have come to add to the list the mobile network and the broadband service providers, the technicians who attend to DTH, the refrigerator, the washing machine, and the RO and so on and so forth.

It seems to me that either our home's fittings and fixtures are aging along with us and they need repair or replacement from time to time or we are finding new ways of feeling unhappy with their performance. But before I conclude I must add that, unlike the real gods in the Hindu pantheon, who normally do not appear before ordinary mortals, the new gods we have now acquired are more condescending and do actually materialize in person. Moreover, unlike RP, I find time to pray to both, although I am able to assign only about ten minutes for the more revered ones.

61 Retirement is a Full Time Job

A year or so after I retired from my last assignment as Secretary-General, Rajya Sabha, several of my cohorts asked me as how I was keeping myself busy. I was reminded of a colleague who after retirement was literally suffering from what could be fairly described as the withdrawal syndrome. In order to get over his problem, he converted one of the rooms in his home into a shadow/surrogate office which, apart from the usual office stationery and other items, was equipped with a call bell, which he could press once in a while by rote to release his tension. No one at home was required to respond.

I did not have any formal assignment but was otherwise kept quite busy. My schedule on a particular day is given below as an example:

Time	Activity
0530 to 0700 hrs	Walk the dog and Morning Walk.
0700 to 0830 hrs	Morning Tea and Newspapers.
1045 hrs	Met the dentist for trial of a new denture and extraction of two teeth.
1200 hrs	Checked availability of a new live-in maid and discussed the terms and conditions of her appointment.
1240 hrs	Visited the District Magistrate's Office for renewal of gun license.
1315 hrs	Shopped for some electrical goods.

1700 hrs	Took the dog for periodic vaccination.
1840 hrs	Participated in a live RS TV show through OB van.
2000 hrs	Attended a friend's dinner party, out of town.

This was in addition to some minor activities, such as getting milk from the milk booth, and checking, replying to (and, more importantly, deleting) emails, WhatsApp messages, SMSs etc. This description may appear very impressive, but I shall let you in on a secret. I could go through with this otherwise 'hectic' schedule quite easily, because I am based in Greater Noida, and all the places visited (except the out of town dinner at the end of the day) are within easy reach, say about 2 kilometres. There was, actually, a slot (2 pm to 5 pm) to watch a movie, if I was so inclined. A great advert indeed for Greater Noida living!

There have been several instances in my life, during my service career, when I had to do a lot of multi-tasking. The first one that springs to mind relates to 1980. I had just landed in Hyderabad after completing my tenure as Under/Deputy Secretary to Government of India and had been posted as Deputy Secretary in the Department of Panchayati Raj, in the Government of Andhra Pradesh. I was straightaway engaged in several activities at the same time including construction of my house, the roof of which was laid immediately on arrival; preparing the manuscript of a book on Indian History for the civil services aspirants; and preparing, within a 3 months' time frame, the final draft (out of nowhere) of the Report of a Committee that had been set up to suggest restructuring of Panchayati Raj Institutions. The third one, for obvious reasons, was finished the first and consequently I was promoted as Joint Secretary in the State and given the responsibility of organizing the conduct of elections to Panchayati Raj bodies in Andhra Pradesh after a gap of 11 years. Everything, with God's grace, was completed well within the expected time schedule.

The second instance was of a more recent origin. As Secretary-General, Rajya Sabha, I was vested with the responsibility of conducting the election to the post of the President of India in 2012. A day before the filing of nominations on behalf of the His Excellency Mr. Pranab Mukherjee (2012-17), we had engaged a maid servant through a Placement Agency. After all the financial matters had been well settled, the next day in the morning (the nomination day) she vanished, in less than 24 hours. So just before leaving for office to receive the nomination papers, I prepared a complaint for filing an FIR against the persons who had cheated me.

Cutting back to the present again, as a retired person, fortuitously, I have had an assortment of assignments. I was made member of a committee, which was required to go into complaints regarding electoral malpractices in a public institution. This assignment lasted about six months. I underwent a major dental procedure which too took about six months and required weekly sittings with the dentist, one of which finds mention in the table given above. Around the same time I was entrusted with the conduct of a Disciplinary Inquiry against a faculty member of an autonomous Government institution, with a mandate to complete the inquiry and submit the report within six months. Having shifted to our own house about 3 years ago, we found several structural and other defects, which needed urgent attention. Again, some major repairs on account of normal wear and tear too had to be carried out.

Of course, there have been other chores to keep me busy all the while. Let us take a look at them. I would like to begin with the mundane but the most daunting task of collating data for filing of Income Tax returns. The assumptions are that you are a retired senior civil servant staying in your own house, with some investments, some 'other income' (called honorarium) for occasional part-time work (such as the disciplinary inquiry I conducted), and want to avoid paying unnecessary Income Tax like the plague. Why fill up public coiffeurs, half of which goes waste anyway for various reasons? So I had to keep all the data and documents relating to various items of expenditure, such as telephone and mobile bills, petrol and parking bills, books and stationery, entertainment expenses, and so on.

There are other routine items such as shopping for groceries, paying bills, visiting malls (mostly for window shopping), watching TV and movies, getting periodic medical checkup done from time to time, going to specialists periodically for re-prescription of regular medicines, collecting monthly quota of medicines from the CGHS dispensary, writing articles like the present one etc. Of course, everything we have somehow needs repair, including us, time and again.

I prefer to pay my bills physically, rather than electronically; it consumes more time, keeps me moving about and provides an opportunity to meet and talk to people. Going to the bank to withdraw the money through cheque, rather than from the ATM, has another advantage. I can get the currency in denominations that I need, particularly in hundred rupee notes in order to pay the daily milk and grocery bills, because the ATMs normally dispense currency in denominations of five hundred and one thousand, which have recently ceased to be legal tender (ha!, ha!). Incidentally, in the initial stages of demonetisation I thought that I had a windfall in terms of using my time standing in the queues of a couple of banks. But very soon the novelty wore off and I took to using my less-used credit/debit cards and making e-payments through net-banking and a couple of e-wallets to avoid having to go to the banks or ATMs to withdraw cash or make payments (such as NEFT) which require visits to the banks.

The list is endless and I do not know how the time flies. Actually, I have been so busy that I could not read any novel for a couple of years. Whereas, when I was in service, I used to read at least a couple of them every year, especially during long international flights. I have an iPad, which I use rarely and mostly to 'Facetime' my son and his family, living in the USA. I had accumulated over two dozen books on teaching of English language to young as well as not-so-young students, in anticipation of my retirement. I have not felt the need to go through them yet. I am a member of a few NGOs, but hardly have time to attend their meetings. I, therefore, consider the question: "How do you keep yourself busy?" quite inane.

I do, of course, realize that over time the sources of so-called official assignments would dry up. But the quota of age and hospital related engagements would perhaps correspondingly increase. The key to keeping oneself busy is having a hobby, focusing on generic expertise in areas of perpetual interest and adding to the skill set, as I did by obtaining a Certificate of Corporate Directorship in 2013 from the Institute of Directors, and successfully completing QMS Lead Auditor Training Course (based on IOS 9001: 2015) from an accredited institution in 2016, which got me new assignments. These have provided some opportunities to me. I spend a lot of time reading for writing and publishing articles on diverse subjects.

I am moderately active on LinkedIn, and have a nodding acquaintance with Twitter; but have kept away from Facebook so far. I have an excellent collection of CDs and cassettes, which I have not used so far. As a matter of fact, a DVD player bought several years ago has not been put to use. I am sure their time will come sooner than later.

62 What are the Options? What a Way to Go!

As one gets closure to the expected date of departure to meet the maker, intimations of mortality start clouding the vision. A report that in the Netherlands a proposal has been mooted to legalize assisted suicide for older people, who are generally healthy but feel that they have led a full life, triggered a chain of thoughts. I mean, about the manner of my death (or 'passing away' or 'sad demise', as the case may be), in a manner of speaking.

Will I kick the bucket in sleep? That would indeed be very nice. One of my lady friend's husband passed away just like that. In the morning, when she tried to wake him up, he was cold. Or another friend, whose wife woke him up in the middle of the night to tell him that she was dying and passed away. It is a good idea; but not quite under my control for execution. In any case, it would devastate my spouse. I do not want to do that under any circumstances.

It could be an accident, you never know. But that might be painful, particularly if I do not die on the spot. I have met with a motor vehicle accident in the past; one of the articles (My Beautiful Teeth) deals with it. It could be messy and may not yield the desired result. I do not like taking chances in matters of life and death.

So, could it be suicide? I have nurtured suicidal thoughts in the past. First time I did it was just like that, when I was holed up in a hotel in Calcutta (Kolkata now) with nowhere to go. It was my first visit to that city, beloved of all Bengalis. But, looking out of the bay window of the hotel, overseeing the bustling street, I somehow felt very depressed, not a very common state of mind with me. May be it was because of the fruitless meeting I had had the previous day or the fear of not making it to the airport in time to catch the return flight. No, I am not cut out for suicide; banish the thought.

Cancer, then? Yes, it is a distinct possibility, the way people are getting it around me. I think it is largely on account of the fact that we are giving a long rope to that ailment simply by living longer than our ancestors did. But if I have a choice, a big No, NO!

No permanent disability; no paralysis, please, God! There is a lot of talk these days about carbon footprints, about leaving the earth better for the generations to come. My concern is a sub-set of that. I do not want to be burden on our children with my disabilities. They should be free to use their time and resources on their children and themselves. Not me.

While watching a movie in a multiplex? I think that is a unique idea; just out of a blockbuster Bollywood movie, which I am sure I would be watching at that point of time (wish it would be good and entertaining; going by the past experience, blockbusters are not always so). After all Adil Hussain, an actor, has said that he would like to die while acting. But, on second thoughts, that would spoil the fun of all other spectators (some of whom would be whistling, while some others are busy on their mobiles), including those accompanying me, because of the 'surgical' removal that would need to be carried out. Not a very desirable option, on second thoughts.

Another option is to have the 'sad demise' or approach of the demise announced on the intercom of a Rajdhani train or a plane. Demise during a train journey would be rather messy. Again, someone may pull the chain of the train, which would delay its arrival at the intermediate as well as the final destinations, where some of the passengers may have an urgent appointment.

The newspapers recently carried a report to the effect that a passenger travelling on a Jet Airways flight from Delhi to Doha succumbed to serious illness, despite the flight being diverted to Karachi. In retrospect, a plane may not be a great place to die in. The passenger(s) sitting next to me may squirm or faint (depending on the gender). The plane making a diversion for emergency landing will definitely disturb the schedule of some of the passengers. It would thus be a spoil sport. No, I do not want to be a pain in the neck of my co-passengers, never. That is not in my genes.

According to the ancient Indian wisdom, life and death are ordained and astrology supports it. Actually my father had worked out the time of his death and used to joke that he was living on borrowed time. How nice it would be if I was told, in advance, the date of my death. Then I could, like Betsy Davies, hold a farewell party for my ultimate departure. The lady in question, of course, being terminally ill, invited her closest friends to say good bye before taking a lethal dose of drugs under the Californian law, which provides for doctor-assisted suicide for terminally ill. No such law is available in India yet, although the issue is being debated in the public domain. Till it happens and one can officially host a sort of 'break-away party', it would indeed be great if, like Bhishma Pitamaha, I could will my death at the time and place of my choice. But in the absence of such a neat solution, I have tried to benchmark my approximate date of departure with reference to my blood relatives, cohorts and colleagues. For example, if a person older than me, say, by ten years is still around then I have time on my hand. It is not a very accurate reckoner; but I know that I am inching closer by each passing day.

Senior citizens living a cacoonish existence, sooner or later, begin to nurse an indescribable trepidation of what will be in store for the survivor. I know a couple, in their late eighties, a conversation with whom is generally about waiting for death. Among other things, there is a grave concern about one of them taking ill suddenly at night, when no help is nearby. There is, of course, the anxiety surrounding the issue: who will go first? It would indeed be great, if the merciful God permitted the couple to 'leave together' after having lived together.

Trent Winstead (88) and Dolores Winstead (83) of Tennessee, married for 64 year, spent their final few moments together clutching each other's hands tightly before dying just hours apart.

The ideal state would, therefore, be to go together in sleep. Have the evening walk; get milk for the next day and keep it in the fridge; watch the favourite programme (serial, ODI or whatever) on the TV; enjoy the home cooked dinner or 30-minute ordered pizza in between; see the latest news at about 10 pm on the favourite news channel; and then retire to bed, at peace with yourselves, before passing away into eternity. But then who will inform 'all concerned'? That is a moot question.

My father died in the process of writing a now-obsolete inland letter. It would be befitting for me to pass away while working at my desktop computer.

When we are born, we start to gel, with the mother or the father or both. Very soon, we started coagulating with and, later, drifting apart from others. We make friends but often fight with siblings. We marry and divorce. In the course of our careers, we make friends, but also enemies. Countries come together and fall away. Stars are formed, but occasionally collide and explode. Galaxies take shape; but, sometimes, converge explosively. Life is subsumed in death and *vice versa*.

In life, we often drift part; but death unites us all. Amen!

तो चलूं

ज़िंदगी में कितने मुकाम आए और गए
ठहरो, अपने पैर कुछ और जमा लूँ तो चलूं।

दिल उब सा गया है, इन बदलते नज़ारों से
इक सुकून भरा आशियाँ बना लूँ तो चलूं।

न जानें कितनी दूर तक फैला है सैलाब यहां,
इसे ज़रा सलीके से समेटूं तो चलूं।

आज तक तन्हाइयों से जूझता आया हूँ मगर,
कुछ कदम रहबर के साथ बढ़ा लूँ तो चलूं।

आज भी कुछ यादें है, जो भूलती नहीं,
इन हसीन यादों को दिल में बसा लूँ तो चलूं।

इब्तदा–ए–इश्क की बात तो सभी करते हैं,
मैं भी दर्द–ए–दिल की बात बता लूँ तो चलूं।

जहां तक देखता हूँ धुआँ ही धुआँ है,
इस धुंधलके को हटा के, कुछ चराग जला लूँ तो चलूं।

दुनियां में मैंने गम के ज़खीरे ही बस देखे हैं,
अब चाहता हूँ खुशियों से सरोकार बना लूं तो चलूं।

Index

42nd Anniversary of Emergency, 52
Aadhar Cards, 127, 129
Abdul Kalam, Dr. APJ, 192
Abhyankar
  And Agnihotris, Brahmin Clans of Maharashtra, 30
  Author's Room Mate, 30
Administrative
  Reforms, 191, 194, 195, 199-201
  Reforms Commission Report, 194
  System and Culture, 33
Advani, Lal Krishan, 57
Aerobic Exercises, 285
Ageing Jaws, 117
Agnihotri, Rati, Actress, 31
Agriculture Sector, 168
AIDS Colony, 175
AIIMS, 55, 99
Alice's Adventures in Wonderland, 260
All India Services, 70, 76
Allahabad University, 33, 144, 186
Allegations
  And Counter-Allegations, 56
  Of Corruption, 58
Alphonsos Mangoes, 63
Ambani, Mukesh, 192
Ambedkar, BR, 212
Ambush Marketing, 270
AN Grover Commission, 59
Anand, Rajesh Khanna's Star Movie, 39
Anantnag, 92
Ancient Monuments, 96
Andhra Pradesh, 33, 34, 145, 179, 251, 253
  AGROS, 168
  Guest Control Order, 165, 167
  Idlis, 275
Annu Kapoor, Film Actor, 248
Annual Collector's Conference, 38
Anti-Hoarding and Anti-Smuggling Drive, 46
Antra, Sr. Citizens Home in Dehradun, 298
Apparel Export Promotion Council, 187
Appropriate Technology, Human Rights Activists, 121
Arjun, 155
Ashoka Hotel, New Delhi, 95
ASI Monuments, 211
Asia House, KG Marg, New Delhi, 61, 100

Asia, Africa and South America, 63
Association of Corporations and Apex Societies of Handloom, 243, 245
Astrology, 161-164
Author
  (Appointed) Officer on Special Duty (OSD) in National Academy of Administration, 52
  Addl. Secretary D/O Administrative Reforms and Public Grievances, 191
  Allahabad University, 33, 102, 137, 229
  Andhra Pradesh Cadre, 1968, 33, 43, 145, 178
  As Returning Officer for Election of President, 53
  As Addl. Development Commissioner, 80, 186, 244
  As Collector And District Magistrate, 185, 232, 233
  As Deputy Secretary, Panchayati Raj, in Andhra Pradesh Government, 303
  As District Magistrate – Paper Loving Boss, 78
  As Joint Director of Academy, 107, 110, 178
  As OSD in 12th Finance Commission, 187
  As Secretary—Ministry of Parliament Affairs, 188
  Association with Gandhi Saga, 100
  Attended Conference of – Business Community Association, 90
  Belief – All Agnihotris are Kanpurias, 29
  Born and Brought up In Uttar Pradesh, 32
  Bought Marks-Spencer Shirts, Cassettee Player, Mixie for Wife and Lego Type Games for kids, 63
  Bought New Fiat Premier Padmini, 14
  Completion of 7 Years in Field of Textiles, 172
  Daily Allowance during Training -Pound Two per day, 63
  Degree from DAV College Kanpur, 136
  Deputation by GOI to Visiting Fellowship in QEH, 276
  Deputed for Course for Senior Hospital and Health Services Administrator, 53
  Development Commissioner of Handloom GOI, 94
  Disposed Fiat in 2012 and Bought New Maruti Wagon R, 144
  District Training, 36
  Education till 12th Standard in Hindi Medium, 135
  Election Observer in Bihar, 118, 182, 278
  Eligible for Foreign Training Program, 101
  Encounter with Happy/ Unhappy Naxalites, 49
  Excellent Command Over Urdu, 41
  Experiences after Joining IAS, 33
  Financing His Tour to Europe (ODA/DFID), 101

Financing Scheme – Holiday in UK By ODA/DFID, 101
First Bonding—with an Eccentric Boss, 76
First Posting as CDM at Mehboobngar, 185
First Posting as SDM in the State of Andhra Pradesh, 46
First Posting as SDM/Asst. Collector, Hyderabad, 36
First Trip Abroad, (UK), 54, 61
Free Access to Bodleian Library, 102
Got Driving License, 141
Got First Royalty for Book Rs. 2000, 294
Got International Driving Licence, 144
In Amarnath Jha Hostel, 137, 229
In BNSD College Kanpur, 225
In British Airways Flight Via Delhi-Doha-Heathrow, 62
In Ministry of Health, 62, 66
In Ministry of Home Affairs, D/o Personnel, 59
In Vishakhapatnam as Collector and District Magistrate (CDM), 73, 74
Introduction into Planets—Constellation, 162
Joined As Asst./Sub-Collector Hyderabad East, 1971, 40
Joined Civil Services at the Age of 23, 29, 32
Joint Secretary in Department of Personnel, 99
Learnt Telugu at LBSNAA during Training, 146
Member of Indian Institute of Public Administration, 101
Memorable Experience of Serving Tea to President of India (VVGiri), 41
Most Horrible Air Travel Experience, 80
Nomination for Foreign Training Program, 61
On Fellowship to Queen's Elizabeth House (QEH), Oxford, 101
Organized an Exhibition in Trivandrum, 30
Part of Anti-Hoarding and Anti-Smuggling Drive in Early Career, 46
Party to Setting of Two Institutions (NIFT and NHDC), 187
Passed Oral/Written Telugu Examination, 146
Ph. D. in Handloom Technology from IIT, 83, 101, 143, 172, 173, 268
Posted As Collector of Vishakhapatnam, 146
Posted as Joint Collector, 47
Posted As Member of Central Administrative Tribunal, 190
Posting as CDM Vishakhapatnam, 143, 243
Posting As Deputy Secretary (Vig. II) D/O Personnel, 113
Posting as Development Commissioner, 172

Posting as Director of Handloom and Textile in Hyderabad, 243, 244
Posting as Dy. Secretary in Department of Personnel, MHA, 55
Posting As US in the Health Ministry, 52
Posting at Delhi, 52
Posting in D/O Personnel and Training, 71
Posting to LBSNAA As Joint Director in 1992, 110
Privilege to have Tea with Presidents of India on Several Occasions, 42
Retirement in 2012, 125
Returned As Secretary General in Rajya Sabha, 190
Returned in Centre, Deputed as Addl. Development Commissioner (Handloom), 99
Returning Officer-Received Nominations for the Post of President of India, 129
Rural Jurisdiction, 41
Selected in IAS, 141
Shifted to LBSNAA Mussorie, 295
Shifted to Private Accommodation in Vasant Kunj, 100
Sold House in Hyderabad, 296
Task to Distribute Taccavi Relief to Farmers, 39
Taught Telugu Language for About a Year, 146
Tenure as Addl. Secretary, DARPG, 194
To Kanpur to Negotiate Deal with NTC Textile Corporation, 99
Toyed With Idea of Writing a Novel, 164
Training in Nizamabad, 146
Visit to Kulri with Wife, 108
Visit to President Elect - Shri Pranab Mukherjee, to hand over Election Certificate, 43
Visit to USSR, 94
Wallets – Mobikwik, Buddy – Pockets (ICICI), 215
With Wife in Oxford for one Year, 276
With NRI of Odisha, 82

Author's
Accident in Car-, 115
Assignment with the Central Government, 143
Beautiful Teeth, 114
Bonding with Paper Boss, 78
Car-Standard Super-10 (1956 Model), 37
Children – Abhishek and Amitesh, 249
Close Friends – Alok and Harish, 250
Contemporary-Shri Ram Naik Kovind in BNSD College Kanpur, 43
Contribution to Cashless Economy, 215
Downloading Paytm, 258
Exposure to UK/US Universities, 252
Family Name – Agnihotri, 29
Father Amateur Astrologer, 294
Father an Electrical Engineer, 135, 161
Father Encounters, 161

Father had Worked out His Death's Time, 309
Father Predicted for Author to be IAS, 163
Field Training at Nizamabad, 232
First Posting as Asst. Collector Hyderabad East, 236
Foreign Training Abroad, 142
Intelligence Test, 226
Jurisdiction, 39
Last Assignment as Secretary General in Rajya Sabha, 190, 297-302
Mis-Adventure, 47
Monthly Budget, 1971, 37
Parents – Late Shri Narayan Prasad and Late Smt. Savitri, 249
Plot in Dwarka, Noida, 295
Posting as Addl. District Magistrate, 165
Posting as Addl. Secretary GOI, Delhi, 296
Posting as Vice Chairman of Managing Dir. of AP State Agro-Industries Development Corporation, 168
Posting in Vishakhapatnam, 30, 186
Rank in IAS Examination, 71
Responsibility as District Revenue Officer, 50
Schedule for Day after Retirement, 302
Son Working in USA, 296
Son's Accident, 53
Supervisory Functions of Jamabandi, 50
Traditional Diwali Gifts to HELPs, 126
Village Training at Mortad, 233
Visit to Moscow, 31
Visit to Nagpur at the Age of 20, 29
Wife Took Teaching Assignment in Primary School in Oxford, 104
Wife – Vijay, 116, 125, 249

Bachua Tewari, 182
Bakhar, The Grain Storage Bin, 279
Ballot
  Boxes, 183, 184, 186
  Paper, 182, 183, 278
Baltic States, 95
Bamboo Test, 228
Bangalore Civil Hospital, 116
Banjara Hills, Hyderabad, 251, 294
Bank Linked Debit Card, 260
Bansilal, CM Haryana, 59
  Defence Minister, 58
Barcelona, 65
Basic Software, 175
Battle of Waterloo, 56
Bhadrachalam Sub-Division, 49
Bharat Darshan, 33-35
Bhartiya Janata Party (BJP), 58
Bhatt, Ila, 192
Bhattacharya, BK (former Chief Secretary Karnataka), 200
BHIM (Bharat Interface for Money), 212
Bhojpur, 103
Bhrigu Samhita, 163
Bhubneshwar, 82
Bihar's
  Rich Culture Heritage, 119

State Civil Services, 119
Black
And White TV, 98
Money, 216, 219, 257, 263
Blair, Tony, 101
BNSD College Kanpur, 136, 228
Bolshoi Theatre, 96
Bomb Blast in Mumbay in 1993, 242
Bonsai to Sushi, 153
Boss Diversity, 66
Bradford College of UK, 266
BREXIT, 219
British
Council in Allahabad, 138
Rule, 135

Cadre
Allotment Procedure, 70
Allotment System, 71
Allotment to IAS Officers, 71
Restructuring of CSS, 200
California Law, 309
Camel Brand of American Cigarettes, 88
Career in Civil Services, 185
Carlos Slim, Richest Man of Mexico, 97
Cash Crunch, 210
Cashless Economy, 219
CBI, 57
Centaur Hotel, 81
Central Pay Commission, Seventh, 199
Central Provinces, 29, 30
CGHS Dispensary, 301, 305
Character Building, 178-181
Chaturvedi, TN, Jt. Director in LBSNAA, 250
Chekhov's *The Proposal*, 114
Chenna Reddy, Dr. M, 40
Andhra Pradesh Chief Minister, 40
Cheshire Cat, 56
Chhagan Bhujbal, NCP Leader, 57
Chief Justice of Andhra Pradesh High Court, 165-167
Chokha, 279
Christ Church College, 137
Cigarette Act, 1975, 66
CIS Formation, 95
Citizen
Centre Governance, 196
Objectives, 196
Civil
Liberties, 57
Services Training Institutions, 192
Clandestine Operations, 48
Collector
And District Magistrate of Vishakhapatnam, 74, 75
Of Old Coins and Currency, 212
Columbus, Christopher, 65
Command and Control Style of Governance, 165
Commission of Enquiry Act, 1952, 58
Companies Act, 245
Computer Age, 241
Congress Party, 58
Constitutional Amendment (73rd and 74th), 179
Conventional Rules of Interpersonal Behaviour, 153
Cooperative
Group Housing Society in Patparganj, Delhi, 295
Society, 46
Corporate Culture, 270

Corridors of Power, 56
Corruption, 56
Craft Festival, 247
Credit/Debit Cards, 258, 260, 261
Cultural Beliefs, 153
Customary Overdrive against Hoarders, 46
Cyber Crimes, 215, 216

Delhi
Bound Flight, 81
Development Authority, 295
Delicacies of South India, 274
Demonetization, 209-220, 257
Department of Textile Technology in IIT, 252
Desai, Morarji, 58
India's First Non-Congress PM, 58
Development Commissioner
(Handicrafts), 186, 187
(Handloom), 186, 268
Developmental Schemes and Projects, 34
Devraj Urs, CM Karnataka, 59
Dhirendra Singh, Author's Colleague, 252
Dickens, Charles, 56, 137
Digital
Economy, 216, 257
Wallet, 216
Discovery of America, 65
District
Bar Association, 165, 166
East Godavari, 49
Hathras, 92
Hyderabad, 40
Khammam, 49, 50, 142
Manager of Indian Oil Corporation, 234
Rajamundary, East Godavari, 34
Ranga Reddy, 39, 236
Training for IAS Officers, 232
Warangal, 49, 211
DND (Do Not Disturb) Scheme by TRAI, 122, 123
Doordarshan
Program, 98, 143, 240
Draconian Law, 165
Driving Lessons, 141, 143
Drugs, 309

Economy, 257
Ecosystem, 172, 269
Education in Convents and Public Schools, 135
Educational Institutions, 107
Einstein, Albert, 225
Elections in USA, 213
Electoral Practices, 304
Electricity for All, 91
Electrification in Haryana, 92
Electronic Voting Machine (EVM), 184, 186
Emergency of 1975, 57
Enforcement
Case Information Reports (ECIRs), 57
Directorate (ED), 57
English to Telugu and Telugu to English Dictionaries, 146
Essential Commodities Act, 47, 165
Ethics in Public Administration—Lecture On, 179
e-Wallets, 260, 261
Export Promotion Zone (EPZ), 155

Fake Astrologers, 162

Farm Mechanism, 168
Farming Community, 168
Fashion
Business Education Centres, (FBEC), 246
Bangaluru—Shillong, 246
Institute of Technology (FIT), 245, 246
Institute of Technology, New York, 85
Fat Tax by Kerala, 263
Fertilizers, 46, 47
Festivals of India, 31
Fifth Central Pay Commission Recommendations, 164
Food
And Agriculture Organization (FAO), 241
Festivals, 247, 275
Grains Scarcity, 47
Security of Andhra Pradesh, 169
Foundation Course, 179

Gandhi, Indira, Shot at, 99, 100
Gandhi, Rajiv,
Death (Demise), 78, 100
Gandhi, Sanjay, Death, 99
General Administration Department, 38, 41
Georgia University, 96
Ghatkesar Station, 41, 42
Giri, VV, The then President of India, 41
Gita/Ramayana, 163
Goods and Services, 217
Gram Panchayat Officer, 118
Grameen Bank in Bangladesh, 219
Grape Wine, 47
Greater Noida Authority, 295
Grievance Redress Mechanism, 196
GST Regime, 263
Guest Control Order, 165-167
Guha, Ramchandra, Historian, 264
Guides and Interpreters, 96
Gulrajani, M, Prof., Author's Benefactor, 252
Gupta, Dr. Akhilesh Das, 167
Guru Dronacharya, 156

Halo Effect, 270
Handloom
And Handicrafts of India, 245
Days, 243-248
Marketing Complex, 187
Products, 243
Rebate Scheme, 187
Sector in India, 243, 245
Technology Tutor, 252
Weavers, 243, 248
Hanuman Chalisa, 103
Happydent Effect, 114
Harappan Civilization, 279
Haryana Model of Electrification, 92
Hassan, 115, 116
To Shravanbelgola, 115
Hawking, Stephen, 225
Health Foods, 262
Heathrow Airport, 62, 63
Herschel,
7th Planet from Sun, 164
A Planet, 164
Fourth Largest Planetary Mass in Solar System, 164
Later Known as Uranus, 164
Third Largest Planetary Radius, 164

Hideouts of Unhappy Naxalites, 51
High
  Level Expert Group (HLEG), 200
  Powered Committee, 179
Higher Secondary Education, 227
Historical Japanese Traditions, 153
Holi, Diwali—Mahabir Jayanti, 278
Horoscope, 163
Hospital Administration, 62
  Program, 63
Hostel Culture, 231
Hota, As Agnihotries, 30
Hota, PC, 252
Hotel Russia in Moscow, 31, 95
House Warming Ceremony, 237, 295
Hyderabad
  Biryani, 275
  Political Circles, 75

Id-ul-Zuha, 278
IIT Kanpur, 173-177
IKAT Tradition, 80
Illiteracy and Poverty in India, 162
Income Declaration Scheme, 264
India
  A Unity in Diversity, 278
  And US, 88
  Small Pox Free Country, 68
Indian
  Administrative
    Service Officers, District Posting, 111
    Services (IAS), 29, 76, 78, 84, 136, 137
  Civil Servants, 194
  Garment Industry, 85
  Institute of Technology, Delhi (IIT), 102
  Intelligence Test, 225
  Largest Democracy, 209
  Lunar Kartik Month, 279
  Political System, 60
  Settlers in Fiji Island, 103
  Textile Traditions, 80
Indira
  Gandhi's Government, 58
  Nagar Residential Colony, Lucknow, 294
Indonesian Decorative Technique, 80
Indo-UK Dish-Chicken Tikka Masala, 275
Indus Valley Civilization, 279
Inkblot Test, 226
Inquiry Commissions and Tribunals, 58
Inspector Raj, 191
Insurance Solicitors, 121
Inter-District Movement of Paddy, 47
International Hospitals Federal Kings Fund College, 54
Island Mentality, 154

Jamabandi, 51
  Operations, 50
Jammu and Kashmir, 92, 275
Janardhan, Dr. G, 167
Janata
  Alliance, 58
  Government, 113
  Ki Adalat Type Program, 196
Japan Bureaucracy, 91
Japanese
  Culture, 154
  Social System, 153

JR Vimadlal Commission, 58
Junk Food, 263

K Brahmanand Reddy, CM Andhra Pradesh, 59
Kamal Hasan, Actor, 31
Kapoor, Sanjeev, Super Chef, 262
Karan Singh, Dr., 52
Kashmir, 92, 275
Kautilya Traditions, 60
KGB (Russian Secret Service), 96
Khanna, Rajesh, Actor, 96
Khullar, Ms Sindhushree, 252
    Nominated Author to QEH Fellowship in Oxford, 252
Knowledge Skills and Attitude, (KSA), 179
Kulbhushan Kharbanda, 248
Kumaraswamy, HD, 57
Kurien, Dr. Varghese, 192

Lal Bahadur Shastri National Academy of Administration, 71, 104, 108, 110, 111, 116, 125, 145, 146, 175, 176, 178, 185, 241, 251, 252, 297, 399, 300
Lalitasana/Raga Lalit/Lalit Gate, 56
Land
    Development, 168
    Scam, 57
League of Mensa Geniuses, 225
Leather Test, 228
Legendary Rice Bowl, 47
Leh (J&K), 88
Liberalization, Privatization and Globalization, 269
Life Expectancy, 200
Lime Rice, 274
Literacy
    Rating System, 31
    Situation in India, 212
Local Words, Phrases and Idioms, Explained, 281
Lok Sabha, 58, 118
Lokayukta of Karnataka, 57
Lokpal and Lokayukta Act, 2013, 264
Lotus-123, 175
LPG
    Connections, 234, 235
    Cylinders, 284

Machhar Jhol, Bengal, 275
Madras Presidency System, 50
Magisterial Enquiry, 40
Maharajganj Samosa, 266
Management of Human Resources Course, 174
Manthan, 248
Maruti Udyog Ltd., 58
Mashelkar, RA, 192
Matsure—Festivals, 154
Meerut and Gorakhpur Culture, 32
Mehrotra, Prof. KK, Head Allahabad University, 250
Mensa IQ Test, 225
Metabolism, 286
Micro-Macro Economics, 269
Migrant Workers, 212
Militancy (J&K), 167
Mill, Powerloom and Handloom Sectors, 268
Minister of
    Health And Family Welfare, 62
    Home Affairs, 59, 113, 195
    Information and Broadcasting, 197
    Japan, 91
    Textile, 187, 190, 245, 268

Textile, Japan Bureaucracy in-, 91
Tourism, 245, 247
MISCIDICI (Make in India, Skilled India, Digital India and Clean India), 191
Mishra, Ajay, 251
Misra, SK,
Development Commissioner Handloom, 243, 244, 247, 248, 251
Posted as Secretary in Ministry of Tourism, 245
Mobile
Banking Vans, 210
Phones, 88
Revolution, 91
Modern Unisex Names, 290
Modi, Narendra, Indian PM, 90
Announcement-24x7 Electricity by 2022, 90
Mantra-Make in India, 191
Modicum of Economy, 269
Mofussil Areas, 37
Mohammed Yunus, 219
Nobel Prize Winner, 219
Mohan Kanda, Author's Friend and Guide, 251
Monetary Quotas of Medicines (CGHS), Dispensary, 210
Moscow Airport, 95
Mother Dairy Booth, 79
Motor Accident Claims Tribunal, 116
Mouth Watering Delicacies, 275
Ms. Madhulika Shukl and Ganga Das, 253
Helped Author to Get Membership in Delhi Gymkhana Club, 253
Mukherjee, Pranab,
Former President of India, 304
President of India, 257
Municipal Tax, 212
Mussorie, 110, 116, 129, 143, 146
Rains, 112

Nagarwala Scandal, 58
Nagela Fabla Village, 92
Nagpur, 29
Capital of Erstwhile Central Provinces, 29
Naidu, Chandra Babu, 193
Naidu, Venkatiah, M (Garu), 43
Narayan, NR Murthy, 192
Narlikar, Jayant, 192
National
Academy of Administration (NAA), Mussorie, 29, 40, 62, 70, 232
Now Lal Bahadur Shastri National Academy of Adm, 32
Democratic Alliance (NDA), 188, 191
Handloom Development Corporation, 99, 245
Handloom Expositions (NHE), 245
Institute of Fashion Technology (NIFT), 85, 88, 89, 195, 245, 246, 248
Act, 246
Science Academy, Delhi, 174
Unity, 154
Naxal
Movement in Andhra Pradesh (NMAP), 49
Operations, 50
Naxalites, 49, 51
Neena Gupta, Film Actress, 248
Net Banking, 260

Payment Option, 259
New
Pension Scheme (NPS), 195, 200
Public Administration And Management, 196
Nicolas, Maduro, President Venezuala, 97
Nish Kama Karma (Gita), 199-201
Nitish Kumar, CM Bihar, 220
Nizam System, 50
Nizam's Rule, 233
Nizami Culture, 41
Non-Officers Strike, 40
North Oxford Overseas Centre Oxford UK, 275-277
NTC Regional Managing Director, 99
Numerologist, 161

Officers Transferred 40 Times in 20 Years of Service, 185
Official Secret Act, 70
Ola, 259
Om Puri, Film Actor, 248
Open Ended Pension Scheme, 200
Operation Jamabandi, 50
Operational Research (OR), 173, 174
Origami, 153
Orwellian Year, 1984, 80
Oscar Wilde, 137
OTP, (One Time Password), 258
Oxford University, 102, 156

P Jaganmohan Reddy Commission, 59
Panchayati Raj, 179, 272, 303
Act, 186
Bodies, Election to-, 186
Institutions (PRIs), 303
System, 78
Panchnama Procedure, 47
Pandavas of Mahabharata, 155
Pankaj Kapoor – KK Raina, 248
Paper Boss, 77
Parliament Questions, 85
Parliamentary Committee, 188
Patan Patola, 80
PDCA, 271
Pension Reforms, 201
Pensionary Liabilities of Central Government, 200
PERT And CPM, 271
PGI Chandigarh, 62
Phase II
Of Training in the Academy, 179
Training, 178
Philanthropic Humanitarianism, 210
Placement Agencies, 128, 129, 304
Pochampalli, 80
Police Commissioner System, 40
Policy Formulations, 179
Political
Parties, 183, 238
Workers, 183
Polling Station, 118, 182, 183
Positive Domino Effect on Economy, 210
Post-Demonetization, 257
Prabhat Kumar, Cabinet Secretary, 252
Prasada Rao (Name Changed), 240, 241
And His Mother Died in Bomb Blast in Centeur Hotel Bombay, 242
In Forest Research Institute, Dehradun, 241
Indian Forest Service, 241

Visit to USA, 242
Pratyeka, (Separate Telugu Movement), 40
Presentation Session of IAS Trainees, 178
Prevention of Money Laundering Act (PMLA), 57
Printing Processes, 212
Professional Education, 245
Programs and Priorities, 77
Pseudo-Experts, 268
Pupul Jayakar (Mrs.), 187

Queen Elizabeth House (QEH), 101-103, 144, 175
Fellowship, 101
Qurbani Song, 237

Radhakrishnan, S, 90
125th Birth Anniversary, 90
Chairman Rajya Sabha, 90
First Vice President of India, 90
Ragging, 229
Raj Kapoor's AWARA Film, 31
Rajamundary, East Godavari District, 34, 49
Raje, Vasundhra, 195
Rajya Sabha TV Channel Loyalty, 57
Ram Manohar Lohia (Wellington) Hospital, 55, 62
Rama Rao, NT, (TDP), 238, 239
Ranjeet Ranjan, MS, 167
Rayalseema
Region, 146
Telugu, 146
Report of Administrative Reforms Commission (ARC), 194
Revenue
And Civil Supplies Administration, 165
Mandals, 50
System, 50
Rice
Bowl of India, 46
Mills, 47
Right To Information Act, 70
Robert (BOB), 88
Roorkee University, 176
Roster System, 250
Rural Electrification Scheme (Deen Dayal Upadhayay Gram Jyoti Yojana), 92
Ryots, 40

SAARC Countries, 247
Safdarjung Hospital, 53, 62
Sai Baba, 170
Sambalpur in Orissa, 80
Samosa, 274
Tax, 263
Samrat Hotel, 89
Sanjay Gandhi Brigade, 53
Sattu from Bihar, 275
Scheduled Castes/Tribes, 170
Senior Citizens, 257-261
Servants Verification Form, 128
Seventh Central Pay Commission, 199
Shabana Azmi, Film Actress, 248
Shah Commission, 58, 59, 112
For Excesses in Emergency, 58
Shankaraguruswamy, D, Author's First Collector under Training, 251
Shastri, Lal Bahadur, 299
Shinto
(Divine war), 153, 154
A Philosophical Study of-, 153

Ethics, 153, 154
Rituals and Festivals, 154
Shiv Khera (Management Guru), 127
Shouri, Arun, 191, 192, 194
Shrines, 300
Shyam Benegal, Film Director, 248
Singh, Dhananjay, P, Director of Estates, 251
Single Tender System (STS), 244
Sisopata, A Monument, 279, 280
Sister Planet Mars, 162
Skill Development, 281
Solankhe, Vilasrao, 192
Spanish Trans-Atlantic Maritime Expeditions, 65
St. Petersburg, 97
State Darshan, 34
Steamed Fish of Assam, 275
Students Agitation, 111
Subramanian, Arvind, Economic Adviser to PM Narendra Modi, 264
Surajkund Lake Faridabad, 247
Swachha Bharat Mission, 153
Swiss
Bank Account, 257
NGOs, 69
SWOT, 185

T. Anjaiah, Congress Party, 238
Taccavi Relief to Farmers, 237
Tank Bund, 39
Tariff Commission, 187
Tata, Ratan Nawal, 192
TCS Software, 175
Telengana
And Andhra Region, 49
Region, 49, 50
State, 40, 49, 145, 211
Telugu Language, 40, 146
Terrorists/Taliban, Good Or Bad, 49
Tewari, Col. SG, 250
Textile Technology,
Department of IIT, Delhi, 172
History, 174
Three Day Working Week, 94
Total Quality Management, 271
TRAI, 122
Transparency in Government, 70
Trump, Donald, US President, 209
Tuglaqi Farman, 212
TV News Readers, 98
Types of Intelligence, 228

UK, 144
Uma Sharma (Dance Maestro), 96
University of
Allahabad, 135
Georgia, 31
UP High School and Intermediate Board, 294
UPA, 188
UPSC, 104-106
USA Older Democracy, 209
USSR, 31, 95
USSR Cities, 94
Moscow, 94
St. Petersburg, 94
Vilnius, 94, 95
Uttar Pradesh, Bihar—Nagaland, 33

Vaghela, Shankar Sinh, Union Textile Minister, 57
FIR – Land Transfer of Mill Land in Bombay, 57
Vajpayee, Atal Bihari, Bharat Ratna, 191
Varanasi, 80

Vegetarian Specialities, 276
Vengal Rao, J, CM Andhra Pradesh, 58
Victor Lal, 103
Vijay Lakshmi,
  Author's Wife, 289
  Vijay Agnihotri after Marriage, 289
Vilnius, Capital of Lithuania, 95
Virbhadra Singh,
  Case of Mis-proportionate Assets, 57
  CM Himachal Pradesh, 57
Vishakhapatnam (Andhra Pradesh), 30, 31
Vodka, 96
Voting Day Tamasha, 182

Water Cycle, 287
Weaver Community, 80
  Famous for IKAT Fabrics, 80
Weekly Faculty Meeting, 110
Weight
  Management, 285-288
  Reduction, 285
Wellington Hospital (now Ram Manohar Lohia Hospital), 53, 55, 62
Whistle Blowers Dilema, 165
WHO, 68
Withdrawal Syndrome, 302
Wool Intelligence, 228
Word Star, 175
World
  Trade Organization (WTO), 80, 263
  Yoga Day, 57
Wyra Tehsil HQs., 50

Yaddyurappa, BS, 57
Year of Citizens, 196
Yoga, 285
Yugandhar, BN, Dir. Lal Bahadur Shastri National Academy of Administration, 252

Zaibatsu, 154